REVENUE

ustomers want to buy

DEPLOY

Put the wheels in motion. Map out their buying process so you can support it at every step. Build an action plan. On the second day of your meeting, you will:

- Build a Buying Process Roadmap for each of your products and services. Each map will show the different stages of your customers' buying process: The concerns they have, the actions they take, the answers that satisfy them, and the best tools to use to provide those answers.

- Build your Revenue Growth Action Plan. The goal is to fix what is broken, and improve what needs improving. Determine which tools you need to create, or actions you need to start taking, to better support your customers' buying process.

- Once you start on the Road, you'll need to make sure you stay there. Use the advice in the last chapter to continue to make customer-centric and revenue-producing decisions.

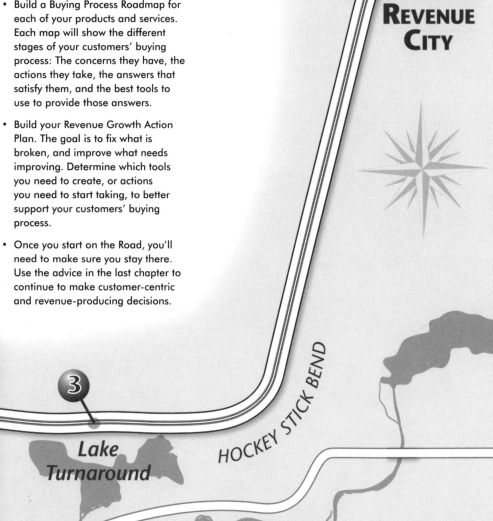

D1272811

REVENUE CITY

3

Lake Turnaround

HOCKEY STICK BEND

ROADMAP TO REVENUE

HOW TO SELL THE WAY YOUR CUSTOMERS WANT TO BUY

KRISTIN ZHIVAGO

BRISTOL
—AND—
SHIPLEY

Bristol & Shipley Press
Jamestown, Rhode Island, USA

ROADMAP TO REVENUE:
HOW TO SELL THE WAY
YOUR CUSTOMERS WANT TO BUY

For information, contact
  Bristol & Shipley Press
  381 Seaside Drive
  Jamestown, RI 02835

To email the author, send an email to Kristin@Zhivago.com.

Roadmap to Revenue: How to Sell the Way Your Customers Want to Buy can be purchased for educational, business, or sales promotional use. Contact BookSales@BristolAndShipley.com.

Roadmap map illustration by Eureka Cartography (www.maps-eureka.com).

Cover design by Bonnie Kellner and interior design by Edward Bolme, both of Lamb Creek Creative Services (www.lambcreek.com).

SECOND U.S. PRINTING

Library of Congress Control Number: 2011922669

ISBN: 978-0-9749179-2-4

*Dedicated to all the hard-working,
honest entrepreneurs and CEOs who feel a
strong sense of responsibility to their customers,
employees, and stakeholders—and who want
to grow their businesses without resorting
to the deceptive techniques used by
the manipulators of the world.*

TABLE OF CONTENTS

Introduction
Your Journey to Higher Revenue Starts Here 1

1 **What You're Doing Now**
... and Why It Could Be Working Better 5

2 **Before and After the Shift**
What Your Business Will Look Like After You Have
Aligned Your Selling Process with Their Buying Process 19

3 **Roadmap Step #1: Discover**
Find Out What They Want and How They Want to Buy It . . . 37

4 **Roadmap Step #2: Debate**
Resolve the Differences Between What They Want
Versus What You Have to Sell, and How They Buy
Versus How You Sell 77

5 **Roadmap Step #3: Deploy**
Document Your Customers' Buying Process So
You Can Support Them Every Step of the Way;
Build an Action Plan 111

6 **How to Support Your Customers' Buying Process**
An Example of a Customer's Buying Process 133

7 **An Overview of the Four Levels of Buyer Scrutiny**
... and the Truth about Marketing Methods
and Channels 151

8 **How to Support the Light Scrutiny Buying Process** 159

9 **How to Support the Medium Scrutiny Buying Process** 177

10 **How to Support the Heavy Scrutiny Buying Process** 197

11 **How to Support the Intense Scrutiny Buying Process** 223

12 **How to Keep Your Company on the Road to Revenue**
Management Strategies for Making
and Maintaining the Shift 253

About the Author 285

INTRODUCTION

We all know that revenue comes from customers.

The problem is, customers are independent-minded. They don't necessarily do what you want them to do. You do everything that you think should work, but the results are discouraging. You get fewer responses than you thought you would.

Those who do respond give you hope. You try to make the sale, but all too often, they don't buy.

You're left wondering what to do. You read blogs and business books, attend webinars and seminars, and hire consultants. You have numerous meetings with your trusted partners. You try one marketing and selling method after another, consuming precious capital and time trying to get potential customers to buy. But the revenue needle doesn't move.

Why not?

Because the answer isn't in the places you've been looking.

Your *customers* are the only ones who know the real answers.

They will tell you, willingly, what they want from you, and how they want to buy it, but only *if you ask them properly, in the right way, at the right time.*

- Don't bother asking when you're selling to them; *nobody* tells you what they're really thinking when you're selling to them.

- Don't depend on surveys or focus groups; both methods have inherent, bound-to-mislead-you flaws when you're trying to find out what your customers want and how they want to buy.

- Nor will social media provide this critical information. Social media certainly gives you a way to see what customers are saying about you, and you can build branded platforms that give your customers and fans a place to converse with each other (such as your own Facebook fan page, or a community/discussion/review section on your site). The information you gather from "watching" online discussions tends to be situation-specific, limited to the context of things your company is doing. While I do think social media is *massively* changing how companies interact with customers—and the very nature of marketing—it is not the most efficient way to uncover the real reasons someone would or would not buy your product or service, what drove them to you in the first place, and the process they went through as they made the purchase. Even social media companies hire me to interview their clients, so they can obtain information about perceptions, preferences, and the buying process.

In this book, I will teach you how to ask customers correctly—in the right way, at the right time. Once you have asked them correctly, and they have told you what you need to know, I will show you how to use that knowledge to change your marketing strategy and the culture of your company from company-centered to customer-centric.

When you become customer-centric:

- You will develop products and services—and positioning strategies—that appeal to your customers and differentiate you from your competition

- You will fix the things that are counterproductive—and costing you sales

- Your people, processes, and systems will be redirected from selling (pushing customers to buy) to making it easy for customers to buy what they already want

- It will be easier for customers to understand what you sell, buy it from you, and tell others about their delightful experience

- Your company will become responsive to customers, to the point where customers will see you as the go-to source for exactly what they need

At this moment, someone is on your website, reading copy that doesn't help him, while looking for answers that he cannot find. Another prospective customer has decided she won't buy from you because of something disconcerting that your salesperson has just said on the phone. In each case, these customers came to you fully intending to make a purchase—and would have been happy to buy from you—but something stopped them. Something they read or heard (or couldn't find) put them off.

Using the methods in this book, you will be able to determine exactly when the customer decides that he isn't going to buy from you—and why. Once you *know* what is keeping your customers from buying, and what they need to happily make a purchase, the solutions become obvious.

Fortunately, the required solutions rarely require a major restructuring. The necessary changes are usually straightforward and not that difficult to make. It's just a matter of knowing what needs to be improved, and then making those improvements intelligently.

As a Revenue Coach, I spend every working day helping CEOs and entrepreneurs increase their revenue by selling what their customers want, and making it easy for customers to buy. I help them reverse-engineer their successful sales, so they can manufacture new sales in quantity.

The methods I've developed and perfected are contained in the pages of *Roadmap to Revenue*. This book is not a collection of theories. Nor is it pushing a single idea that worked once, in a particular situation, or describing a "silver-bullet" solution—the kind that gurus have been selling since snake oil was invented.

This book contains a *system* that uses proven methods that have worked, in every situation where they were applied—no matter what was being sold, or who was buying it.

The system is straightforward and logical, but there's a lot to it. There is some learning to be done.

After you put the system to work, it will become easier and easier to make sales.

- Your buyers will help you, and spread the word for you

- You will be able to short-circuit the usual internal political battles, including the ones that employees have managed to keep off your radar

- Your marketing, sales, product/service development, product management, and top managers will all be driven by the same strategic program, which will satisfy your customers' wants and needs—and fill your coffers

I'm thrilled to be going on this journey with you. Nothing is more satisfying than helping yet another business leader escape from the marketing and selling maze, leaving behind the methods that simply didn't work, and experiencing a whole new level of revenue growth. It's one of life's most rewarding adventures.

How to get the most out of this book

This book requires a change from the usual way of thinking about sales and marketing. You'll be carrying out a process, and anyone who joins in, in the middle of the movie, won't understand what's going on. They might then impede or even sabotage your efforts.

For that reason, it's best that your fellow change agents—managers and key employees—also read *Roadmap to Revenue* before you embark on your journey to higher revenue. You will find, as my clients have, that once your managers and employees understand that you are going to use a sensible, proven method to satisfy customers and increase revenue, they will be eager to participate.

One last note. I've written this book specifically for and to entrepreneurs, CEOs, and other business managers. I've purposefully left out the usual academic folderol so you can get the point, then get to work. Everything in this book comes from experience, tested and perfected in the real world.

WHAT YOU'RE DOING NOW

1

... AND WHY IT COULD BE WORKING BETTER

The usual methods of selling a product or service suffer from built-in limitations. Marketing is supposed to bring in leads (lead acquisition). Salespeople—or your website—should be converting those leads into closed sales (lead conversion).

Marketing staff and vendors consider it their job to help you bring in the leads. As a rule, however, they don't consider it their responsibility to make sure those leads convert into sales. There is a disconnect. Marketing can easily make promises that are subsequently broken—by your processes, policies, products/services, or people. No one person "owns" the marketing *and* selling process, viewing it as a single effort supporting the *customers' buying process*.

I'm often brought in after an entrepreneur or CEO has tried a number of methods and has struggled with the disconnect between marketing and sales. In spite of a lot of effort and investment, the needed conversions have not occurred, and the revenue needle hasn't moved in the right direction.

Why don't these efforts bring in the desired results? Because marketing and selling have nothing to do with what your *buyer* is trying to do, and your buyer is the one who determines whether you will be successful or not.

MARKETING AND SELLING IS WHAT *YOU* DO. *BUYING* IS WHAT YOUR *CUSTOMER* DOES.

The two activities—your selling and their buying—are worlds apart. The misalignment between what you are doing, and what your customer is doing, is costing you. You are losing sales you should be making. You're also wasting money. Your marketing and selling activities aren't making it easy for customers to find you, to understand what you're selling, to see how it could help them, and to buy what they need.

Your customers have a buying process that they follow. If you properly interview a representative sample of your existing customers, you will be able to document their buying process in all its vital details.

You will know:

- Where they looked for you

- How they looked for you

- What they were looking for—and the words they use to describe it

- What they found

- How they made their buying decision

- The concerns and questions they had about your products, services, and company

- How they think about and describe your products, services, and company

- Why they decided to buy

- Who was involved in their buying decision

- The roadblocks in the buying process that almost stopped them from buying

- How long their buying process took—from search to purchase

- The trends they see that will affect their buying behavior in the future

- What they wish your company would do or change

- What they think of your competition

- The price they would be willing to pay for your product or service

- How helpful or unhelpful your website and/or salespeople were as they were making their buying decision

Armed with this information, you can adopt the correct marketing and selling methods and accurately target your messages.

Barriers to the sale

Companies actually make it *difficult* for customers to buy from them. Here are just a few examples of "barriers to the sale":

- Failing to include needed and helpful information on product packaging and in product documentation

- Neglecting to properly train and support third-party sellers, such as distributors, system integrators, installers, retailers, etc., so they can properly answer customer questions

- Not understanding why people actually buy the product or service and how they use the product/service—so the customer's real actions are not addressed in marketing, packaging, and documentation

- Omitting important information from the website, information that the customer must have before making a purchase

- Allowing—or worse, training—salespeople to attempt to bully the customer into buying

- Deceiving customers—usually by omission, but sometimes via out-and-out misrepresentation

- Keeping business hours that make it difficult for a customer to contact the company, to ask a question, or make a purchase

- Responding slowly or not at all to customer inquiries, questions, requests, and complaints, so the company earns a word-of-mouth reputation for not caring about customers

- Using complex, confusing pricing schemes, or pricing models that don't match the realities of the customer's usual method of purchasing and using that type of product or service

- Not staffing up, or failing to create systems and processes that meet customer needs

- Not making the product or service available where customers would expect to find it

- Misunderstanding or neglecting search engine optimization, so that customers don't find the product or service on the Web when they type *their* search terms into Google

- Insulting customers in subtle or even overt ways

- Failing to provide visual information on the website and on packaging, including clear pictures, close-ups, different views, and diagrams—so the customer can accurately assess the product's features and functions

- Using a voicemail system that "greets" customers with a phony, "we care about you" recording that really tells the customer that the company *doesn't* "care" about him, and will probably *not* give him an option that matches up with what he wants to do. The minute the customer hears that all-too-familiar "press one for this" recording, he's dreading his experience with the company.

- Using social media and other electronic tools in a deceptive way—such as having employees or other imposters pretending to be "satisfied customers" on public online forums, in testimonials, and in reviews

- Subscribing to multiple "trend spotting" sites and feeds, and believing that these sources are revealing what potential customers are thinking and doing, and making decisions on the misleading data

- Using the latest technological marketing technique or tool without considering how it will impede or assist the customers' buying process

- Hiring a consultant or employee who only knows how to sell to one type of audience, or who has a pet approach—and assuming it will work for the company's customers

- Writing promotional copy that describes the customer's *problem* in great detail, rather than saying how the product or service will solve the problem

- Creating really "cool" or "gross" ads that get attention—but then don't make it clear what is being sold or how the product or service will help the customer

MONEY IN HAND, CAN'T BUY

Here's an example of "making it difficult to buy." A blogger, Chris Heuer, had received a $500 gift card from social media sponsorship company Izea on the condition that he use it to go shopping at his local Sears store, and then blog about his experience. He and his wife, Kristie, went shopping—with $500 burning a hole in their pockets. Chris describes his experience on his blog:[1]

> We headed straight for the electronics department and found the karaoke machines. We found the one Kristie wanted on sale at a great price, only $90, down from $150. Though we couldn't find the extra microphones or music, but that's another story.
>
> Knowing we had more shopping to do, we asked a nearby sales associate if there were shopping baskets available. Her English was poor and she couldn't understand the question, even after asking it several times—this is something I have become used to in Miami retail, and while unfortunate [it] is not uncommon—I wish I spoke Spanish fluently, but I don't. Realizing there weren't shopping carts available and not wanting to carry it all over the store, we left the karaoke machine and headed a few aisles over to the video games where ...
>
> We didn't find any Wiis ... so we found another sales associate who told us they were sold out and didn't know when they were getting it in. Bummer, but this has often been the case with Nintendo for the past year plus, so that is not entirely Sears' fault. In fact, when we got back I ran across [an] article about November being the biggest month of video game console sales ever.
>
> At this point, we said, ok, lets go check out the noise-canceling headphones—unfortunately the choices were limited and I didn't see the headphones I wanted. We did find something suitable though, but then I couldn't get it off the rack (it was locked in somehow). With these frustrations mounting, we realized we should just wait to get the Wii from sears.com and since we had to fly home anyway, [we] should get the karaoke machine online too. After all, why spend $25 to check an extra bag? Or waste the time going back when you can just order online and get free shipping.
>
> Of course, in going to look at buying it online, they are only

[1] http://www.chrisheuer.com/2008/12/15/sears-grants-a-wish-for-my-wife-and-perhaps-you-sponsored/

offering it in one of those silly packages designed to make you buy games you don't really want—really not very good marketing on their point (Nintendo's) in building a good relationship with folks like me—we are seriously considering a PS3 now, but I digress …

You probably recognize many of these impediments to purchasing because of your own buying experiences. How many times have you walked into a store or visited a website, fully intending to buy something, and they made it difficult—or impossible? How many times have you had a conversation with a salesperson, and you just couldn't get the information you needed to make a buying decision? How many times did the salesperson not know the answer, so he faked it? Or, he didn't want to tell you the truth, because he believed it would have kept you from buying? How many times did you attempt to "try out" the product, only to find that the store or website prevented you from doing so?

Your company could easily be making these same mistakes. You won't know which ones, and you won't be able to fix them, if you're not talking to customers. Your salespeople and customer service people won't tell you; they may not even know. They could even be part of the problem (due to incompetence), or they might be handicapped by faulty procedures, poorly conceived company policies, insufficient training or poor supervision. There is a whole range of possibilities.

THE ESSENTIAL CONCEPT:
IN ORDER FOR YOU TO SELL,
SOMEONE NEEDS TO BUY.
IF YOU MAKE IT EASY,
THEY WILL BUY FROM YOU.

Consumers work so they can buy the things they need and want. Business people buy systems, supplies, and services. Both types of buyers come to sellers with money and a set of expectations. Make it easy for them to accomplish their goal—meet or exceed those expectations—and you will make the sale. Make it difficult, and they will buy from someone else.

So far, this sounds like plain old common sense. What's the big deal?

THE FUNDAMENTAL PROBLEM:
WHEN YOU THINK LIKE A SELLER,
YOU'RE NOT THINKING LIKE A BUYER.

If you're not thinking like a buyer, you won't be able to support your customers' buying process. You'll unintentionally set up barriers to that process. You will *think* that you're doing everything to "make sales," when in fact you are *impeding purchases*.

At this point, you might be muttering to yourself, "That's not happening here. I know what my customers want and how they buy."

Are you sure? Who do you spend the most time with, every day? Your employees, or your customers?

One of the most impressive things about Lou Gerstner, when he was at the helm of IBM, was that he spent an average of 40% of his time with customers—in spite of the fact that he was managing a huge, complex public company with about 300,000 employees.

I was doing consulting work for IBM while Lou was in charge, and afterwards. While Lou was CEO, the employees at IBM were more market-aware, less political, and more customer-driven than I had seen before, or have seen since. Their decisions made more sense from the customer's perspective, and the company was a more formidable competitor. Potential customers who had turned away from IBM came back. Their selling partners and customers alike were encouraged—as confirmed by my interviews of partners and customers. It made a real difference. No manager is perfect, but Lou thought like an IBM customer because he had *been* an IBM customer. And, after he took the helm, he went out and talked to customers, and brought their perspective back in to the company.

When you spend the bulk of your time with employees, you will end up making faulty assumptions about what your customers are thinking, and what your employees should be doing. When you begin spending more time with customers, you will start to realize that you weren't seeing the true picture, nor were you hearing about the problems that customers were having with your products/services, processes, or people.

I've seen this *so* many times, in companies of all sizes. The CEO thinks he knows what is going on, but when he finally does get out among customers, he is surprised. Things that he thought were "fine" are actually quite broken.

If you spend more time with customers, you will also uncover opportunities for new products and services. You will identify new sources of revenue that you didn't know existed. You'll realize that you have more opportunities for growth than you had thought.

Your customers' perceptions and needs will begin driving your decisions. You'll be able to say, in a meeting, "I know you think that product function is important, but the customers I talked to have absolutely no interest in that function. What they really want is X."

Until you force yourself to spend more time with customers, you can't imagine how much it will change your thinking—and give you a whole new level of confidence in your decisions. Because of your first-hand interaction with customers, you will know what will work and what you should do.

In most companies, decisions are driven by what employees say. Information about your customers is coming to you second-hand, through an agenda-driven filter. Often, the person delivering the message is a salesperson, who tends to be too positive about the reality of the situation, and who is also unaware that buyers never, ever tell salespeople what they are really thinking. The information you get from these internal sources will not result in sound revenue-growth decisions.

Talk to customers, and you will understand what you really need to do. You will be confident that customers and prospects will respond positively, because you are giving them what they are asking for.

NOTHING GETS THE ATTENTION OF A CUSTOMER OR PROSPECT MORE THAN GIVING THEM WHAT THEY WANT.

WHEN THEY GET WHAT THEY WANT, THEY ARE RELIEVED— AND HAPPY THAT SOMEONE HAS ACTUALLY SOLVED THEIR PROBLEM.

Your customer is coming to you in the hopes that you can say, "Ah, yes, of course, I have just the solution for you. Here it is. Here's what it will do for you. Here's the price. We have plenty in stock."

In order to say that to the customer, you have to:

- Have what they want (because you *already knew* what they wanted)

- Successfully describe what you're selling, in your marketing and packaging, on your website, and via your salespeople and social media channels, so that you answer *all* of your customers' questions

- Have prices that are easy to access, understand, and afford or justify

WORLDS APART

Your list of problems has absolutely nothing to do with your customer's list of problems. What you wrestle with all day, every day, is worlds apart from the problems your customer is hoping to solve with your product or service.

That's why, if you don't go out of your way to make the customer's problems *your* problems, you will continue to be worlds apart, and the decisions you make will end up obstructing their buying process. You will be hurting your own sales levels, just by doing what comes naturally—by doing what anyone would do, in your position.

You have to decide that you're *not* going to stay in your comfort zone. You have to make a conscious decision to go out of your way to spend more time interacting with customers, personally and meaningfully. It may be difficult at first (especially if you are somewhat shy), but soon after you start, you will come to think of customers as your friends, and they will start to feel the same way about you.

You can't afford for your company and your customers to be worlds apart. You can't afford to frustrate customers. Your business—any business—needs all the purchases/sales it can get.

Proceed with caution—myths perpetuated by sales and marketing gurus

One of the vulnerabilities built into the heart of every business owner is the tendency to believe fast-talking marketing and sales gurus.

It's not that these gurus are so great at selling; it's just that what they're promising is so attractive to you. They *know* what your need is—to grow your business. They know your need is strong, even all-consuming. It's easy for them to take advantage of your need as they pitch their method or service—even if it has no chance of increasing your revenue. Here's what you need to know so you don't fall prey to their pitches.

MARKETING GURUS: When my husband and I ran an ad agency in Silicon Valley years ago, we had a competitor who was the perfect example of the slick marketing guy. He could convince his clients to spend incredible amounts of money—on things that were never going to work.

He did quite a lot of work for publishers of trade magazines. Publishers were easy marks for him, because most publishers had started out as advertising salespeople and moved up. They were good at selling. No offense to any salesperson reading this, but salespeople are suckers for a good pitch. It's a professional admiration situation. When we meet someone who is good at what we do, we want to spend time with them, and learn from them.

This slick agency guy would produce expensive, oversized, glossy, gorgeous brochures aimed at media buyers (agency people who bought ad space for their clients).

He told his client that the oversized brochure was "too big to file" on purpose. He would explain that because the brochure was too big to file, it would stay on the media buyer's desk, where she would be constantly reminded of the publisher's publication. The client bought that concept, and the brochures were produced.

In the real world, media buyers received these oversized pieces, looked at them briefly, realized they couldn't be filed, and then *threw them away.* I know that because I *was* a media buyer, and also because I had interviewed scores of media buyers for my trade publishing clients. They all said the same thing: "If it's too big to file, it goes in the trash."

The slick guys always know how to do one thing well—make the client feel good about *himself.* It is the easiest sales job in the world.

WEBSITE DESIGNERS: In today's market, it's quite common for a clever website designer to create a "look" that he thinks the client will like—rather than what the client's customer likes or needs. The resulting site is a navigation nightmare for the serious buyer. Unnecessary Flash animation. Non-searchable catalogs, where the images are scanned in from the printed catalog (don't laugh, every industry has these). Hard-to-follow pathways to the individual products and the shopping cart.

Next time one of these design guys makes you drool because of the cool factor, remember that Google is one of the busiest sites in the world, and there's really nothing cool about it, from a "designer's" point of view. Cool doesn't sell. It gets in the way of buying.

SALES GURUS: The myth perpetuated by most sales gurus is that you are in control of the sale. They'll give you all sorts of advice about *how to manipulate the customer into buying.*

Their basic premise is deeply flawed. When a customer comes into a store, who's in charge? Who's got the money? Who can *walk out* at any moment, if he doesn't see what he wants, or the salesperson frustrates or irritates him?

Obviously, the *buyer* is in control of the buying process. No amount of clever manipulation—which buyers are wise to, anyway—will change this basic fact. Besides, it's rude—and it's the fastest way to lose the trust of the buyer, who will then go out of his way to avoid you in the future.

RELATIONSHIP GURUS: Every industry has its fads. In the marketing industry, relationship consultants have tried to convince CEOs that the key to successfully marketing and selling is to build a relationship with the customer.

The problem is, it's the *seller* who wants the relationship. Buyers don't start interacting with sellers because they want a "relationship." Relationships are what you have with your family and friends, not salespeople.

When buyers go to a seller, they want the seller to do what he is supposed to do: provide products or services in a professional, helpful way. In other words, they just want to buy a car from someone who is honest and helpful. *They don't want the car salesman showing up for dinner.*

Of course there are complex business services where the seller and the buyer interact for a long time. Yes, you could call this a relationship. Yes, it is possible to make friends with your vendors. But assuming there's a desire for a relationship on the part of the buyer is not realistic. It permits the seller to feel as if he has more power than he really does.

Long-term interactions between buyers and sellers are much more about *the performance of the seller* than any kind of relationship. As long as the seller is performing to the customer's satisfaction, the customer will want to continue interacting. As soon as the seller starts to slip, the customer will look elsewhere.

LOYALTY GURUS: Can you "create" a loyal customer? Do you think that a customer will stay loyal to you, no matter what? Think again. You can't control customer loyalty. But you *can* control your organization's behavior towards customers. If your behavior pleases your customers, they will stay loyal. There's no need to create a special "loyalty program" when you're successfully meeting customer needs.

HARD-SELL INTERNET CONTENT GURUS: There are some bright guys who have learned how to sell content on the Web. They sell other things, too, but educational content is their specialty. They have developed an infomercial-type approach, complete with testimonials, video, and a sense of urgency and scarcity. They make good use of affiliate marketing programs, compelling landing pages, hurts-less pricing techniques ("only 12 monthly payments of $197.99"), and other tried-and-true late-night-TV techniques. They do make money.

All well and good, if you are selling something similar to what they are selling, and if you follow their techniques to the letter. The problem is, their methods may not be right for your product/service and your customers. It could be the *exact opposite* of what will actually work.

LATEST GREATEST GURUS: As I am typing this, social media is all the rage. It's the Latest Greatest. The latest greatest gurus scream that you must be there, wherever "there" is. And, in fact, social media (or the latest hot marketing channel) definitely *could* have a rightful place in your marketing mix. It might even be the most successful way for you to get the word out and interact with your customers.

Social media may also be a colossal waste of money, no matter how much time and effort you put into it, if your customers simply aren't there or you aren't using the media in a way that works for *them*. You can't afford to guess about this. You don't want to risk your marketing budget and opportunity window because you're guessing. You need to *know*.

My mantra about social media is, "Ask not what social media can do for you; ask your customers what they want you to do for them, using social media."

There is no question that social media is changing the way companies interact with customers. I think it is profound; companies used to be the dog wagging the customer tail, and now customer-created content is becoming the customer dog wagging the company tail.

It is likely that you will find a way to monetize social media, given the new tools that are emerging and taking hold. However, if you *start* with the customer, and find out how they want you to utilize it, you will be supporting their efforts to buy your products and services. They will reward you for doing that. If you jump into it because it is sexy or "everybody's doing it," you'll end up with more regrets than revenue.

I've watched dozens of "latest greatest" fads come marching down Main Street, band blaring. Most of them continued marching, right out of town, never to be seen again. Only a few have stayed and become part of the commercial community.

How can you know, ahead of time, what will work for your customers? What will pay, and what won't?

Your customers will answer these questions for you, *if you ask them correctly.*

THERE ARE DOZENS—EVEN HUNDREDS— OF WAYS TO MARKET YOUR PRODUCT OR SERVICE.

ONLY YOUR CUSTOMERS CAN TELL YOU HOW THEY WANT TO BUY WHAT YOU SELL.

Your potential buyers *may or may not* respond to the latest marketing techniques. You can spend your entire budget thrashing around in the dark, trying this, and then that. You can go out of business using the most up-to-date marketing methods. Many companies do just that.

Or, you can make the entire process straightforward, by understanding what your customers need and how they want to buy it, then putting those things in front of them. You will eliminate the uncertainty and guesswork. You will make a series of informed decisions that lead to increased revenue. And, you will sleep better at night, because what you are doing will make sense.

BEFORE AND AFTER THE SHIFT

2

WHAT YOUR BUSINESS WILL LOOK LIKE AFTER YOU HAVE ALIGNED YOUR SELLING PROCESS WITH THEIR BUYING PROCESS

Shifting your organization from company-centered (marketing and selling) to customer-centric (supporting the customers' buying process) makes perfect sense.

Your customers are driving the buying process. They are in charge of the interaction. They know what they want and how they want to buy it. They hold all the cards. They can walk away at any moment.

If what you say and do supports the way they want to buy, they will stick with you through the process. You will make the sale. If you don't support their process, they will simply take their money elsewhere.

MAKING THE SHIFT: BEFORE AND AFTER

Making the shift from company-centered to customer-centric is a journey. You'll be starting where you are, and you will end up in a new place. In this chapter, we will look at where you are now and where you will end up.

From this point forward, I'll be referring to the shift from company-centered to customer-centric as "The Shift."

One more thing. Many books on marketing and sales devote about 80% of their content to the breathless pitching of their solution. Page after page is devoted to describing how your life will change forever if you adopt their techniques. The other 20% of the book (if you're lucky) talks about how to put their advice to work in your organization.

I'm not going to do that in this book. I'm going to invert that ratio. I'm going to devote this *one* chapter to describing "Before and After," so you can clearly see what the happy ending looks like, if you use the methods in this book. The rest of this book will be devoted to the step-by-step instructions—both strategic and tactical—that describe exactly what you need to do.

The following "After" descriptions show what will happen after you make The Shift. You won't be "marketing and selling" anymore. You'll be supporting the customers' buying process, systematically removing barriers to the sale, and selling more.

ENDING THE CIVIL WAR BETWEEN SALES AND MARKETING

Before:

Right now, in your pre-Shift state, there is surely a civil war going on between your marketing people and your salespeople. Neither group has much respect for the other. They might be polite enough in meetings (especially when you are present), but in private conversations, each group thinks the other group is clueless.

Salespeople complain that marketers don't understand customers, and that the materials they produce are off the mark and useless in an interaction with a real customer. So salespeople produce their own materials.

Marketing people groan when they see materials that the salespeople produce, because those materials break *all* the marketing rules—branding, "look and feel," product and service positioning, legal protocol, and corporate messaging.

Your company is a house divided against itself, riven by the acrimony between these two groups. You are handicapped in the marketplace, because the very people responsible for making you look good to your customers are at war with each other.

After:

Focusing both of these groups on the customers' buying process eliminates the civil war between marketing and sales. As part of The Shift, you will spend a day or so mapping out the customers' buying process, which will include a list of needed materials and processes at every critical step. As you do, you will see the energy in the room change from two camps with different agendas to one camp with one agenda, working together in concert. Your customers' needs and preferences will become the ultimate arbiter, shifting the focus from internal politics to customer-satisfying strategies and tactics.

Everyone will understand their role in the customers' buying scenario. They will see where they can provide value and how they can help each other. They will have new respect for each person's role, because each person will be doing their part in the accomplishment of a single mission. You will see teamwork energy in your company, without having to endure any of those silly teamwork exercises (e.g., "Catch me when I fall!").

ANSWERING CUSTOMER QUESTIONS

What is the fundamental essence of marketing and selling—from the customer's perspective? In other words, if marketing and selling are working for the *customer,* what happens?

The customer finds what he's looking for—and gets his questions answered, to his satisfaction.

Yes, it is that simple, conceptually speaking.

Simple in concept, tough to implement. Why? Because everyone in your company thinks that the customer has one set of questions, when, in fact, the customer has a completely different set of questions. This is one of the most common barriers to the sale.

Before:

Even if you are answering the same questions the customer is asking, the answers that you're giving probably aren't *satisfactorily* answering the customer's questions. In other words, you may *think* you are answering the question, but the customer is not finding *his* answer in the answers that you provide.

Disappointed, the customer feels compelled to contact your salesperson for more information, or search the Web for his answer (looking not just on your website, but also in discussion groups, forums, blog articles, customer reviews, and on your competitors' sites). In other words, if *you* don't answer his question, he will look elsewhere, and what he finds may not be very complimentary. It may cause him to decide that he doesn't want your product or service after all. You will lose your chance to explain why you do something a certain way.

Here's an example. Let's say you're selling a high-end DVD juke box system. You show the physical dimensions of your juke box on your website. In your mind, because you have posted the dimensions on your website, you believe you have answered the question, "How big is it?"

But that's not really the customer's question. The customer's question is, "Will this DVD system fit in the space I've reserved for it in my home entertainment hutch?"

Your DVD player has cords that must be plugged into the back. How far do they stick out?

Have you *ever* seen any equipment manufacturer answer this important customer question about the various cords that must be plugged into the unit, and the distance they stick out? I haven't.

It's as if there is an imaginary boundary line drawn around the product, at its physical edges. Anything outside that boundary line—such as the reality of the environment in which that product will be installed—does not concern the seller of the product.

As the customer searches in vain for the answer on your site, he can almost hear the greasy, overweight, cigar-chomping peddler saying, "Hey, that's not *my* problem, buddy. The plugs and your hutch are *your* problem. Do you want to buy this unit, or not?" You may not feel like you're this greasy guy, but when the customer can't get the answer to this question on your website, you may as well be.

Same product, different example. Let's say your DVD player has a remote. You say so, on your website. You even show a picture of the handheld remote, with call-outs explaining all its buttons. However, what the *customer* needs to know is, will the remote control signal work though the glass doors on the front of the hutch?

See what I mean?

You and your marketers *think* you've answered the customer's questions about dimensions, just by posting the width, height, and depth of the product on your website. You *think* you've answered questions about the remote, because you've described its functions and displayed a photo with call-outs. But your customer, who is ready to buy if he gets his questions answered satisfactorily, still can't buy. He doesn't really know if your DVD player will work for him, the way he needs and wants it to, after he brings it home.

This is what I see, in all markets, with all products and services, and all sizes of companies. It's been this way for years, and the situation is getting worse as buyers depend more heavily on websites for their pre-purchase research.

Companies spend incredible amounts of money attracting qualified buyers. Those buyers come to the company's website with money, questions, and a desire to buy. If they can't find the answers there, the sale that could have been made—and the lead that cost so much to acquire—is now lost.

After:

You could actually bring in fewer leads and make *more* sales, if every single person coming to your website or contacting your salespeople got their questions answered. Not the questions you think they are asking, giving them the answers you think they want, but the *actual* questions they are asking and the answers that satisfy them.

You could try guessing, as most company managers do, but guessing is a sure way to miss the mark. The only way to know what the questions are, and which answers will satisfy your customer, is to ask your customer. There is no other way to get this right. The good news is, if you get this information from your customers, you will be miles ahead of your competitors, who are probably still guessing.

We all think we know our customers, and we don't think they can teach us anything new. Use the methods in this book, however, and you will discover that you were missing incredibly important information. Once you have that information, you can make powerful, revenue-producing decisions that you could not make before.

Copywriter sees light; writes to real people now

When I coach copywriters, one of the first things I do is teach them how to interview customers by phone. It always has the same effect. It astonishes them and changes them. They realize how irrelevant their copy has been to real customers. Finally, they can correctly envision who the customer is, and what his specific needs are.

This awareness brings new vitality and relevance to the copy they write. Instead of making vague, general, anyone-can-make-them promises that no one pays attention to anymore ("increase your productivity, lower your costs"), they can make specific promises that will resonate with their customers ("reduce part count and simplify assembly").

Customers can tell the difference. Customers know when someone knows who they are and what they are struggling with. It is basic human nature to know when someone actually understands you, versus someone who is pretending to understand you and is telling you what they think you want to hear.

I recently got an email from Rob Sims, a copywriter who worked for me at Dow Jones when I was working there as a "rent-a-VP." Back then, I insisted that Rob interview customers by phone before writing copy.

Eight years after we worked together, Rob is still employing the "get to know your customer before you write to them" methods that I taught him. In the email to me, he said, "Since we worked together, my dives into customer experience drive most of the copy that I write."

I'll never forget Rob's face after he made that first customer call. He looked like a man who had just discovered a long lost treasure. He was sitting in his cubicle, mind racing, concepts crystallizing. He suddenly knew who he was writing to, and what he needed to say.

All selling involves communication between human beings—and communication is mostly done with words. Those words will be downright irritating if they don't ring true for your customers. In other words, you will go to the same trouble and expense to produce and deliver that off-the-mark selling copy, without getting the results you need.

If you're writing to "anyone," your words will be meaningless and empty. If you're writing to someone you know, your words will come alive—and will be meaningful to that person. Actual communication will take place and sales will follow.

Google-driven buying

Before Google, buyers got about 20% of their questions answered prior to contacting the selling company—then called the company to get the remaining 80% of their questions answered.

Now, with Google, people go online when they're looking for a product or service, and do a search. They get about 80% of their questions answered, using a variety of online sources. Then, only a couple of *very specific* questions remain. All their general questions have been answered. They then contact the companies offering potential solutions, and ask their particular questions.

Salespeople, unfortunately, are trained to answer *general* questions. Customers coming to them, in our Google-equipped buying world, have already gotten the answers to those basic questions, and now need information that the salesperson doesn't have. By the time your customer comes to your salesperson, thanks to diligent and motivated online pre-purchase research, she often knows more about the product than your salesperson does!

When asked a specific question that he doesn't know the answer to, your salesperson will brush off the customer with something he makes up on the spot. Or, he will answer a question the customer didn't ask, the one that he knows the answer to. It's the old politician's trick—answer the question you want to answer, not the one they asked.

This doesn't lead to a sale. It leads to a disappointed, frustrated buyer, a salesperson who can't close the deal, and a company that could have increased its revenue, but didn't.

Similarly, your website may answer general questions well, but not the specific ones that your real customers are asking. You are losing sales because of this.

Your Web content has to work harder and be more relevant than ever. Yet Web content is something that CEOs often marginalize. It's an afterthought for many CEOs, who assume that their professional-looking but generic brochure-like website is sufficient for today's buyers. Instead, it doesn't satisfy the buyer. It just teases him. It looks like it's going to answer his questions, but doesn't answer the questions that must be answered for the sale to be made.

How can you find out what your customers' specific questions are? Ask them! When you interview them, ask, "What questions or concerns did you have, as you were considering our product?" Also ask salespeople and customer service people what questions customers are asking. Document the questions and concerns people have. This information is critical to increasing your revenue.

All of the questions that customers ask—and their appropriate answers— should go into a searchable database, along with the answers that actually satisfy customers. That database should be available to everyone in your company. It should also be available on your website, in a form that makes it easy for customers to use.

Want an example? Think Amazon.com. Jeff Bezos has built a whole business on databases made available via a customer-friendly website. It's so well designed that the technology is invisible. You just do what you want to do, without ever thinking, *OK, how do I do this next step?* That's how easy it should be for your customers to get their questions answered.

Right now, your marketing plan is crippled by insider subjectivity. Marketing plans built by non-customer-driven people end up being a hodgepodge of pet methods and channels, previous successes (almost always irrelevant), appealing vendor offers, and marketing fads. Let's look at how these bad marketing decisions affect your sales.

PET CHANNELS

Before:

"I'm really good at search engine marketing. That's where we should be putting the bulk of our budget."

"I read *The Wall Street Journal* online. It's a great way to reach top executives like me. We should be advertising there."

"Email is the only way to go. We should be using email to reach our potential customers."

"We absolutely must be in all the social media spaces. Everybody is there now."

I've heard those comments, word-for-word, dozens of times. In psychology, it's called "projection." We assume that because we like something or do something, our customers will also. These subjective, personal preferences infect every marketing plan. They seldom, if ever, result in increased sales. Meanwhile, your customers are somewhere else, looking for a product like yours.

After:

It doesn't matter what you—or anyone who works for you or influences you—finds compelling. All that matters is what your customers prefer, and what they actually do. Where are they? What are they reading and viewing? How do they want you to communicate with them?

Asking customers will give you the answers to these questions. Their answers will make it possible to profit from the right methods and safely avoid the ones that won't pay off.

PREVIOUS SUCCESSES

Before:

A company hires a new marketing manager. She is hired because she was successful at her previous company. Unfortunately, her new situation is completely different—even if the new company is in the same industry, and sells the same kind of product.

Why? Because companies are unique. One of a kind. The CEO is different, so the character of the company—and the decisions the CEO has made while building the company—are different than any other. The people he hires, and the way they do things, is different. The way the company does things is what determines how the customer is treated, and how the product or service is designed, created, promoted, and supported.

So many CEOs make the mistake of thinking that if they just imitate some other company, they will succeed as the other company did. It never works. Yes, I said *never*. I'll say it another way: it is guaranteed to fail.

When the new marketing manager starts her new job, she begins by doing what she knows how to do—what she did at the last company. It won't work in the new company the way it worked in the previous company.

It takes time—and money—for the failure to become obvious, which is one of the problems with marketing in general. Mistakes aren't immediately apparent.

By the time the CEO realizes that the marketing manager's program is not working, serious opportunities have been squandered. Potential customers have gone elsewhere because their needs were not addressed. The CEO will have to scramble to get everything back on the right track.

The first thing the CEO will do is fire the marketing manager and hire someone new. Someone who was successful at another company, using a specific method. Someone who will now attempt to apply that method to this new situation.

The pattern repeats. If this keeps up long enough, no amount of financing will be sufficient to keep the company alive in the absence of real incoming revenue from customers.

After:

You will use your own previous successes with your own customers and your own product/service to determine what your customers expect from you and how they want to buy from you. What you will be doing is reverse-engineering a successful sale so you can manufacture similar sales in quantity.

Of course, when you use your own successes to create further successes, you will avoid hiring someone who will take your company for a ride down their own inappropriate and unprofitable memory lane.

APPEALING VENDOR OFFERS

Before:

You're listening to a very intriguing voicemail. Someone named David, a producer for a cable business program, wants to feature your company on the program! Well, that makes your day. When you call him back, he describes how he's selected your company in particular, how he's going to send in a video crew, and how your company is going to be featured on a business program that runs on X number of cable channels. Plus, when you're done, you'll have your own video to use however you like. You're thrilled.

It isn't until the very end of the conversation, after you've set a day for "the shoot," that David mentions "a small production fee." That small fee turns out to be $17,000. You gulp, but you think, *may as well, it will be worth it,* and you go ahead.

Too bad. You've just been suckered into one of the most successful scams going. The "professional crew" will consist of a second-grade videographer and one assistant. They won't do a good job, and the video won't be worth anywhere near what you paid for it. Yes, your video will run on the promised number of cable channels ... at 4AM, on a program that is obviously a string of infomercials. A program that none of your prospective customers are watching.

This scam is just one example. There are dozens of others. Companies selling media space—in print and online—can make some very attractive offers, tempting because of all the exposure they promise, and for an unbeatable price. But what if your *customers* never go there—or pay attention? What if they never respond to that type of ad? Getting a bargain price on something that your customers won't pay any attention to isn't a bargain. It's an expensive mistake.

After:

You will consider vendor offers only *after* you have interviewed customers and you *know* what they respond to. Where did they look for you? How did they look for you? For example, you will know that they aren't watching business cable channels at 4 AM. You will know that they go to Google first, and you will know the search terms they are typing in.

Once you have the answers to these questions, you will be able to go to the specific vendors whose media channels will place you in front of your customers. Your own customers will have told you that this is where they would expect to find you. You'll still be able to get some great deals. Media outlets are always hungry. You will also be able to avoid channels (anything on which your message can be displayed) that simply aren't going to work for you.

MARKETING FADS

Before:

Means of reaching customers come and go. Some stick—as a portion of the marketing mix—while most quickly fade into oblivion.

These means are the tools of the trade for marketers. Consultants and in-house marketing people *must* jump on the bandwagon when a new channel emerges in order to be a part of the in crowd. They cannot stand—or afford—to be left behind, for the sake of their careers. They will tell you, sounding like a teenager talking to her parent, that "everybody is doing it." They will use your budget to play with the new toy. Will those efforts pay off? Maybe. Probably not. You won't know until after the money has been spent, and your opportunity window has closed.

As you and others try to deal with the realities of a new fad—and experience the limitations of the method—the same bloggers and reporters who breathlessly touted the method will start to trash it.

Meanwhile, all through this cycle, one thing never changes. Customers are always trying to buy products and services from companies, and companies are making it difficult, partly because they are distracted by marketing fads. It's as if customers come to your "store," hoping to buy, and you're too busy to pay much attention to them. The message they get from you: "Don't bother me right now, I'm working on my social media strategy."

After:

When you interview customers, you'll discover how they search for—and buy—products and services like yours. You'll find out which sites or communities they turn to when they start their buying process. You'll learn what they care about and what they do in pursuit of a solution. You'll still need to test different approaches within each type of channel, such as headlines, copy, and frequency.

You will still need to test different ways of interacting with your customers—and test different ways of letting your customers interact with each other, because just changing a few words can have a significant impact on response. But because you are driven by what your customers have told you, you will at least be spending money and effort where it will do you the most good.

When you interview customers, you'll ask them which terms they used when they started their search for your solution, and the refinements they made to those terms as they went along. Once you have their answers, you can test those words and phrases in paid ads, in addition to adding them to your search engine keyword list. Paid search engine ads make it easy to test and perfect your concepts and copy.

Fads come and go. Stay in touch with your customers and you will know which new methods they are adopting or ignoring as they make purchases.

Be where the money is—
get a head start on your competition

Interviews I conduct for my clients give us deep, early insights on industry trends. We know what is going to happen, *two to six months* before others get wind of the trend. Yes, even now, in this age of instant communications.

Why? Because customers tell us what they're thinking and what they're going to do. Then they do it. In time, those customer movements become obvious to everyone. Meanwhile, my clients are taking advantage of the new trends, because they know—before anyone else does—what customers are thinking. They know what their customers' needs are, what their customers wish someone would do to meet those needs, and where those customers are looking for solutions to their needs.

Customer perceptions, needs, and concerns are what move markets one way or another. If you know what they're thinking and doing, you will know where your market is going next. And you'll be way ahead of your competition.

Don't mistake general trends in the broader marketplace for the trends that will help you in your own niche. General trends may or may not be important to the growth of your business. They could be a major, money-losing distraction! What you need to know is what *your* potential customers are thinking.

When potential customers are *thinking* of moving in a certain direction— when they begin to feel a specific need—it's time to gear up your business to meet that need. That's the right time to jump onto the new trend.

It's invigorating and profitable in the middle of a river of revenue. Rivers change course; when they do, you have to change with them.

EVEN THOUGH IT MAKES PERFECT SENSE TO ALTER YOUR ORGANIZATION SO IT SUPPORTS THE CUSTOMERS' BUYING PROCESS, IT WILL NOT BE EASY

All of the momentum in your company—in any company—is always heading toward the company-centered direction. Keep this in mind as you move forward, so you are prepared when you meet resistance, and have a complete program in place to overcome it.

Companies are like private clubs. The customer is just another outsider, unless the company's leader makes a concerted, ongoing effort to bring the customers' needs and perceptions into the organization. This book will give you the tools you need to do that, but you'll still have to make the effort, and stick to it when you get "push back."

That's what Lou Gerstner used to call it, when he'd come back from his customer visits. He would share his new customer-centric insights with his managers at IBM, and then he'd get "push back." He probably heard what I've heard from IBMers—and people in all other companies:

- "We can't do that. We only know how to do it the way we do it."

- "We can't do that. We're not set up for it."

- "We can't do that. It's too hard to change our systems."

- "We can't do that. We tried it in 1987 and it didn't work."

- "We can't do that. The VPs will never go for it."

- "We can't do that. No one is doing that now. Everyone is doing [some other thing]."

Someone has to represent the customer to your organization. That someone has to have the political clout to give the customer a powerful voice, inside the company. A voice that employees will pay attention to. That someone should be you—the leader of the company. No one else has as much political clout as you do.

I've seen product managers, sales managers, and marketing managers try to represent the customer to the company. They all failed. They just didn't have the political clout to overpower that insider's club mentality and momentum. If the CEO isn't speaking up for the customers, there's nothing that anyone else can do—regardless of their position—that will turn the company into a customer-centric organization.

So it's really up to you. It's your job. It may even be your most important job. Everything comes from revenue, and all revenue comes from customers. If you have enough revenue coming in, you can do whatever you need to do.

That's the end of the Before and After pictures. Now we will begin the step-by-step instructions, so you can create your own roadmap to higher revenue.

THE WORK AHEAD

You can't make The Shift from company-centered to customer-centric without interviewing your customers. But there is more to it than just finding out what they want to buy from you and how they want to buy it.

You have to analyze that knowledge, turn it into an Action Plan, and get everyone in your company involved.

If you don't, you won't really be making The Shift. You'll still be "marketing and selling," while *trying* to make The Shift. You'll still have all the problems I've listed in this chapter, plus the complication of everyone thinking, *the Boss wants us to do this Shift thing, but I'm not clear what I should do, and I have a deadline to meet right now.* You'll be confusing matters, instead of bringing wonderful new clarity to your revenue-generating activities.

Here's the entire Roadmap to Revenue process. There are three basic steps. While subsequent chapters describe the steps in detail, this summary provides the big picture of the Roadmap as you make The Shift—aligning your organization with your customers' buying process.

ROADMAP TO REVENUE: THE THREE STEPS

Step 1: Discover. *Find out what they want and how they want to go about buying it.*

You will interview customers to find out what they need and how they want to buy. During the interviews, customers will also give you additional critical information, such as their perceptions of your company, products, services, and website; trends they see; how they're using technology to make purchases; and what they think of your competition.

The information gathered in the initial interviews will be turned into two reports: a Conversation Report and a Summary/Recommendations Report. The Conversation Report will contain the customers' comments, categorized by subject. The Summary/Recommendations Report will contain summaries of what your customers said and recommendations on how the company can solve the problems raised by customers.

These reports will reveal what is broken and what is working. You will know what customers want to buy from you, how they want to buy, and which aspects of your product or service they find most appealing. It is never what you assume; customers will say things that surprise you, and make you realize you've been moving in the wrong direction in some areas of your business.

Step 2: Debate. *Resolve the differences between what they want versus what you have to sell, and how they buy versus how you sell.*

Once your "brain trust" has read these reports, it's time to hold a Brainstorming and Planning Meeting. On the first day, you will:

- **Analyze, discuss, and prioritize what customers have said.** The findings of your customer research will be presented to the people in the room (usually consisting of top management, sales, marketing, product management, and Web folks). Use Post-It® easel pad sheets to list the issues most important to customers—and all of the other issues, trends, perceptions, needs, and buying process data uncovered in the interviews. Everyone in the room will now be aware of what customers want, the problems that need to be solved, your strengths and weaknesses, and the barriers to the sale.

- **Agree on the essence of your promise to customers.** Customers are attracted to companies and their products or services because they expect to find a solution there. Promises are made, by the company, to the customer, about the company and its products/services. The customer expects those promises to be kept. This is where you will identify and articulate the promises customers *want* you to keep—and ones that you *can* keep.

Step 3: Deploy. *Document your customer's buying process so you can support them every step of the way, then build an action plan.*

On the second day of your Brainstorming and Planning Meeting, you will:

- **Build a Buying Process Roadmap.** Using the information gathered in interviews, and the experience of your salespeople, marketing people, and Web people, you will build a Buying Process Roadmap for each of your products and services. The Roadmaps will show the different stages of the customers' buying process. For each stage, you will list who is involved in the buying decision, the concerns they have and the actions they take, and the tools you will use to address those concerns, answer their questions and make it easy for them to take the next step. The Buying Process Roadmap will align your sales, marketing, and Web teams. Everyone in the room will understand their role in supporting the customers' buying process.

- **Build your Revenue Growth Action Plan.** You'll want to fix what is broken and improve what needs improving. You will create a master "to-do" list. Each item on the list will have a description of the issue, the recommended solution, the steps involved, the owner, the due date, and the status.

As you go forward, with the Buying Process Roadmap as your guide, you will build, implement, and then fine-tune your lead acquisition and lead conversion activities. You will institute methods for obtaining customer needs and preferences data. After the meeting, you'll have weekly meetings where everyone can report on their progress (or completion). If anything is falling behind schedule, you'll figure out how to get it moving again. The Action Plan must include the processes and systems for continuing to interview customers and gather data from customers when they interact with your customer-facing people. Processes must then be set up so the data leads to action.

The revenue-killing momentum caused by insider mentality is like a boulder that must be pushed up a hill. Stop pushing, and it will roll over you. Over time, as you make The Shift from a company-centered mentality to a customer-centric mentality, the boulder will decrease in size. Don't be surprised if it takes a year for The Shift to take place. Don't relax even then. There will always be negative forces at work, trying to separate you from your customers' realities. You can't afford for that to happen. Customer realities drive your revenue.

Of course, even the small, immediate changes you start to make will make it easier for people to find you, understand what you are selling, and buy from you—even before you have fully instituted The Shift. Their questions will be answered in a way that satisfies them and takes them comfortably to the next step in their buying process. One by one, their concerns will be addressed and eliminated, and they will gladly make a purchase.

The initial, incremental changes in the way you market and sell will move your revenue needle in the positive direction.

Note that the Roadmap to Revenue method is not a one-time fix. As you make changes using these methods, new issues and situations will arise. You won't know about them unless you are continually interviewing customers and incorporating their input into the way you run your business.

That's the overview. Now on to the specifics.

ROADMAP STEP #1: DISCOVER

FIND OUT
WHAT THEY WANT
AND HOW THEY WANT TO BUY IT

Your journey to higher revenues starts with customer interviews. This chapter will tell you how to do the interviews correctly, so you obtain the information that you need.

You should conduct at least five of the initial interviews yourself. This will help you personally understand your customers, their situations, and their buying process. It will also help you manage anyone who may be conducting additional interviews for you.

Once you have overcome your initial hesitation, you will find that you enjoy doing the interviews yourself. You will also find that the results of the interviews will help you see your business in a new light. Don't be surprised if you want to conduct many additional interviews yourself.

Once you have interviewed customers, you will be able to confidently represent the customer, inside your company. You will know when something that an employee tells you about customers rings true (or not), because you have heard what customers say—yourself.

Customers will tell you things when being interviewed that they will never tell you while you are selling to them—or even in any other type of situation, such as a social event. People only reveal this information when asked and asked in the right way—a way that makes it easy for them to give you all the important details, and to tell you the whole truth.

To make this section as readable as possible, I will write as if you are the interviewer. Anyone who interviews your customers should also read this chapter. You and the interviewer should discuss these instructions and advice, prior to the interviewer calling customers.

You only have the opportunity to interview each customer once. You won't want to waste that invaluable opportunity. It's important to do it right.

The methods described and recommended in this chapter have been conceived, tested, and refined over the course of thousands of customer interviews, across dozens of industries, for hundreds of companies. If you follow the instructions carefully, your customers will react as predicted, and you will achieve the results you need to make revenue-increasing decisions.

This chapter is fairly long and detailed, because the interviews are a foundation of the revenue-growth process. There are also a number of techniques that will ensure your interviews are successful.

In this chapter we will cover:

- Whom you should interview

- How many customers you should interview

- How to make appointments for the interviews

- How long each interview should last

- Who should make the calls

- How to behave during the interview

- How to record the conversation

- The questions you should ask

- Examples of customer comments

- How to get the conversations transcribed

- How to organize conversational transcriptions into a Conversation Report

- How to build the Executive Summary and Recommendations Report

- What you can expect when you distribute the reports

Before we go into the specifics of the Roadmap to Revenue interviewing technique, I need to address one question that often arises: "Why the telephone? Why not email or some other form of interactive communication?

Especially now—in the age of social networks and instant messaging?"

Because you want to *hear* the person. You want to *get to know* the person. That person is one of the most important people in your life, because that person holds the keys to your financial future. The best way to get to know someone is to have a conversation with them.

I have tested all types of surveying methods. I have concluded that:

- People talk most freely if they are on the phone, in their comfort zone, sitting in their home, car, or office

- People are very hesitant to reveal everything they're thinking when conversing in person, in any setting. Too many psychological factors come into play when you're face-to-face.

- People tend to be more confident and more willing to state their opinions when they're talking on the phone

- People will say things on the phone they wouldn't dream of saying in an email or text message, an online survey, or a social media site. This is especially true if you are selling a business-to-business product or service, but it applies to any type of consumer. People know that emails and instant messages are permanent and public forms of communication. They know that whatever they say in text form could well be "on the record." So they hold back.

- In-person interviews are essential when you're hiring someone. But when you are trying to determine a buyer's deepest concerns and perceptions, the phone is a superior investigative tool.

Check-the-box and multiple-choice surveys are flawed from the start because the questions are composed by people who haven't been talking to customers. The real issues in the customer's mind are not addressed in the survey. How many times have you been surveyed—online or by phone—and your real, honest answer wasn't included in the choices offered? When I've said to a surveyor, "None of those answers match my situation," the surveyor replies, "Well, I'll just say choice B, then." I cringe, because I know that these flawed results are going to be used by company executives to make flawed decisions.

Focus groups are inherently problematic:

- Focus groups gather strangers in a room, in an uncomfortable, stilted environment—a far cry from your customer's personal and private work or home environment. The participants know they are being watched, and it makes them nervous and guarded.

- The most influential customers typically decline to participate in a focus group. Getting a stale sandwich and $75 for a half day is not even close to being an attractive offer to a busy executive or consumer.

- Once the participants are gathered, a group dynamic develops. There is the "dominator," who starts to lead the group. There are plenty of wallflowers who are more than happy to let the dominator dominate. There may be people with interesting and helpful things to say, but they are not going to say them in front of the other people in the room.

- Yes, there are superior focus group moderators who can still extract some useful information from focus group participants, in spite of these drawbacks. But they are rare. When I've sat with clients behind the one-way glass, the moderators often fail to drill down on the important hints that participants are dropping.

- People will not say everything they're really thinking while sitting in a focus group. They certainly aren't going to admit anything that might embarrass them or their company.

- The real truth remains hidden, which means the results are misleading—and the decisions made using these results will not lead to success

- Bringing up a problem in a focus group does not hold the promise of something being done about it. On the other hand, if the CEO or someone who has been hired by the CEO is conducting an interview, the person being interviewed will believe that something positive will happen as a result of the interview. This always encourages the person to tell you everything he or she thinks might be useful.

Social media sites and platforms give you great ways to have two-way conversations with your customers. But those conversations don't convey the full picture, nor the relative importance of each issue. They contain bits and pieces of disconnected information. It is easy to become so distracted by the latest discussion or crisis that you never focus on the big picture that will get your ship moving in a customer-pleasing direction. In order to do that, you need to understand all the forces at work. You need to aggregate all the issues into a comprehensive picture—a snapshot in time—that will be valid for months to come. And, most importantly, you need to understand their thought patterns during the buying process. You can't get this from social media.

The interviewing techniques in this book will help you hear the small inflections that can lead to new revelations. The person you're interviewing on the phone might answer your question with a hesitant "yes." You will—and you should—pick up on the hesitation. The customer is inviting you to pursue a problem that they are reluctant to bring up without some encouragement. You'll say, "You don't sound completely convinced. Was there a problem?" The customer will then feel free to tell you the *real* story.

No matter how automated the world gets, it is still human beings who buy your products and services. Interacting with them impersonally through your keyboard will not give you the data you need about customer perceptions and buying decisions.

Even though I am constantly assimilating new technologies, I have *still* found that a properly conducted telephone interview is the most efficient and reliable way to get the data you need to grow your revenue. That is why it's an essential component of the Roadmap to Revenue method.

WHOM YOU SHOULD INTERVIEW

If you are an established company already selling a product or service, you should interview your current customers. Your customers will give you the information you need. You should interview current customers because:

- They know more about your company than you think they do

- They will be able to describe their buying process, their concerns, how you allayed their concerns, what they like about your product or service, and other information that is essential to revenue growth

- They will have good suggestions for you, because they have thought about what you could do to improve

- They will be glad that you will be doing something useful with the data, and that the data will help others

- They have an interest in your success, because they are already somewhat dependent on your company, due to their purchase

So many times, as I've presented interview results to top executives, they're amazed at how much customers know about their business. At first, it is unsettling to them, but then they start to realize the value of knowing what customers are thinking. They recognize that it is far better to know—and be able to do something—than to continue operating without that knowledge.

If you are starting a new business or are introducing a new product or service, you (obviously) have no current customers. You will have to find and interview prospective buyers. How to do this is covered on page 43. For now we will assume you have a list of customers or prospects you can call. Once you have that list in hand, the procedures are the same.

If you are selling one type of product or service to one type of customer, and there are no significant differences in their buying processes, there is no need to divide customers into categories.

If you are selling to several different types of customers, or have several product lines, you will want to divide your customers into categories to make sure that you understand the buying process for each one. Every business is unique, so these categories should be adjusted to fit your business and situation.

Here are some examples of categories my clients and I have used. We typically end up with two or three categories from which we draw the list of customers. That will probably be true for you as well.

- Product or service purchased
- Size of customer's business
- Length of time they are engaged in the buying process
- Type of person (by title, role, etc.)
- Amount of purchase
- Length of relationship with company
- Geographic location
- Industry
- The customer's satisfaction level
- Repeat or one-time customer
- Salesperson associated with the customer
- Division associated with the customer (for large enterprises)

The customer categories you decide on must reflect the mix of customers served by your business. If the data are skewed in favor of one group over another, you won't be able to sell effectively to the short-changed groups.

Since your goal is to reverse-engineer successful sales and then manufacture them in quantity, you will want to make sure that the majority of the people you interview are your most profitable customers—those who purchased most quickly, bought the most, and/or required the least after-sale assistance.

You will want your customer interview list to include unhappy customers as well as satisfied customers, so you know the problems you should be solving. However, the bulk of the people you talk to should be satisfied, because you are going to be building a buying process model that reflects a successful sale.

If the bulk of the people who make the buying decision for your product are IT managers in large businesses, at least 60% of the people you talk to should be IT managers. If they must get approval from a CEO or CFO before they can make the purchase, at least 30% of the people you talk to should be in this "approver" category.

All of this is just common sense. The main point is, you will want to make sure you consider the categories carefully as you create the interview list, selecting and weighing the participants, so you end up with a representative sample of your company's customers. You won't want to conduct a number of interviews and then realize, in the next phase of the process, that you overlooked an important group.

The response rate you get to your initial survey request email will be one out of every three customers you contact, so the list should contain three times as many customers as you hope to talk to, in total.

Build your interview list using a customer calls spreadsheet. Columns should include the name, title, company name, email, phone number, the category (or categories) the customer fits into, a little information about the customer, and the status of your interviewing efforts.

Name	Title	Company Name	E-mail	Phone number	Category	Addl Info	Status
Joe Smith	President	Blast, Inc	JS@blast.com	555-555-5555	Contractor	Sale took 3 weeks, came in via Google	9/25 - Sent interview request e-mail

What if you don't have any customers yet? Obviously, if you are already selling an existing product or service, and those *same* customers are prime candidates for your *new* product or service, you can call your current customers.

If you're just starting a new business or introducing a new product or service to a new set of customers, you won't be able to interview existing customers. You'll have to find likely prospects to interview. Your goal will be to learn how they buy products and services that are similar to yours.

Fortunately we live in an age where social networks make it easy to put the word out. Now you can tell many people that you're looking for people to interview about their buying process for your type of product/service. You should also ask your family, friends, and business contacts to refer you to people who might be interested in your type of product/service. Another technique is to produce a document that describes your product or service, and offer it on your website. Those who sign up to download it will make good interviewing candidates.

Once you know whom you are going to call, create the interview list and the call status spreadsheet, just like the one shown above for existing customers. Create an interview request email using the methods described below. If someone referred you to a person you want to interview, obviously you will want to mention the person who referred you as part of your email. I recommend including that person's name in the subject line.

Your response rate to your emails to prospective customers will probably be as low as one out of ten, so you'll have to work extra hard to obtain enough people to interview. And, because they won't have specific experience with your product/service, their advice won't be as helpful as it would be if you were calling current customers. Again, make sure you talk to enough people so that you are seeing definite trends. You will know you've talked to enough people when you hear them say the same things, using the same words and phrases.

When you come across really good interviewees, invite them to participate in the evaluation of the new product or service. As soon as you have created something people can use, contact these people. You should also invite others in your social network to test it as well. It's up to you how many people you involve in your market test. You'll want to strike a balance. Too many, and you're basically giving the product or service away to those who would have bought it. Too few, and you won't have the market data you need to proceed. You'll need to interview at least ten people in a given category to start getting useful trend data.

Once you've acquired customers, and they've had enough time to try out the product or service, it's time to make further calls.

The input you get will keep you on the right path in the early stages of your business and beyond.

What if you sell through distribution channels? Some products aren't sold directly to customers. They are sold through retailers or distributors. If that is your situation, how do you find customers to call?

One way, of course, is to obtain customer information from the retailer, if they are able and willing to give it to you. If that isn't possible, include an offer in the packaging of your product that gives customers some incentive to contact you or register with you. Incentives can include a free accessory, tips on how to use your product, or a chance to win a prize of some sort. (Keep in mind that any sweepstakes or contest will need to conform to legal requirements for such activities.)

When they contact you, respond to them immediately. Their purchase will still be fresh in their minds, and they will be impressed that you responded so quickly. Depending on the type of product you sell, or the type of customer you sell to, you may wish to contact them by phone rather than emailing them first. Be respectful of their time; if you must call them at dinnertime, use that call to set up an appointment that will work better for them.

If you can, sell a version of your product through your own website, in addition to selling it through distribution channels. Offering some version of your product directly to customers will supply you with a steady stream of customers who will give you their contact information. Of course, you will want to make sure that you aren't undercutting your distributors on price. Always offer your products for full price when you sell them direct.

How do personas factor into the Roadmap method?

Personas, in case you're not familiar with the term, are the character profiles you can build to represent a typical or most desirable customer. For example, a persona might be "Sally," a 30-ish career woman who is the prime buyer for your product or service. Or, "John," an IT manager at a large company.

Personas are usually used to make decisions about the design of e-commerce sites, so that the sites do a good job of meeting the needs of the typical or most desirable customers.

As with all things marketing, they can be useful—and they can also be misused.

When and how personas are useful:

- Building personas helps to make customers "real" to company insiders.

- Using a persona to represent a type of customer whom you want to reach, but are not currently reaching, can be helpful until you have real, live customers that you can actually interview. At the very least, it will get everyone thinking about the customers' perspective and needs. It can also be helpful when you are designing a product or service.

- It's easier to discuss various product/service and marketing changes when you are talking about "what Sally would want," rather than discussing customers in vague, generic terms.

When and how personas can be misused (and misleading):

- It's quite common to make incorrect assumptions about Sally and what Sally would do when you're building the Sally persona. For example, you might assume that Sally won't read a long landing page because she's a really busy person, when in fact, because of the complexity of your product/service and the importance of the buying decision, Sally may want you to publish more information, not less. People are perfectly happy to scroll if the information is essential to them.

- Creating a persona is not the same as hearing from real customers, who are having difficulties as they try to buy or use your product or service. It's humbling to find out that your shopping cart is frustrating or that your search function doesn't really work for them. These are the issues that are driving your customers crazy now. These issues won't come up in any discussions about a persona, because personas are created by company insiders. I've also seen company insiders create either unflattering personas, or personas that are far more patient and accommodating than their real customers are. Inaccurate or disrespectful personas can lead to incorrect and costly decisions about website navigation.

- Before you even think about going after new types of customers, and establishing personas to represent them, you need to make sure that you have eliminated the barriers to the sale encountered by your current customers. Doing so will help you as you start selling to new customers.

- Real customers are real people who will surprise you. Personas that we create are not going to surprise us, because we created them. Real customers surprise real sellers all the time—and real customers are the only real source of revenue. Pay more attention to real customers than you do to the perfect customers floating around in your imagination.

No persona is complete without a Buyer Scenario

Yes, it's important to know who your customer is. It's even more important to know what your customer wants. Every buyer, as he starts his buying process, has a "scenario" in his head. He is imagining the perfect solution, and the perfect buying process. This is the Buyer Scenario.

How close you come to the ideal Buyer Scenario will determine how successful you are in selling to your customer. Let's imagine that Sally wants to buy a pair of denim stretch shorts. Her perfect Buyer Scenario is to type "denim stretch shorts" into Google, and the perfect pair appears, right on top, at a fantastic price—let's say $15 a pair.

Sally types "denim stretch shorts" into Google and is immediately faced with the fact that most denim stretch shorts are hip-huggers. Sally prefers more coverage. So now she has to figure out what the fashionistas are calling shorts and pants that reach up to the waist, not ones that fall short.

After some digging, she finds the term: "natural waist." She adds "natural waist" to her search phrase. Now she starts to see more relevant results. She finds a pair that looks pretty good, at NewportNews.com. They have shorts in her size, in the style she wants. She decides to order one pair, and if she likes that pair, she will order more later.

She wants the checkout process to be fast. It is. She gets the shorts in a couple of days, they fit perfectly, and she goes back to NewportNews.com and orders more.

Problem solved—as she hoped it would be.

You can know every little detail about the Sally persona, but if you're not living up to her ideal Buyer Scenario, you're not meeting her needs—or making the sale.

HOW MANY CUSTOMERS YOU SHOULD INTERVIEW

If you interview customers correctly, you will only need to interview seven to fifteen people in each of your categories. Because the interviews will be in-depth conversations, you will start to see definite trends after the fifth complete interview. In other words, you will hear the same basic issues raised by each customer. Customers who have never spoken to each other will even use the same exact phrases to describe a perception or situation. By the tenth interview, the main themes will be firmly established. By the fifteenth interview, there will be no doubt in your mind about the big issues. You will also start getting ideas about how to solve the problems people are having with your website, products, policies, and people.

This "five/ten/fifteen" rule holds true no matter what you are selling, the complexity and length of your sales cycle, the types of customers you sell to, or the industry you are in.

If you have multiple categories of customers, at the *minimum,* you will want to have good interviews with five customers in a given category. To be safe, make it ten. If you really want to make sure that you aren't missing anything, talk to fifteen.

Not all customers will respond to your request for an interview. As I mentioned earlier, I have found that about one third to one half of the people you contact via email will respond, provided you use the right subject line (see below). Because of this normal response rate, as I mentioned, you will want to send your email to three times the number of people you need to interview.

If the email comes directly from you, the business owner or CEO, you may have a higher response rate.

Testing Solutions

One of my Fortune 100 clients was so accustomed to doing things on a large scale that they weren't comfortable with me speaking to "only" fifteen people in each category. They insisted that I talk to forty people in each category, in spite of my protests. As I predicted, the five/ten/fifteen rule held true.

By the time I was talking to the twelfth person in any category, I had started to formulate solutions. I was able to start testing these solutions on the subsequent calls—after the customer I was interviewing had given me all of his input. I only offered these solutions after hearing everything the customer had to say in answer to my interview questions.

Customers' reactions to the solutions I described were always positive; it's only logical, since the solutions resulted directly from earlier conversations with customers who were having the same problems.

HOW TO MAKE APPOINTMENTS FOR THE INTERVIEWS

Send an email to the person asking if you can interview her. Ask her when it would be convenient to talk.

Here's what an email would look like if it was coming from you, in your role as the head of your company:

Subject line:

Would like to interview you

Email text:

Dear Susan:

I am making sure I hear what our customers have to say. I would like to interview you at your convenience, to find out how you feel about our product, hear about your experiences with our company, and ask you what trends you see in your industry right now.

Would you be able to talk sometime next week? I can call you at the time we agree to. The number I have for you is 550-557-5555.

John Smith

CEO of WebWidgets, Inc.

Here's what an email would look like if it was coming from an interviewer you had hired for your company:

Subject line:

Would like to interview you for WebWidgets

Email text:

Dear Susan:
I have been hired by John Smith, the CEO of WebWidgets, to interview some WebWidgets customers. I would like to interview you to learn how you feel about the WebWidgets product, hear about your experiences with the company, and ask you what trends you see in your industry right now.
Do you have any time over the next week? I can call you at the time we agree to. The number I have for you is 550-557-5555.
Thanks,
[your first name]
[your official company signature]

The subject line tells Susan what you expect of her. The "interviewing" aspect is a bit flattering. And, the mention of the company name helps, since Susan is a customer of WebWidgets. She will know that this isn't spam. All of these factors will make it more likely that Susan will open up the email.

When Susan responds to your email, you can set up the appointment and update the customer call spreadsheet. Obviously, you will then call the person at the preferred number, at the appointed time.

If you are selling a "business to consumer" product, the second sentence in the first paragraph would read: "I would like to interview you to learn how you feel about the WebWidgets product, hear about your experiences with the company, and ask what trends you see with our type of product."

HOW LONG EACH INTERVIEW SHOULD LAST

A complete interview should last about an hour, give or take fifteen minutes. This is the norm, if you are doing your job correctly.

If the interview takes less than an hour, because the person just doesn't have much to say or ended up in a time crunch, I count it as "half" or even a "third" of an interview, and make additional calls to make up the difference.

An hour is the normal amount of time for a business meeting. Any business-to-business customer who sets up a time to talk will agree to set aside an hour, if you ask properly.

If you are interviewing consumer-product customers, the amount of time will vary depending on the complexity of the product and the depth of their passion for the subject. You might be surprised at the amount of knowledge your customers have about your product, your competition, and, of course, their own buying process. It's easy for an interview to fill an hour, even for "simple" products, when the knowledge and passion are there.

If you're a busy executive, listening to several customers for an hour each may seem almost impossible. But you're already having dozens of hour-long meetings each week in which decisions are being made without the benefit of this revenue-driving information. My own experience has convinced me that once you bite the bullet and invest some time, you will wish you'd done it sooner.

WHO SHOULD MAKE THE CALLS

As the leader of your company, you should make at least five of the first calls yourself. You should also insist that others involved in marketing (marketing managers and product managers) make at least five calls each.

Make the calls until you are comfortable doing it, are enjoying the interaction with customers, and are hearing the same basic issues raised in each new call. At this stage, it is safe—and even advisable—to turn some of the interviewing over to an outside consultant.

When customers talk to an outsider, they will open up more. People are always a bit reserved while talking to company insiders. The words they use and the emotions they display will be subdued when they are talking to people who are directly involved with the product or service. They are trying to be nice. When they talk to a consultant, their words and emotions will be much stronger. The stronger responses will be helpful in getting everyone to understand the seriousness of the deficiencies.

I had a situation once where the customer was *furious* because my client's product—a large manufacturing machine that the customer had spent millions on—kept breaking down. He was absolutely livid in the interview call; when the machine was down, he was unable to produce products and fill orders. His business was basically dead, because the machine wasn't working. Since his problems were so acute, I asked him if he would like to talk to the company's CEO (I already knew the CEO would want to do this). The customer consented.

I got them on the phone together, and when I did, the customer was about 70% less furious. He still described his problem in detail. He didn't leave anything out. But the seriousness of the situation certainly didn't come through as clearly as it did in the original call.

This is why I recommend that you make some calls, and your in-house people make some calls, but that you also hire someone you trust to make some—or a majority—of the calls. It's the best way to make sure that you get the whole, unvarnished picture.

I should also mention that salespeople should not make these calls. Even the best salesperson will have a very hard time simply "listening," without jumping in to correct any misperceptions that the person has. Plus, the customer will feel as if she is being sold to, albeit covertly, if a salesperson is the person asking the questions.

Choose your interviewer carefully. Make sure that whoever makes these calls is a professional—not an interview-fatigued, working-by-rote automaton call-center person.

The interviewer should be:

- **Knowledgeable** about your product or service. If the customer being interviewed realizes that the person knows almost everything about your product or service, he will talk freely. If the customer discovers that the interviewer knows very little about the product or service, he will quickly lose interest and terminate the call. It won't take more than a minute or two for the customer to determine how knowledgeable the interviewer is.

- **Personable and friendly,** without being too effusive or affected. The right interviewer is the kind of person whom others naturally trust and confide in.

- **Perceptive** enough to be able to detect subtle openings during the call. The customer will test the interviewer at the beginning of the call, answering a question with a short, but emotionally tinged answer. There is an assumed "but." The customer will then pause, waiting to see if the interviewee will get the hint. A perceptive interviewer will say, "Well, you just said you were satisfied, but it sounds like there was a little doubt in your voice. Was there a problem?" The customer will then go into detail. The interviewer will have passed the test, having earned the trust and respect of the customer.

The idea of getting on the phone with customers may be a daunting prospect if you prefer to communicate via your keyboard. The good news is, you don't need to talk to a lot of people, and you'll be conversing about things you know a lot about. You'll be in your conversational comfort zone. All you have to do is have a few phone conversations, and you'll be miles ahead of where you would have been without that information.

Just to encourage you, at the end of every single interview I've conducted, customers always thank me for interviewing them. They also say, "If you have any other questions, please feel free to contact me." Often, a customer will say, "It really says something about the company that the CEO cared enough to have you call me." Rather than seeing it as an intrusion, they are pleased that someone cared enough to call—and to listen attentively. They are confident that their comments will be heard and heeded.

HOW TO BEHAVE DURING THE INTERVIEW

Interviewing correctly means that you:

- **Actually listen—with your full attention.** If the person you are interviewing thinks, for even a second, that you are bored or disinterested, she will lose interest as well. In an instant, the mood can change from "This has been interesting, so far," to "I must attend to other things now. Sorry I can't talk any longer."

- **Don't let anything distract you,** such as incoming emails or calls, people stopping by your office, instant messages popping up on your screen, and so on. Conduct your interviews in a distraction-free environment.

- **Take notes as she is speaking,** even if you are also recording the call. That way you will have backup data in case you have a problem with the recording, and you can also help the customer get back to her train of thought if she gets interrupted or distracted at some point during the conversation. She will be impressed that you are able to repeat her words back to her, because you had written them down. This will signal to her that you really *were* listening. She'll open up even more.

  Take notes by hand, because the sound of typing in the background will distract the customer. She will start to focus on—and even obsess about—the typing sound. She will wonder: *Am I talking too fast? Is this person managing to get down the important details of everything I'm saying? Is this person pretending to type what I'm saying, but is really just checking email?*

- **Tell her, up front, that all of her comments will go into a report that is categorized by subject, so it is completely anonymous.** Of course you will keep this promise. This allows the person to relax (I often hear customers give a little sigh of relief when they hear this), and she will tell you more than she would otherwise.

- **Don't get defensive,** even if the customer is telling you something that you know isn't true—or that you have since corrected. Let her tell her whole story. At the end of the conversation, you can go back to this subject and explain what you know about that subject, or what has already been done to fix the problem. But don't do that until the end of the interview.

  If you respond while she tells her story, or even right after she tells it, you will appear defensive—even if you try to be calm and dispassionate. Your customer will decide you're not able to hear the truth, and she will clam up.

  Staying silent will take a lot more character and self-discipline than you would think. You will be *burning* to blurt out, "We fixed that two months ago! Didn't you get the email announcing it?" But silence will do you more good than a rant. You'll have to face the fact that if she didn't get the message, a lot of other customers probably didn't either. And, if you are quiet, she may give you a solution that she wouldn't have had a chance to share with you if you had interrupted her.

  Interrupting her will effectively end the interview. She will decide that you aren't really that interested in her needs, perceptions, experiences, and suggestions, and she will find a way to politely—but firmly—end the conversation. Again, at the very end of the interview, bring up the subject, and explain what you have done to fix that particular problem. Ask her what she thinks of the solution.

- **Have your list of questions in front of you,** and move on to the next one once the customer has finished answering the previous question. If the customer answers an upcoming question in the course of answering an earlier question, don't ask the upcoming question. You've already got your answer, and the customer will be seriously disappointed if you ask a question she's already answered.

Some researchers offer the interviewee monetary compensation. I've never done this. I've found that current customers are more than happy to talk, especially when a) they know their comments will be heard at the highest level, b) they will be dominating the conversation, and c) they are free to speak their minds anonymously.

If you want to reward them in some way afterwards, that's fine. A little token of some sort might be entirely appropriate, such as a product sample or discount, or a useful gift. Of course, you could really blow them away and send a hand-written thank-you note—with or without a gift.

You'll be surprised at how helpful people will be, if approached correctly, without any mention of a reward. People like to be helpful when they think it's going to make a difference.

HOW TO RECORD THE CONVERSATION

If you are located in the United States, you should know that some states in the U.S. require that both parties know the conversation is being recorded; others require only that one person knows. U.S. Federal law also requires that one person knows. Because there are penalties involved, please check the information on call recording in your jurisdiction.[2]

Customers will be a little nervous if you tell them you're recording the conversation, but if the law says you must, do it. At the very beginning of the conversation, after you have explained that their comments will go into a report that is anonymous, tell them that you are recording the conversation for your private use only, so the conversation can be transcribed for the sole purpose of accurate transcription, and it will be erased when it is done. Keep these promises.

If you can, use a landline, to ensure a top-quality recording.

To record calls, I use a small earbud mic called the Olympus TP7, available on Amazon.com for about $15.00. I plug it into the mic jack on my personal computer or laptop, and place the earbud mic in my ear. I then use an over-the-ear headset when I make the call. The earbud mic detects both my side of the conversation and the customer's side.

Instead of using an earbud mic, you can pick up the sound directly through a headset plugged into your computer.

This is only the mic, though, which picks up the sound and gives you the *ability* to record. You still need recording software.

You can record the conversation with voice recording software such as ExpressDictate from Australia.[3] There are dozens of recording programs on the market. ExpressDictate has the advantage of an associated dictation playback program called ExpressScribe, and it stores the files in a special

---

[2] www.rcfp.org/taping/states.html

[3] http://www.nch.com

format (believe it or not, it's in the QuarkXpress dictionary file format—.dct). These ".dct" files are much more compact than digital audio files, and can be emailed easily to a transcriber who has the ExpressScribe transcribing software. The ExpressDictate files can also be converted to standard digital audio files, if you wish.

Voice over IP technologies, such as Skype, also often include recording applications, although some of them can act strangely—such as limiting the recording to fifteen minutes, and terminating the call when the software stops recording! Not good. Another problem with computer-based recorders is they don't always give you a visual indictor that the conversation is being recorded.

Whatever you decide to use to record the conversations, test the setup thoroughly before making an actual interview call. It's heartbreaking to have a wonderful conversation with someone, filled with useful insights, and then realize that the recording didn't work. One author I know, who interviews doctors and other business professionals, uses a Skype recording program, but then also records on an old-fashioned cassette recorder, just in case.

Always keep the recorded conversation file on your hard drive until you receive the transcription and are satisfied that the transcriber captured the conversation accurately.

THE QUESTIONS YOU SHOULD ASK

The questions I list below have been refined over the course of thousands of interviews and always result in rich, interesting responses.

Use these questions as the basics. You may want to add others. However, you won't want to ask more than about ten to fifteen primary questions in a one-hour interview. That's all you'll be able to squeeze in. You don't want the person to get question fatigue. It's better to ask fewer, more general questions—which are designed to extract as much relevant information as possible—than to ask many specific questions that might cause you to miss important, high-impact perceptions.

This is not a survey with dozens of questions, which people find boring. This is a *conversation* with someone who will help you to plan a profitable future for your company.

It's fine to ask secondary questions during the course of the conversation, especially if the person says something that you want to learn more about. Ask for more detail or clarification. Make sure you truly understand.

The questions shown below are listed in normal order. Feel free to ask them out of order if it makes more sense to do so in the flow of the conversation.

Again, if the person answers one of the later questions while answering an earlier question, do *not* ask the later question. The interviewee will think you weren't paying attention. She will *immediately* shift into "bored" mode, and find a way to terminate the conversation.

Also, as you listen, make sure she knows you are listening. Do what psychologists do. Say "uh-huh," and "that's interesting." In addition to the questions listed here, ask "drawing out" questions when appropriate, such as, "And how did that work out?"

The primary questions to ask are:

- **What do you think of our [product or service]?** You want as much detail here as possible. Since this is the first question, your interviewee might assume you're looking for a very short answer, such as, "It's good." Tell her to feel free to go into more detail. This will give her permission to do so—and you'll get the information you need.

  If you're selling a product that is used to accomplish a task, usually the interviewee will discuss the usability of the product while answering this question.

  You can also ask her this secondary question: "On a scale of 1 to 10, with 10 being highest, how would you rate the usability of the product?" This will help you determine if you have a problem in this area. If the number is low, make sure she explains the nature of the problem.

- **Have you had any interaction with our customer service? How was it?** If you have a problem with after-sales support, this is how you'll find out about it. Perhaps the customer sent an email or submitted a Web form, and didn't get a response. Or maybe there was never anyone available to "chat" with when she came to your site with a question. It could be that the answer she received didn't help her. It's very important to identify the specific weaknesses in your customer support system. How you treat customers after the sale is often the main topic of conversation when customers share information about their experience with your company.

- **If you were the CEO of [our company] tomorrow, what's the first thing you would focus on?** The answer to this question provides invaluable information, as it reveals what is most important in the customer's mind. It will tell you where you should focus your attention first. I have found that customers are very consistent in their responses to this question. After even just a few interviews, you will see a definite theme.

- **What problem were you trying to solve with our product/service?** Successful marketing starts with an understanding of the problems that your customers were trying to solve. More specifically, it starts with understanding how your customers perceive and talk about that problem. Their descriptions will help you write relevant, meaningful marketing and sales copy using the same words and phrases that your customers use when they think about the problem. This will also help to ensure that your search engine phrases are the same phrases customers type when searching.

  When your customers read your copy, they will recognize themselves. They won't need to translate your company's jargon into the words and phrases that they naturally use. You will have more customers coming to you via search, and more of them will buy, all because you understand the problems that they are trying to solve.

- **How did our product/service help you solve your problem?** The customer may have answered this question while answering the question above. If so, don't ask it.

  The answer to this question will also help you create relevant marketing copy. For example, you might claim that your product makes the customer "more efficient." That kind of copy falls into the "empty, boring phrases that everyone uses" category. The customer, on the other hand, might say that she was able to complete her tasks in two steps instead of eight. Or, that she used to spend three hours on a task, and now gets it done in ten minutes.

  The customer's specific description of her increase in efficiency is far more compelling than the usual over-used boilerplate market-speak.

- **What was your buying process—what were the steps—and what questions or concerns did you have, as you were considering our product/service?** You need to understand what they did at each step in their buying process, the questions that had to be answered, and the answers that satisfied them enough so they were ready to go to the next step in their buying process.

  Make sure you know where they began their search. Did they go to Google first, or talk to other people? Make sure you find out who else was involved, what their concerns were, and their respective roles in the buying process.

The answers to this question will help you fill in the details of your Buying Process Roadmap, ensuring you show up with exactly what buyers need when they are looking for your type of solution.

- **If you were looking for this type of product/service again, and you didn't know about our solution, what would you type into Google?** This question assumes they would use Google, a safe assumption. If they use a different search engine, they'll tell you that.

  It's important to ask the question this way, because now that the customer already knows about you, they would search differently than when they first started looking.

  Obviously, the words and phrases they give you in answer to this question will direct your search engine strategies. You will find that all of your customers tend to use the same phrases, and that those phrases aren't necessarily the ones that you have been using.

  You could also ask what they first typed into Google, but they may not be able to remember. Asking the question this way will get you as close as possible to their original search terms.

- **What do you think is a fair price for this product/service?** I have tested dozens of ways to ask this price question. Asking the question just this way—asking what they think is the fair price—will result in a price that includes a profit margin. If you ask them what they'd *like* to pay, there won't be any profit margin in their answer.

  If you sell a complex product, or one with multiple levels of pricing, also ask how they think the pricing should be structured. Confusing price structures will cost you sales.

- **What is your biggest challenge right now?** If you are selling your product to businesses, I usually add, "… in your work," to the end of this question. Otherwise, they may laugh and ask you, "You mean in my personal life, or at work?"

  The answer to this question will reveal market opportunities. They may have a problem that you can solve, that you weren't aware of until you conducted these interviews. Or, you're already able to solve this problem but didn't think it was a big deal to your customers.

  Their answer will also help you write better selling copy. You won't bore them talking about things that don't matter. As they read your copy, they'll know you understand what their problem is, and that you're offering a solution that will work for them.

- **What do you think of our competition? Is there anything we can learn from them?** As much as you may hate to admit it, your competitors do some things right—and knowing what those things are can help you improve your own business.

  You also need to remain aware that even though you have captured that customer, your competitors haven't given up. They're still trying to steal that customer away from you. You can learn from their efforts.

  Asking the question this way will encourage the customer to give you valuable information. For example, you may learn that the competitor is sending out an email newsletter that your customers find useful. Signing up to receive it will help you see that useful content for yourself.

- **What trends do you see with this kind of product/service?** If you are selling a business-to-business product or service, I would ask the question this way: "What trends do you see with this kind of product—and in your own industry?" I always get interesting and enlightening answers to this question. Again, the answer to this question will reveal opportunities. You'll find out which trends are mostly media hype and which trends are real and relevant in the lives of your customers. You will discover that many of the articles in the press, including online articles, completely ignore trends that affect your customers' buying decisions—and your bottom line.

At the very end of the interview, just in case, ask one more question:

- **Is there anything I should have asked you, that I didn't ask?** This last answer often contains well-stated and prescient responses that will be very useful as you develop your strategy.

  Because you're asking this question at the end of the interview, the person has had time to think about the subject as she was answering your other questions. Her answer may be, "No, I think we covered it all." But even then, the customer may add, "I guess the main thing is that ...." She will then proceed to go into more detail about a point that she made earlier, to make sure that you understood it—and its importance to her. She may also summarize her comments for you. "So, overall, everything has been fine, but that one shopping cart problem really should be solved."

  What she chooses to elaborate on is always the most important issue in her mind.

EXAMPLES OF CUSTOMER COMMENTS

Here are some snippets of conversational reports, for several different software products. I have edited them slightly to ensure the comments cannot be attributed to any company or person. My goal here is to help you see how frankly people speak and see the difference between "happy" and "unhappy" customers. In the unhappy examples, my client needed to make changes to their product. Other clients had problems related to processes, people, policies, marketing and selling messages and methods, service, and systems.

Unhappy Customer 1

"This accounting program describes functions in a way that is different than the way we describe those functions. So, when we were evaluating the program, we kept asking, 'Does it do this?' The salesperson told us, 'Yes. It does do that.' Now we see that the product *almost* does what we want, but it really doesn't. For instance, the product lists everything in unit prices, and we are used to doing it in quantities. Little things like that. We could adjust the way we do business to accommodate the program, but we'd rather not. Their terminology and conventions are different than ours, which made it tough to evaluate the program properly, and now we're having to make adjustments we'd rather not make. This is the product's biggest downfall."

Unhappy Customer 2

"My biggest concern is that we end up entering something twice. So I tell my gal here, 'Always enter the exact invoice number from each invoice exactly as it is printed on the invoice. If we do that, and don't try to abbreviate things, there is no way that we can duplicate an invoice.' But then we realized that this program has a limit on the number of characters allowed in the invoice number column. This drives me nuts, because it forces [the gal] here in the office to decide how she's going to enter the invoice number. She will be asking herself: 'Do I enter the first six characters, or the last six?' Then when I do something with the invoice, I wonder, *Did she use the first six or the last six?*"

Happy Customer 1

"When I was looking for this program, I found that most programs are only good in one area. I got discouraged, because I thought I would have to use three or four programs to do what I needed to get done. And then I would have three or four companies that would be holding me hostage, so to speak, simply because I needed that one function they did well. It could be the scheduling. It could be the payables, or the receivables, or job tracking. I would have to jump from program to program, with four screens open all the time, which would make it very difficult for my employees to learn—and use properly. That's the problem I needed solved. This program gives me all the functions I need, in one place."

Happy Customer 2
"I never have had this level of service with any other company. It's really great. When I call them they immediately say, 'Let's set up a meeting where I can see your screen. We'll do a guru session. Let's figure it out.' This is good. Fantastic. A lot of times when you call to [a specific Fortune 100 company], they say, 'Send this or that report and then I'll get back to you.'"

As you can see, if you were the CEO of any of these companies, and all of the customers interviewed raised these issues, there wouldn't be any doubt in your mind about your strengths and weaknesses. In other words, you would know what you should be promoting and what you should be fixing.

The phrase that sums it all up

When I submit the Summary and Recommendations Report to my clients, I always include a statement that sums up the company's main strengths— and weaknesses. The statement is always a "They're really good at this, but not so good at that," kind of statement, extracted from the answers customers gave me.

Here are some real-life examples of these "sum it all up" statements, and the obvious next steps.

Software buyers who had purchased a fairly technical program said: "I want to be able to use this program, and I understand what it can do for me, but I can't seem to make it work."

In this case, customers purchased the program and started to use it, but became frustrated. Some of them had managed to solve one problem with it, but couldn't figure out how to solve others. Some had gotten everything set up, but the results they got were inaccurate, and they couldn't figure out what they had to change to fix the problem.

We also discovered that buyers weren't sure which version of the program was right for them. There were too many choices, and the website wasn't clear enough about which version would work best to solve each type of problem.

The obvious next steps: Simplify the product line, create tutorials and examples that would help buyers use the product, and set up a customer support consulting service to help customers when they had difficulties.

Women who bought makeup from a boutique makeup company said: "The products are fantastic—no chemicals, and they actually work. And the owner is an amazing woman. But no one knows about the company, and the website is difficult to navigate."

The company had very loyal customers, but the website made it difficult to find the products they wanted. The illogical navigation was especially irritating when they just wanted to reorder a favorite item. The founder is a brainy, shy scientist type who needed some help marketing her products—including the website, packaging, and branding.

The obvious next steps: A makeover. First we helped her organize the entire product line so that the website navigation would make sense to potential buyers. Then, a new logo, packaging, and website, with the help of several talented designers. This was done over time to make it affordable for the owner, but it all got done. The result is lovely. As I write this, we are now working on raising the company's visibility, now that the website and products are ready for prime time.

Engineers buying telecom fiber optic systems said: "Their products are great, but they aren't a barn-burner when it comes to marketing."

The phone company engineers who bought these products were very happy with them, but not enough people knew about the products in the first place. The engineers trying to buy this company's products had difficulty convincing their upper managers that this was a reputable product, because their managers hadn't heard of the company.

The company (my client) was being run by talented engineers who put their energy into product development, assuming their excellent products would "speak for themselves," since the phone company engineers who bought them were so happy with them. The telephone companies that had purchased these products gained a competitive edge over their competitors. The products were easier to install and maintain, making it easier for the phone companies to come up with new types of services and rate structures.

Unfortunately for my client, the engineers inside the phone companies were not about to tell their competitors—engineers inside other phone companies—how much of a difference my client's systems were making. So they were not "spreading the word" for the client.

The obvious next steps: The company needed to get the word out that these products provided a competitive edge, and they needed to support the buying process of the phone company engineers—and the top executives who would approve the purchase. We instituted a new marketing campaign, complete with trade journal cover stories, articles in the business press, and memorable product branding. Even the top managers still read the trade journals in their industry, and being on the cover didn't hurt. Awareness among top managers went up.

The company started to post record double-digit increases in earnings, winning an award as one of the top ten turnarounds in the industry.

Surgeons buying metal and plastic implants said: "Their representatives do a good job of selling the implants to us for use in surgery, but the insurance companies don't always pay for the surgery when we use those products. Often it is a matter of how we describe the procedure to the insurance company."

In this case, we had initially set out to determine what the sales reps could do to convince the doctors to use the company's implants. It turned out that most of the doctors were more than happy to use the company's implants.

But after they performed surgery placing the implants in the patient's body, and submitted the claims to the insurance companies, the insurance companies balked. They sometimes paid very little or nothing at all.

Obviously, this caused the doctors to avoid my client's implants when they did subsequent surgeries, using a competitor's implants instead.

The real barrier to the sale was not the doctors. They liked my client's implants. The barrier was the insurance company payment processes. In essence, the insurance companies were the real consumers of these products—not the doctor or the patient.

The next obvious steps: We needed to interview the insurance companies and find out why they were resisting "buying" the product, and see how the problem could be solved.

Owners of marine retail stores, selling an iconic sailboat with a worldwide following said: "I have to sell [this brand of boat], because the sailing class is so large, and people come in asking for them. But doing business with the manufacturer is a nightmare."

My client was the manufacturer of the popular sailboat. The company's processes were convoluted and difficult for employees to implement. That was one reason it was a "nightmare" for their dealers to do business with them. The other was a manager in a pivotal position who tended to take a very negative, unhelpful approach.

The dealers, trying to get boats shipped to them in time for local regattas, too often found themselves apologizing to their customers for non-delivery. Imagine being one of those dealers at the regatta, apologizing to families for the fact that they couldn't enter the regatta because the boats didn't arrive. It was the worst possible scenario for the dealers, emotionally and monetarily.

The obvious next steps: Fix the processes, and address the "unhelpful manager" issue.

We spent several days working the kinks out of the shipping and accounting processes. The "unhelpful" employee was very involved in that process. It turns out she had become quite negative because the convoluted processes had made her cranky, inflexible, and frustrated.

As we worked on the processes, the employees—many of whom were just as frustrated as the dealers they were trying to serve—started to realize that positive changes would be made. Everyone was encouraged, even the most negative person.

Unfortunately, just as the new effort was gathering steam, the company was sold. The CEO who had brought us in left the company, and the new managers were not interested in a customer-centric strategy. Dealers still contact me, asking if I am still involved (I'm not), because they became hopeful when they started to see the positive changes. But now things were getting worse, not better.

I include this example because it reveals how a company can "go positive" due to increased customer awareness—and can also suffer when new owners decide they are smarter than their customers, dealers, and/or distributors.

It's very important to institutionalize a customer-centric system so the company can continue to prosper in spite of unfortunate management changes. People who don't care about customers can destroy any company, but institutionalizing customer-centric systems will make it more difficult for them to do so. If these company-killers are replaced by customer-centric managers before the competition gets a foothold, the company will survive.

Business partners who sell software for a Fortune 100 company: "They produce a lot of selling materials. But it's too hard to find the particular ones we need in the portal they've provided for us."

This company sells half of its software products through resellers, who generate billions of dollars in revenue. These partners are hard-charging sales organizations that need the right information, fast.

Imagine the business partner, on the phone with a hot customer. The customer has said, "If you can just answer this one question about the ReallyBigExpensiveProgram, I'll give you an order right now."

The business partner does not know the answer to the question; the ReallyBigExpensiveProgram is one of 300-plus products that he sells.

He knows that the customer has already tried to find the answer on the ReallyBigExpensiveProgram website, so he doesn't bother going there. He goes to the Business Partner Portal, where he hopefully (and frantically) starts searching for the answer to the question. Meanwhile he tries to keep the prospect on the phone with boilerplate small talk.

But the navigation on the Portal is not organized by product. It's organized according to the "packages" created by the company selling the ReallyBigExpensiveProgram. Only some of the packages include an explanation of the ReallyBigExpensiveProgram. Worse, when he first logs on to the Portal, he sees that the site is now dominated by the latest, hottest marketing campaign, which adds yet another barrier between him and the information he's seeking.

Still stalling for time, the salesperson resorts to asking the customer questions while furiously searching. He types ReallyBigExpensiveProgram and a word that relates to the customer's question into the Search box on the Partner Portal.

He gets 1,299 results, and a quick scan shows him that he's not going to find his answer any time soon.

By now he's run out of small talk.

Now he and the customer *both* know that he didn't have the answer, and he hasn't found the answer. The business partner knows that he is losing a major opportunity. He knows that right after the call ends, the customer will call a different business partner, who will make the sale if he can provide the answer.

My client's business partners needed a way to find useful information — more than could be found on the company's main website — in seconds. Unfortunately, as with most large companies, the navigation of the Business Partner Portal was driven by internal politics. The current hot solution always rose to the top of the navigation hierarchy, until the Portal became a disorganized collection of once-popular solutions. It no longer made any sense to the business partner, for whom the site was built.

The obvious next steps: Reorganize the navigation so it made sense to the company's business partners. First I interviewed dozens of partners. I then presented my findings and a new navigation schema that presented the information exactly the way the business partners wanted it to be organized. We got approval from all the interested parties in the company (a massive job in itself), and lab-tested a mockup of the new navigation with real business partners.

Once it was refined using the testing data, I built a huge tree-structure mindmap to represent the new navigation, then mapped the existing 3,000+ pages to the new navigation. This mindmap guided the company's internal website programmers, showing them where to place existing content in the new portal design.

The result: The new portal made it possible for the resellers to find the information they were looking for, in a couple of seconds. No more dead ends, or head-scratching confusion about where to find that essential piece of data needed to close the sale.

In all of these cases, the CEO or entrepreneur knew there were some problems in these areas, but considered these problems no more important than the many other issues they were dealing with at the time. They didn't realize how much these problems were preventing them from bringing in more revenue, and how much more they could make if these problems were fixed.

HOW TO GET THE CONVERSATIONS TRANSCRIBED

Once you have recorded the conversations, they need to be transcribed. There are plenty of transcription vendors in the world, and (obviously) they don't have to be close to you geographically.

I've had the best luck with self-employed people who love to transcribe, work out of a home office, and have some familiarity with my clients' industry. One woman worked with me for more than ten years, before retiring. She used to be a programmer at IBM, so did a great job on even the most technical interviews.

I have tried the larger services—a company in New York, for example. The problem I had there was a high rate of turnover. Transcribers working on your interviews become better at it with experience; the longer you work with an individual transcriber, the smoother it goes.

Each person who works on the files must sign a non-disclosure agreement. The information in the conversations is powerful stuff that should not end up in the hands of a competitor. They should delete the audio and text files from their computers after they have transmitted them to you safely.

Of course, if you're the CEO of a larger company, someone inside the company can do the transcribing.

Whoever you choose should be intelligent, detail-oriented, and trustworthy.

HOW TO ORGANIZE THE CONVERSATIONAL TRANSCRIPTIONS INTO A CONVERSATION REPORT

Once the individual conversations have been transcribed, each conversation needs to be categorized and "anonymized." Again, someone you trust should take the paragraphs—or blocks of paragraphs—from the transcriptions and insert them into the proper categories in the final Conversation Report. The questions asked during the interviews should serve as the category headers in the Conversation Report.

If you are a one-person business, you'll be creating this report yourself, so you can present it to your brain trust. Or, you may have a vendor you trust who can organize the information.

If you run a larger company, I suggest that you ask a product manager to do this. Whoever does it must be intelligent enough to know how to edit the information so that the customer's identity is not revealed, while the essence of what the customer is saying—and the details of the useful information—remain intact.

Keep the promise of anonymity

As you distribute this document, people will ask, "Was that Joe Smith talking, on page thirty-four? Sounds like him. He's always complaining about this."

You will be tempted to say, "Yes, it was." Don't. Don't reveal who said what. Instead, tell everyone reading the report that "who" doesn't matter as much as "what." Why? Because if they know who it is, they might dismiss those comments—and, in doing so, lose the motivation to carry out their part of the solution.

Sometimes the customers who are the most "irritating" to the organization are that way because they are the most passionate about your success. It doesn't always feel that way, but it's true. Consider your own personal relationships. Strangers couldn't care less about your success. But those who care about you do—and they make their opinions known. Even if the customer is just the kind of person who likes to complain, pay attention to what he's complaining about. It could be that your less grouchy customers have allowed you to slide in that area, an area that is actually costing you sales.

The other reason you should never reveal "who's who" in the Conversation Report is because you promised your customers, as you were interviewing them, that you would not reveal who they are. You must keep your promise.

Keeping this promise will help you establish credibility quickly with those you interview as you go forward. You'll be able to say, truthfully, that "I've never broken this promise, no matter how many times people have asked me to reveal who is speaking."

Here is a section of a Conversation Report page, taken from the doctors we interviewed for the healthcare company that makes metal and plastic implants. Each new person talking is separated with a line.

As you read their comments, you'll see there's a definite theme.

WHAT IS YOUR BIGGEST CHALLENGE RIGHT NOW?

My biggest challenge right now is getting paid. Part of it is the insurance companies. And part of it is that I use an outside billing source and they have undergone some changes in personnel lately. So I'm trying to make sure that we bill appropriately for what we do and that we are getting paid appropriately for what we bill.

In general the insurance part has been getting worse. The insurance companies tell you up front that they're going to pay you—and then they don't. They'll say, "We'll give you these incentives. We know you have had trouble in the past. We're going to make this commitment to you that if you send in a clean claim, then we're going to pay it in fifteen days, or ten working days." Then, every time that we don't get paid, they say, "This wasn't a clean claim." We respond: "Yes it was. All of the information is there." They say: "But there wasn't a period in block 42." There is always something that they don't like. And it's like trying to hit a moving target, because we are not told all of the rules up front.

The biggest challenge in my work right now consists of "driving through" the insurance world and getting things approved and having the guarantee that the reimbursement will be there when the treatment is given. You have to have all of the documentation. Everything has to be justified and you have to make sure all the steps are there, so that when you give the treatment, there is no argument about what was given and why I used this instead of something else.

What is my biggest challenge right now in our practice? Reimbursement. Everybody has the same issues.

Processing the reimbursements requires a multi-faceted approach. You have to deal with the short-term, immediate issues, which consist of trying to get them to pay you. That means hiring more staff. And then the doctors need to be as thorough as they can with documentation. We have to make sure that they understand coding, that they are coding properly. We have to make sure that we have enough of the right people in place so that we can code properly and then get the bill sent off, as is appropriate, however they want us to do it. And it's making sure that they actually pay us, which is a frequent problem. They either just don't pay us, or they deny payment, for whatever reason, which means resubmitting.

If you interview 10–20 people, the Conversation Report may be as short as 50 pages or as long as 200 pages, assuming that you interview each person for an hour.

HOW TO BUILD THE EXECUTIVE SUMMARY AND RECOMMENDATIONS REPORT

Once I am done creating the Conversation Report, I build a second report containing summaries and recommendations. This Executive Summary and Recommendations Report can be more widely distributed, and serves as an excellent tool for your upcoming Brainstorming and Planning Meetings.

I build a table for each category. Each cell in the table contains a paraphrased comment.

How do you feel about (name of company and name of product)?
Everything has been fine.
Service has been good. We get answers to our questions. They don't keep us waiting.
There was a learning curve with the software, but I got it up and running faster than other programs. I don't have a lot of time.
They are doing a good job. I'm happy. I want them to keep up the good work, to keep making it simple for us.
We bought the software last year but didn't get it up and running until January, because we didn't have the time to migrate the data. I don't think they could have helped us speed up that process.
I like the software. Overall it's great. It was missing some functions that we needed, but they have added them over time. Some of them are really, really important to our business. We needed point-of-sale functions, refund capability, and credit card processing – with a barcode reader.

Creating this table is a lot of work, but it's worth it. Reorganizing and presenting the information this way is incredibly powerful. The person doing this work—it could be the same person who "anonymized" the Conversation Report—will internalize all the comments made by the customer. This person will become an expert on everything that customers said.

Company executives can scan this table and easily see the big picture. The important issues and trends become very clear. Each new cell is one person talking; if the person has many things to say on this subject, I add more rows below the first one and indent the text so my client can see that the same person is talking and providing more detail on that particular subject.

At the end of each section's table, you will want to summarize the information contained in the section's table, identifying the problems and kudos that customers mentioned in their conversations.

This is also where you should list your recommendations. Again, if you or a product manager do this work, the solutions will become obvious to you as you create the tables, summaries, and recommendations. Some of the recommendations will come straight from customers—they will make recommendations to you about how you can improve your products/services, your selling process, and your interactions with them.

Here is an example of just a few of the recommendations made for a software company, at the end of only one of the sections. They had not yet been prioritized. They were intended to serve as ideas for the Brainstorming and Planning Meeting.

Recommendations:

- Develop a list of possible new functions and send the list out to customers so they can vote for their favorites. Ask them to prioritize their choices for you. Set up a program of improvements. As each new function is developed, and ready for market, promote the new features to your current and prospective customers.

- Develop training videos for specific tasks and job functions.

- Consider having a trainer go to customer locations for large installations.

- Customers are thrilled with the technician scheduling function in your program, but it is barely mentioned on the home page and product pages. We need to bring it front and center, so that prospective buyers will know—when they first come to your site—that the scheduling function in your product will drastically streamline their operations.

Whoever is summarizing and making recommendations should be constantly asking himself:

- "What is the big picture here? What trends do the conversations reveal? What keeps coming up—in one form or another (such as barriers to the buying process, product/service problems, and problems with customer service)?"

- "What is the most important need that must be met? How can we efficiently and profitably meet that need?"

The goal of the Executive Summary and Recommendations Report is to get you prepared for building your Action Plan. It's the raw material for the brainstorming, prioritizing, and planning that will come next.

WHAT YOU CAN EXPECT WHEN YOU DISTRIBUTE THE REPORTS

At the very least, top executives will be surprised. The CEO is always shocked that customers know so much about the company, and that the customers tend to share the same concerns.

In the hundreds of times I've presented this information, in every single case, the company's leaders were focusing on issues that the customers didn't feel were that important. Customers were focused on other areas. As long as the company's leaders were focused on issues that didn't matter to customers, no amount of effort would result in increased revenue.

Knowing what your customers are concerned about will get you and your entire company pointed in the right revenue-producing direction.

Once the interviews are conducted and the reports are created and distributed, you're ready to move on to the next step: The Brainstorming and Planning Meeting, which we'll cover in the following chapters.

Review of the Roadmap to Revenue steps in this chapter:

1. Create your "people to interview" list in a spreadsheet you will use to keep track of your email request, appointment, and call status.

2. Send email invitations to the interviewees.

3. Make appointments for the interviews.

4. Conduct the interviews. Record them (mindful of laws regarding recording), and also take detailed notes.

5. Ask these questions:

   - What do you think of our [product/service]?

   - Have you had any interaction with our customer service? How was it?

   - If you were the CEO of [our company] tomorrow, what's the first thing you would focus on?

   - What problem were you trying to solve with our product/service?

   - How did our product/service help you solve your problem?

   - What was your buying process—what were the steps—and what questions or concerns did you have as you were considering our product/service? (Who else was involved? What were their concerns?)

   - If you were looking for this type of product/service again, and you didn't know about our solution, what would you type into Google?

   - What do you think is a fair price for this product/service?

   - What is your biggest challenge right now?

   - What do you think of our competition? Is there anything we could learn from them?

   - What trends do you see—with our kind of product/service, and also within your own industry?

   - Is there anything I should have asked you, that I didn't ask?

6. Have the interviews transcribed.

7. Create the Conversation Report, organized by question, with each person's answer to that question in the proper category.

8. With the Conversation Report in front of you, summarize the customer comments in the Executive Summary and Recommendations Report, and make recommendations based on customer input.

9. Distribute the reports to those who will be involved in the upcoming Brainstorming and Planning Meeting.

ROADMAP STEP #2: DEBATE

4

RESOLVE THE DIFFERENCES BETWEEN WHAT THEY WANT VERSUS WHAT YOU HAVE TO SELL, AND HOW THEY BUY VERSUS HOW YOU SELL

DAY ONE OF THE BRAINSTORMING AND PLANNING MEETING

The last chapter was very tactical. Now we're going to get more strategic, right after we briefly cover the best way to set up your Brainstorming and Planning Meeting.

The Executive Summary and Recommendations Report from Chapter 3 will serve as the framework for your discussions. Using this report, you should:

1. **Give the Conversation Report and the Summary and Recommendations Report to everyone involved, and give them time to read them.** Busy executives will need about a week to digest these reports. Those involved typically include the CEO and managers from marketing and sales, Web managers, and product managers. Others may be added to this core group, depending on how your company is structured and the personalities involved. In meetings I've held, other participants have included the chief financial officer, the head of product development, the company's chief operations officer, chief customer experience officer, chief revenue officer, and a variety of other VPs. Of course, if you're just

starting out, or you are a sole operator, the only attendees will be you and your brain trust. They should also read a copy of this book.

2. **Set up a two-day Brainstorming and Planning Meeting to discuss the reports and build your brand promise, Buying Process Maps, and Revenue Growth Action Plan.** The meeting is best held off-site, to minimize distractions. It doesn't have to be an exotic, expensive location; a nearby hotel conference room works just fine.

Here's what you'll need for your two-day Brainstorming and Planning Meeting:

- A competent moderator

- Your brain trust—the people who will help you make decisions and carry them out

- Easel and easel paper (easel-sized Post-It® pads are best)

- The ability to display a laptop's screen so everyone can see it

- A fast, well-organized typist to take notes, which will be distributed to everyone afterwards

The two-day Brainstorming and Planning Meeting should be divided into four sections, two per day:

Day One:
Covered in this chapter

- **Analyze what customers have told you.** List, discuss, and rank (in importance) the issues raised in the reports.

- **Build the promise you can keep.** Agree on the promise that your company is currently making (branding), the promises that your company is currently keeping (your brand), and the promises you will be keeping in the future (your new, real brand).

Day Two:
Will be covered in the next chapter

- Build your Buying Process Roadmap(s)

- Build your Revenue Growth Action Plan

DAY ONE OF THE BRAINSTORMING AND PLANNING MEETING

Analyze what customers have told you. List, discuss, and rank the issues contained in the reports.

Someone with a strong moderator's personality should be responsible for writing on the large easel-sized sheets and keeping the meeting moving. You will be discussing a lot of different issues, so expect to use all the wall space. You'll need to see all the notes and you'll be referring back to earlier discussions as the meeting progresses. It is going to be a complicated and sometimes heated meeting.

This is the part of the meeting where the moderator lists the issues raised by customers. Don't prioritize them yet; just list them. They should be prioritized only after they are all listed.

It's a good idea to create one easel page for each of the following categories:

- Needs, perceptions, and concerns
- Market trends
- Competition
- Problems customers are trying to solve
- Customer experiences—as they tried to buy and use our products and services
- Any other important categories, such as:
  - Our website
  - Our product packaging, documentation, usability or pricing
  - Customer interactions with people in our company, including sales, marketing, service, etc.
  - Misperceptions about product functions or how the services work, pricing, or other issues
  - Our marketing and sales methods
  - Partnerships with other businesses

Every company is unique. Your customers may have brought up other issues that need to be listed. The issues you list will be determined by the things your *customers* thought were important.

The goal here is for this "customer reality" to end up on the walls, where everyone can see it and start to internalize it. It will be as if your customers are in the room. Their reality will become your reality.

For many company managers, this will be a first. You will see a variety of reactions to this customer information, as you look around the conference table. The obstructionists will be scowling, with their arms folded. Some will argue with the customer perceptions, rationalizing them or dismissing them. Others will be thrilled that this information is out where everyone can see it, and will be eagerly contributing to the conversation. Some will be thinking about themselves—how this information affects their job, what's in it for them, how they can take advantage of the situation, how they can look smart about it, and so on.

Take note of who's who—it will help you manage your way through The Shift to a customer-centric organization after the meeting. These first reactions reveal your managers' true attitudes about your customers and their needs. This will also tell you who is genuinely with the program and who is likely to be sabotaging it behind your back, while pretending to be enthusiastic.

After all the "big issues" have been listed, they should be prioritized. Priorities should be based on two factors:

1. **What did customers consider the most important issue**—the one brought up by the majority of customers, the one they talked about the longest, and were most emphatic and emotional about?

2. **Which issues are the most likely to be the biggest "barriers to the sale"?** Which issues are keeping current customers from recommending you? Which issues are keeping new customers from understanding what you sell and preventing them from buying from you?

These high-priority issues should be starred or highlighted on the easel sheets where they appear, and also listed on a separate easel page.

Now that the meeting tactics have been explained, the big issues are front and center, and the customer is in the room with you, let's spend a few minutes discussing strategy. It's time to focus on the essence of your business: Your brand.

BUILD THE PROMISE YOU CAN KEEP

My branding philosophy has been quoted in a variety of books, articles, and websites since I first articulated it in 1994:

"BRANDING" IS THE PROMISE
THAT YOU *MAKE.*
YOUR "BRAND" IS THE PROMISE
THAT YOU *KEEP.*

These two sentences sum up the difference between your "insider" reality and the customer's "outsider" reality. The Roadmap to Revenue is really the method that takes you from your reality to their reality.

Customers come to your company expecting certain things. I call these "Industry Baseline Promises."

For example:

- Boats are supposed to float.

- Airplanes are supposed to stay up in the air until it is time for them to land.

- Food you buy in a store or restaurant is not supposed to make you sick.

- When you pick up your clothes from the dry cleaners, the clothes should be clean—and not damaged by the cleaning process.

- Search engine optimization experts are supposed to know what the top search engine companies are doing, and the latest search engine optimization techniques.

- Website designers should create websites with clickable links that work. The clickable links should take you where you expect to go.

- Social media sites aren't supposed to crash every couple of weeks, nor violate the privacy of their members.

- Packaging should be easy to open.

- Tools should not break.

- Electronics should plug and play (amazing how rare this is!).

Your industry has its own set of Baseline Promises. You know what they are. At minimum, you should be keeping these promises. If you are not, you are not even meeting the basic standards in your industry. If you don't make changes fast, you are history.

List the Baseline Promises that are assumed for your industry. If the interviews revealed that you are failing to keep a Baseline Promise, fix that problem first.

Most of the companies I've encountered are able to keep the Baseline Promises. What they need to focus on, then, is the next level up: the promises that distinguish them from their competition in the customer's mind.

These are the unique promises that you can keep—that your competitors are not keeping, or, even better, cannot keep. Why? Because they haven't built the company you've built. They haven't hired the people you've hired. They haven't created the processes you've created. And, their products and services are not like yours.

You may have known all this before, but now you're sitting in a room where you are surrounded by lists of things that are important to your customers.

What will distinguish you in your customers' minds—and make them glad that they did business with you?

1) You will be distinguished from your competition because the promise that you make is the promise that matters most to your *customers*.

2) They will be glad they did business with you (and refer others to you) because you actually *kept* that promise when they did business with you.

This is how great companies create loyal customers. They know what promises their customers want them to keep. They make those promises. And they structure their companies so that those promises are kept.

Here are some of the best, customer-oriented promises that companies have made—and kept—over the years.

"When it absolutely, positively has to be there overnight."—FedEx

"You're in good hands with Allstate."—Allstate Insurance

"When you care enough to send the very best."—Hallmark

"It never varies."—Dewar's Scotch Whiskey

"Finger-lickin' good."—Kentucky Fried Chicken (KFC)

The visual moment of satisfaction

"Finger-lickin' good" was the slogan that Kentucky Fried Chicken used from the time the restaurants were founded in the '50s, until 1999. It was then revived by the company in 2005 for select stores, and used by the company's London ad agency starting in 2008. "Finger-lickin' good" is one of the best brand promises ever.

These three words describe what I call the "visual moment of satisfaction"—the moment when the customer is most glad that he bought the product. It's all about fried chicken, which you definitely eat with your fingers. It's all about licking those fingers because of the special, spicy grease. It's all about how you feel immediately after licking your fingers—before you get indigestion.

Every great product (or service) has this "peak moment." Yes, KFC had problems with the slogan in China, because it was translated as "eat your fingers off." But it was truly the company's most memorable promise. Even while they had stopped using it, news stories about the company continued to contain it.

Years ago, one of my newsletter subscribers, a marketer at a high-tech company, was sitting in a conference room full of engineers, trying to come up with a tagline. Of course, his first mistake was brainstorming with the product developers rather than talking to customers first.

The engineers in the room wanted the tagline to focus on one of the more challenging-to-create aspects of the product. Or, they tried to be "slick," and they came up with meaningless slogans, such as "Limited Only By Your Imagination."

Frustrated, the marketer finally burst out, "You know, if you guys were selling Kentucky Fried Chicken, your headline would be, 'Dead Chicken Parts,' and the subhead would be, 'Fried in Grease at 350 degrees.' Not one of you in this room would have thought of 'finger-lickin' good.'"

The best promises are very specific. They describe how the company, product, or service is going to deliver exactly what the customer wants.

Back to the Brainstorming and Planning Meeting. What is the "peak moment" for your product or service? How did your customers describe it? Why were they glad they bought your product/service, and what did they find most valuable about it?

This is the promise you are *already* keeping. This is your real brand. This is a good place to start. Rather than trying to be something you're not, capitalize on the promise you are *already able* to keep. Articulate it, using your customers' own words.

Make a list of the phrases that describe this promise. Don't judge them; just write them down. The "duds" may lead to a great promise. Don't expect to come up with the ultimate promise in this meeting; just make progress. At the very least, agree on the big idea. The words don't matter as much as achieving consensus on what your promise is.

Why is creating the right promise such a critical component of the Roadmap to Revenue method?

- **It's not a slogan. It's a *solution*.** We're not talking about a slogan or a mission statement. This is not about your "image." This is about what you do and how you do it. It's really about making it easy for customers to recognize that your company has the solution they've been seeking.

- **It will unify your troops.** Remember the emphasis on ending the civil war between marketing and sales (in Chapter 2)? This is one of the ways you will do it. If, in this two-day meeting, you all truly agree on the promise that your company can keep, then all of your marketing, selling, development, and customer service efforts will be unified under this one conceptual umbrella. Salespeople will lead with this promise. Marketers will use it in their materials. It will be the first thing people see when they come to your website. Those who serve customers every day will know that this is the promise they must keep. The most successful companies are those whose people are all working in the same customer-pleasing direction.

- **No one else can make your promise.** This is the big difference between you and your competitors. It communicates what is special about your company—and everything associated with your company.

- **It will put the focus where it belongs.** People who are focused on meeting the customer's needs will make decisions that lead to higher revenue. If everyone knows that the customer must be satisfied, they won't have to ask for permission in order to do something helpful for that customer. They will just do it. The customer will be delighted—and your promise will be kept.

Google has a well-known promise: "Don't be evil." Though not displayed on its famous Web page, this promise has become part of the company's folklore. This is an important promise for Google to make, as the company expands its franchise into Web-based applications and other tools—and also because it is competing with Microsoft, the company everyone loves to hate.

Zappos.com, the online shoe and apparel store, has a promise under its logo: "Powered by service." All employees go through four weeks of customer service training, where they personally interact with customers and learn how to meet customer needs. Here are some typical testimonials from thrilled Zappos customers:

This is a note to inform you how wonderful your staff is. We buy from other companies and they might have one or two exceptional people to talk to. The staff of your company is all exceptional and a real pleasure to speak and deal with. They are very patient and understanding since I am a little hard of hearing, especially on the phone and even though they might have to repeat a few times, they never sound as though they wish I got off the phone. If I had to rate them 1 to 10, with 10 being the highest, I would rate them with a 20. I don't know what else to say, except to say keep every one of them on your payroll. Yours truly, Joel K.

Dear Zappos, I don't know how you guys do it. I placed my order late in the day. I received my daughter's sunglasses the very next day by UPS. I remarked to the UPS man how fast the package arrived. The UPS man simply replied, "These guys are good." I just wanted to let you know that not only did you impress me, you also impressed my UPS man. This was not my first or last order from Zappos. Congratulations to you and your amazing team. Jan

---

I am so impressed with the way that your company handles everything. My original order arrived in no time at all and any contact that I had on the phone with your people was outstanding. They were all so friendly and so helpful. THEN ... to receive this email to let me know that my return merchandise had arrived is wonderful. I don't have to wait to see my Visa bill to see if the items arrived safely. Thank you so much! Gwen S.

I'm sure you can think of examples of promises that companies have made and kept—or broken. Promise-keeping is at the heart of all interactions between customers and companies.

One of the reasons I focus on the concept of your real brand being a promise is to put *control of your brand* back into your own hands. I want to save you from the terrible waste of money and effort that usually goes into the typical branding effort. Branding experts will tell you that your brand is your "image" or your "look and feel." That's what they sell. Sure, you will have to get a professional and talented graphic designer involved at some point. But an empty or meaningless promise, even when it is accompanied by a logo that's beautifully designed, is still an empty or meaningless promise. It will do very little to raise your revenue.

When the suits and ponytails are in charge of your branding, you don't think you have much control over it. That's not good, because the suits and ponytails at design companies don't keep (or break) the promise every day. You do. Your products/services do. Your company does.

THE TOOLS YOU USE TO KEEP YOUR PROMISES

We're getting closer to being able to define the promise that you can keep. Before we can do that, we have to look at the tools you have available to you, to keep the promise you're going to make.

You keep or break your promise with the five tools listed here. I will cover each one in turn.

- Processes

- Products/Services

- People

- Passion

- Policies

When I help companies increase their revenue, I often find that the process area needs the most work.

The product or service usually has enough customer-pleasing attributes to be competitive. On the whole, the people are smart, hard-working, and want to do a good job. The CEO is passionate about the company and its prospects. The policies are fine if the CEO is a decent person, who cares about customers and employees (frankly, I don't work with any other type of person).

In the spirit of dealing with the worst things first, let's start with processes.

PROCESSES: PROMISE-KEEPING TOOL #1

There are a few companies in the world today that started out as process-oriented organizations. Amazon.com comes to mind. Their infrastructure was their distinguishing characteristic. Over time, Amazon.com was able to move beyond books to sell any type of product, because the infrastructure was sound—and scalable.

I can confidently predict that your employees, customers, and partners are frustrated by one or more of your processes. It could be that you just haven't paid a lot of attention to that part of your business, throwing together systems and processes as the company grew. But over time, if your processes are not "owned" by someone, and if you are not constantly improving them, they will start to break down. They will act as an obstruction to efficiency—and a barrier to sales.

When my husband and I founded our company years ago, we made a conscious decision to grow the business without adding employees. My husband had managed as many as 70 employees as a design engineer and manufacturing plant manager. He knew that if we hired employees, we would end up spending our time managing, rather than applying our talents to the creative work for our clients, which was what we really wanted to do. It was easy for me to add new clients—obviously, I know how to bring in business—so the challenge was to constantly improve our processes so we could handle an ever-increasing client and project workload.

At our peak, the two of us were billing the same annual amount as competitors with eight to ten employees. We had a great time working together. Our clients *loved* the personal involvement of the principals. It was our processes that made the difference.

I have to credit my husband for pulling the business out of my vest pocket, so to speak. Being a typical entrepreneur, my answer had always been to work harder and faster—but not necessarily smarter. As he (and later, we) kept improving our processes, our systems became so efficient that in about an hour I could place millions of dollars' worth of advertising each month for our clients, using a grid we developed that showed me exactly which elements of the complicated media-buying process I had already completed and what remained undone.

He turned me into a process fanatic.

Years later, when I reinvented myself as a rent-a-VP for large companies, hired to turn around struggling marketing or sales departments, I always turned my attention to the processes first. At Dow Jones Interactive, we were able to increase the number of projects completed by the marketing department by 500% in the first five weeks—using the same number of people. Once the processes were efficient, I was able to focus on the quality of the creative work and making sure the right people were in the right positions.

If your sales and service people are struggling to do their best work because of substandard processes, your customers will be frustrated by the service they receive. Salespeople won't get back to customers fast enough, causing customers to click over to a competitor. Quite often a competitor will be able to close the sale before your salesperson gets back to the customer. This is one of the most common revenue-reducers.

When customers come to your service department with a complaint, and leave unsatisfied with the response, they will warn others to stay away from you. Their opinions will show up in places where potential buyers are researching your type of product, such as the reviews on sites where your products/services are sold, discussion groups, or social media sites. Negative word-of-mouth (or word-of-mouse) is a major revenue reducer. Sales you could have made will be lost to a competitor.

When people are ready to buy, they expect you to make it easy. They expect you to *want* to take their money.

Yet, as a consumer, how many times have you felt that the company you were contacting just wasn't that interested in your business? The usual culprit is the company's processes.

You simply cannot keep your promises (or compete effectively) if your processes are substandard. You will want to analyze the following:

- **Employee processes:** What your employees do as they work for your company, and how they do it

- **Employee training:** Do you train? If not, you need to start—and all training should include testing, to make sure that each employee properly absorbs the training.

- **Employee management:** How you manage your employees, including policies, contracts, reporting, and reviews

- **Vendor processes:** What your vendors do for your company, and how they do it

- **Vendor instructions:** Who gives instructions to the vendors, and how they do it. Instructions should be clear and complete. Projects should proceed in a linear fashion without major changes in direction.

- **Vendor management:** There should be an effective process, used by everyone in the company, for finding, evaluating, and hiring vendors.

- **Project management:** A process should be in place for efficiently selecting, prioritizing, and managing projects, from initiation, through ongoing activity, to completion.

- **Systems:** All systems should be streamlined, including accounting, customer service, fulfillment and shipping, customer relationship management, email, and auto-responders. The company should have an intranet that makes it easy for employees to get their work done. Most companies' employees struggle to get their work done using isolated, incompatible software systems. Many companies often attempt to create their own systems from scratch. Unfortunately these projects drag on forever and seldom reach even the usable-but-with-bugs stage.

The best systems I've seen are those where a talented group of programmers has created a soup-to-nuts system for a specific industry. If no such system exists in your industry, there are companies that specialize in integrating otherwise incompatible business programs. You can use best-of-breed business software—or whatever you're already using—for each departmental function (accounting, CRM, logistics, etc.), and then have the business integration company write software that ports data from one system to another.

SOLVING PROCESS PROBLEMS

The two-day Brainstorming and Planning Meeting is the right time to identify and list the process problems that customers brought up in the interviews. But it's not the right time to solve them.

Solving your process problems should be a separate, but concurrent effort. Focus on the customers' problems first, then work on your internal processes. Once you have solved the process problems that made customers unhappy, you'll have more revenue coming in, and you will be able to pay for improvements to your internal processes.

There will be a temptation to think that it's not necessary, because you're busy and profitable. Don't fall for it. Anything could happen—changes in your industry, unexpected new regulations, shifts in technology. Money will get tight again. Your remaining internal process problems will only make your situation more precarious.

As you move quickly to patch the most pressing process problems, in the back of your mind you should be designing the ultimate integrated, streamlined system. As much as you can, make the patches modular so the work that went into creating them won't be wasted and you can integrate them into the new, more rational system. This will also help your employees feel better about working with a patch that is a bit kludgy, because they will know that a better system is being created.

Here is how the most successful process improvement projects are carried out:

1. **Conduct a process audit.** Assign an analytical person to investigate your current processes. The analyst should interview everyone carrying out your company's processes. He should discover which aspects of the processes are most frustrating or confusing to the employees. He should then create a report that diagrams all of the steps in all of the processes, the aspects that are most frustrating to the employees, and the processes that are affecting customer satisfaction.

2. **Hold a Process Improvement Meeting.** The meeting should be attended by the people who actually do the work. Each task should be represented. The analyst should present the diagrams to the group. The analyst should point out which processes the customers are complaining about, and corrections should be made to those processes.

3. **Identify the inefficiencies that are causing the biggest problems for customers.** Whatever is keeping customers from understanding, buying, and using the product or service should be the highest priority. Perhaps customers are not getting the products on time. Or, the products are shipped improperly. Or, services are not being performed as customers expect them to be. Or, customers are confused by invoices or the online shopping experience. These problems should be fixed as quickly as possible.

   To identify these inefficiencies, ask yourselves these questions:

   - What do customers expect to happen, and what has been happening instead?

   - What is the actual goal of this process—from our perspective? What are we trying to accomplish?

- How can we reduce this process down to a couple of steps?

- Better yet, is there a way to eliminate this process entirely and still achieve our goal?

4. **Look for obvious redundancies.** About 30% of all process problems are due to duplication of effort. Look for places in the diagram where something is being done twice. Figure out how you can eliminate these redundancies. Once these problems are solved, employee morale will improve (people hate doing things twice). Customer satisfaction will rise, due to improved efficiency and morale.

5. **Agree on the other process problems that need to be solved.** After you have identified the redundancies and customer-facing problems, you will want to agree on the other areas that need improvement. Decide what the new processes should look like.

6. **Diagram the new processes, get agreement on them, then put the new processes in place.** If you can start fresh without trying to incorporate all the old data into the new process, by all means, do so. Too many process improvement efforts get bogged down—and never reach their full potential—because everyone believes that the old data must be in the new system. You can always go back into the old system to retrieve the old data. Assign a caretaker to the data in both the old and the new systems. Put a process in place to monitor the efficiency of the new data system.

7. **Make sure everyone knows about the new process, including your partners, vendors, and customers.** Customers who had been avoiding your business because of your broken processes will be glad that you "heard" them, and, if they're still in the market for your product or service, will decide to give you another try. Vendors who had warned customers to stay away will tell customers that you used to have problems, but they're fixed now—and they are happy to recommend your products or services again. Employees who thought you would never improve those terrible processes will be thrilled that something positive finally happened, and they'll come to work with a new, positive attitude.

8. **Make sure that the new process is fully adopted and working smoothly.** After the process has been in place for some time, do another Process Audit, refining it further. The time period between audits could be hours,

days, weeks, or months—it depends completely on the nature of the process and the volume the process supports. You'll most likely have a good sense for the amount of time that should pass before another audit is required.

Employees—and business owners—will put up with terrible processes for years because "we've always done it this way," or "the VP insists that we do this," or "this is how everyone in our industry does it." Meanwhile, customers with money in hand, ready to buy, are driven away, turning to your strongest competitor because it is so much easier for them.

You don't have to be a victim of your own processes. You can turn your processes into one of the main drivers of your revenue.

Now let's look at the other resources you use to keep your promises.

PRODUCTS/SERVICES: PROMISE-KEEPING TOOL #2

Almost all products/services are the result of a thorough, conscientious effort by skillful people. The problems usually lie elsewhere. However, if your survey results say quite clearly that your product/service has serious problems, solve those problems first.

THE ROADMAP TO REVENUE METHOD WORKS TO HELP YOU IDENTIFY *WHAT* THEY WANT TO BUY FROM YOU, AS WELL AS *HOW* THEY WANT TO BUY IT.

You can use the exact same method I describe in this book to identify what the customer really wants to buy from you. You can then make the necessary improvements in your product or service so it more perfectly meets customer requirements and satisfies their preferences.

If the product or service is substandard, the word will get around. *Marketing won't be able to save it.* The Roadmap to Revenue system is designed to get people together with *good* products and services, not to trick people into buying bad products and services.

You'll note that I tend to focus on software products in this section. I'm doing this on purpose. First, it's an area that is very familiar to me, so I can easily speak from experience. Second, we all use software, so it is a type of product that we can all relate to. Third, software is one of the most complex and "invisible" products sold, making it particularly challenging. It's a good "worst case" example.

Fixable product problems—for all types of products—typically fall into three categories: the product/service itself, the documentation, and a confusing product line.

1. **The product/service itself.**

     It is too difficult to make the product do what it is supposed to do. This happens frequently in the case of complex software products. One person inside the customer's company—a "champion" for the product— buys the program, finally masters it, then tries to get others in his company to use it. However, no one else is as dedicated or determined as the champion, so the additional sales never materialize. There is no momentum.

     As a result, the software manufacturer who sells this product has to struggle for every sale. Obviously, the solution is to focus on making the product more usable, by simplifying the user interface and creating educational resources. We have also created "roll-out kits" or "adoption kits" for the champions to use, to increase adoption by others in the champion's company. Poor usability is a common barrier to the sale, and a common cause of software company failure.

     This problem is not limited to business products; any consumer tool or appliance can have the same problem. One dedicated person in a family might learn to use it, but no one else will take the time and effort. Or, a consumer might buy it, find that it is too difficult to use, and just let it sit there—a reminder of failure. Next time he wants to buy a similar item, he's going to resist buying it from the vendor whose appliance or tool was too difficult to use.

     The product is poorly made. If the product breaks soon after it is received, it will certainly disappoint customers. Disappointed customers feel like jilted lovers. They believed, were deceived, and now they are angry. They will tell other people exactly what happened. This story, told by all those who have the same experience, will become the product's true brand, in spite of all the marketing money being spent on more positive aspects of the product.

Potential customers will always trust another customer more than they will a seller. No amount of marketing on a seller's part can overcome a word-of-mouth reputation for shoddy products.

Shoddy products get that way through a series of shoddy processes and policies. A shop foreman we know, running a factory in a country where low-cost labor was common, was telling us why he fired a worker he had hired. He said he hired the worker to do a job. The worker went to work on the project. "A week later," the foreman said, "when I checked on the work, he was doing it all wrong."

My first thought was: *Why on earth did you wait a week?* I have a rule about putting employees to work on new projects. I check back in 10 minutes, then a half-hour, then two hours, then 5 hours, then a day, then a couple of days, then a week. A manager who sets someone to work on a project, and then doesn't check in until a week later isn't a manager at all. He's simply not doing his job.

The only way to fix this problem is to bite the bullet—as Ford did years ago—and make quality a priority throughout the entire company. Someone has to be put in charge of the effort, and that person has to answer to the CEO and other top managers. Give the person the authority and support needed to accomplish the turnaround—and a reasonable but aggressive deadline.

2. The documentation.

Product documentation for physical objects—such as appliances and electronic devices—has gotten better over the years. At least, the information is available and organized in a fairly logical way. If the product works as it's supposed to, this documentation is usually sufficient. However, if the user runs into a problem, the documentation almost always falls short.

I experiment constantly with new software programs. When something doesn't work as I expect, I go first to the Help function built into the product (which sometimes takes me to an online Help resource). I'm lucky to find the answer there *one time out of ten.* I am usually forced to go to Google where I type in the name of the product and the nature of the problem. I then hunt through discussion groups and blogs until I find the answer.

Why is product documentation so poor? Because companies don't do usability tests, documentation isn't written by people who actually try to use the product, and the documentation isn't updated to include new issues raised by customers who are trying to use the product.

You might argue that doing all this is too expensive. It wouldn't be, if you were set up for it. If your systems and processes included these essential steps, and you performed them efficiently, you'd actually come out ahead overall. You'd end up spending less money and time trying to convince people that your products are easy to use. Your customers would find that out for themselves—and tell others. You would have more customers, and more money to pay for the improved documentation. You'd spend less on customer support.

3. **A confusing product line.**

Product lines tend to grow over time, usually in an illogical fashion. This is especially true for complex products—including software. A programmer will realize that he can add a feature to the program. He either knows or assumes that it might be appreciated by at least one customer, so he adds the new feature. A new version of the product is created called Product + New Feature.

After a while, the company ends up with too many products and too many confusing names. What's the difference between the Magnus Plus, Magnus Pro, and Magnus Premium? If potential customers have to pore over complex tables with checkmarks in them, your product line is too complex.

You'll sell more—and have more money to spend on promoting your products—if you simplify your product line using more logical product delineations and meaningful names. Magnus Small, Magnus Medium, and Magnus Large would make more sense than Plus, Pro, and Premium. Unfortunately the marketers in your company would be horrified if you wanted to use those names.

It would be better to find out which functions in each product are most needed and appreciated by your *customers,* and base your product names on those functions.

Which brings us to the Critical Characteristic.

THE CRITICAL CHARACTERISTIC

Perhaps you've actually done a great job of creating your product. It works as promised and it is well-made. But no one knows about it. This is a very common situation when the head of the company is an experienced product developer.

Count your blessings. This is a relatively easy problem to fix.

The first thing you have to do, through your customer interviews, is identify the *Critical Characteristic.*

THE CRITICAL CHARACTERISTIC IS THE FUNCTION THAT IS SO IMPORTANT TO THE CUSTOMER THAT IT COMPELS THE CUSTOMER TO BUY THE PRODUCT.

Usually product developers assume that the most important function is the one that was the most difficult to develop. Unfortunately, that same function may be a shoulder-shrugger for the customer. Promote this function, and the customer will not be interested. They'll never visit your website. You'll never even know they were trying to buy your product.

If your competitor promotes the Critical Characteristic, he will make the sale, and your customer will end up with your competitor's shoddy product. Find out which functions really grab the customer, and you will be on your way to higher revenue.

I'll give you an example. A software manufacturer we work with was promoting integration with QuickBooks as an important feature. Competing programs were also compatible with QuickBooks, but their integration wasn't as elegant as the integration that my client had achieved. The CEO, my client, was proud of the way he and his development team had made the program compatible with QuickBooks.

However, customer interviews convinced me that customers *assumed* that all the competing programs worked well with QuickBooks. It was a Baseline Promise. The subtle differences between my client's program and others were not that meaningful to them.

What did impress these customers—all of them very busy small business owners—was the fact that you could enter data once in one part of the program, and that same information flowed *automatically* to the other functional areas in the program. They loved this aspect of the program, because they hated entering data more than once. They knew that double entry was a profit-killer.

We rewrote the copy on the website so it focused on this Critical Characteristic. We also found in our research that clients wanted more help understanding how to use the program. I helped the client find someone who could rewrite his product documentation, and the client created some video demo tutorials and posted them on the website. Conversion rates increased 40%, during a severe economic downturn.

The revenue-increasing solution was not a massive company-wide transformation, but just the right tweaks. They simply weren't aware of the Critical Characteristic and how important it was to the customer. Once they understood, they could make the right decisions and the right changes, and revenues went up.

When your customers come to your website or product listing, the Critical Characteristic should be the first thing they see.

PEOPLE: PROMISE-KEEPING TOOL #3

No matter what you're selling, your employees will make the difference between satisfied, happy customers and unhappy customers. Your people will either reduce your revenue by their behavior, or raise it. You are only as effective and efficient as the people you hire.

Jim Collins, in the book *Good to Great,* found that the leaders of the great companies made sure they had the right people in the right positions (which also meant that they let the non-performing people go), before they even set their strategy. I should also note here that he mentions a "culture of discipline." Collins says: "When you have [hired] disciplined people, you don't need hierarchy. When you have disciplined thought, you don't need bureaucracy. When you have disciplined action, you don't need excessive controls."

How do you make sure you hire people who are going to keep your promise? Here are some of the things I've learned:

1. **Hire people who are high-energy and positive.** There are two kinds of interviews: energizing or draining. I always take note of my energy level after I interview a candidate. Did I feel more energetic and positive after the call, or did the call drain my energy? People who are enthusiastic

about life will work much harder, naturally, than those who are ambivalent or pessimistic. They will look on the positive side of every situation. They will lift others up. You want people like this in your organization. They will make you look forward to coming to work every day. They will give your company revenue momentum. They will create revenue opportunities simply by being high-energy, positive people. When customers interact with these employees, they will think highly of your company and want to find ways to do business with you again.

2. **Don't rely solely on phone interviews.** If a candidate passes the phone interview, and you can't interview the candidate in person, interview them via video. How a candidate carries herself and how she interacts with you will speak volumes about her character and motivation. Video isn't as effective as in-person interviews, but it will get you 80% of the way toward assessing the person's character. Many people can be sociable and pleasant on the phone, especially in an interview. In person, you will discover character traits that you simply can't pick up in a phone conversation, such as excessive vanity and nervousness.

3. **Try before you buy, if you can.** No matter how much you interview someone, and how many references you check, until they are actually doing the job, you can't really tell how well they will perform in the long run. It's not as easy to fire someone as it used to be. It's also the most painful part of being a manager, for anyone with a conscience. To be sure you won't have to let the person go, build a trial period into the employment agreement, along with specific goals and milestones. Three months is usually sufficient.

4. **Make sure that you interview the candidate's peers and underlings as part of your evaluation.** It's quite common for a two-faced person to kiss up to management and treat everyone else poorly—including your customers. These folks can rise to high positions in poorly managed companies. A good question to ask those who worked for or with the candidate: "Did this person make it easier or more difficult for you to get your job done?"

5. **Use my "jerk test."** I have developed a jerk test which is quite reliable. When you're interviewing the candidate, pick an appropriate moment to make this statement: "We have a policy at [our company]. We don't hire jerks."

If he is *not* a jerk, he will laugh. Nice people like this idea and find it amusing. They are relieved and encouraged when they hear this, because it means they will not be working with jerks.

If the candidate *is* a jerk, he will be offended. His reaction will be subtle; body language is your best indicator. He may raise his eyebrows and then shift in his chair, so that he is no longer looking at you head-on. He may cross his arms or shift to some other "closed" position. If he does laugh, it will be a nervous laugh, and he will scowl even as he is laughing. He will study you more closely.

If he is a master manipulator—the most dangerous type of jerk—he will know why you made that statement, and will deflect it in some way, as if it doesn't apply to him. He may lean back and chuckle a little. "Very interesting policy," he might say. "Smart."

A jerk is a jerk because he has decided to be a jerk. Jerks know they are jerks.

If you are suspicious that you have a master manipulator on your hands, be extra thorough as you check references. Don't just call the references he gives you. Ask for other references when you call the references he's provided. Keep digging.

Obviously, you'll want to make sure there are no jerks in your customer-centric company.

Once you've hired the person, you'll want to be sure that person always behaves in a customer-friendly manner, and keeps the promises that your company is making. This requires effective management.

Here are some real-world observations on management.

1. **Everyone must be managed.** People need direction. Even the best employees get off track if left alone too long. Get to know everyone. Take an interest in what they're doing. Drop by unannounced. Encourage them to speak freely. If someone lodges a complaint, do some investigating and find out if others feel the same way. Only then should you confront the manager who is responsible. Make sure everyone has what they need to do their job well.

   Publicly recognize good work. Criticize in private.

2. **Diligently carry out your leadership role.** For good or ill, you set the tone and the standards in your company. Not just with your direct reports, but with everyone who works at the company. Behave as if a skeptical customer, considering a huge order, is always in the room with

you. If a customer saw everything you said and did, would she want to do business with your company?

3. **Make sure everyone understands what your customer-centric goals are.** It is so common for "the leadership team" to come to agreement in a meeting about the company's direction, and feel as if they are "done." They then fail to tell the troops—the people who will actually carry out the plan. Oh, there might be an email from the CEO, which will get opened, but that's not enough to change a company's culture. You will need to communicate frequently and consistently. You will need to make sure everyone is getting the message and acting on it. One message is never enough.

Be on the lookout for situations where an employee has agreed to the changes needed to support the customers' buying process, but isn't doing what needs to be done. The employee may discover there are problems with the new methods, but may not bring it to your attention; she will then fall back into old habits. Her results will not be what the customer needs. When you discover this, you will need to find out what is wrong and fix it.

4. **Monitor how customers are treated.** Use call monitoring techniques, which are completely acceptable if your employees and customers know the calls are being recorded. Continue to interview your customers, using the methods described in this book. Use online social media channels to monitor customer experiences in the marketplace by setting up automated "readers" to watch for mentions of your company, product, and services in online forums.

Put someone in charge of monitoring the posts, helpfully responding where appropriate, and alerting you to any serious issues. Solve those problems quickly, and respond back to those who lodged the complaint. Your "monitor" should also submit a report to everyone once a week, so you can track trends.

These three methods—recording calls, conducting interviews, and "listening" to online discussions—will tell you what you need to know about how customers are being treated.

How your employees interact with customers will have a big impact on your revenue. During your Brainstorming and Planning Meeting, make sure that everyone in the meeting understands the importance of the new customer-driven direction, and that they are on board.

If you sense reluctance from someone in the meeting, keep an eye on them as you move forward over the next few weeks. Do what you can to help bring the person on board, but if they continue to resist, let them go. They will only drag down the others who are trying to make The Shift, and replacing the resistor with a customer-friendly person will bolster everyone who is making an effort. It's always better to lose a surly employee than to lose good employees—and good customers.

PASSION: PROMISE-KEEPING TOOL #4

People who start companies are naturally passionate about their company and its products/services. They have to be, because it takes a lot of guts and determination to start, build, and run a company.

The question is, are you passionate about solving your customers' problems—or something else? One CEO we worked with was most passionate about his standing in the technical community. He had a very high opinion of his abilities as an engineer. He was brilliant; no question about that. But his real passion was to prove to other CEOs in his industry that he was smarter than they were. Once it became clear that he cared more about his engineering reputation than solving his customers' problems, we bailed. He failed, ultimately filing for bankruptcy and selling off portions of the company.

Even a newborn knows if it is being cared for—or not. As a human being develops, this awareness only becomes more sophisticated. We can tell in seconds if a person cares about our welfare or couldn't care less. People who work for jerks know that the jerk doesn't care about them. Customers doing business with the company can tell that the CEO doesn't care about his employees—or his customers. He views them as a "revenue stream" or a way to satisfy his own needs.

CEOs whose passion is helping customers meet their goals are the ones that stand out in the business world. Their passion is infectious. Customers enjoy buying from them, partners enjoy doing business with them, and employees enjoy working for them.

Steve and Lori Leveen, co-founders of Levenger ("Tools for Serious Readers") do a great job of listening to and interacting with customers. Even negative product reviews get a response from the company. Mixed right in with the product reviews on their site are the responses from the company. Not defensive, "you're just not using the product right" responses, but apologetic and mature responses, such as: "In response to a number of customer comments regarding advancing the lead in our mechanical pencils, we've asked our manufacturer to remove the ¼-inch starter lead that caused some confusion." In other words, several customers complained about a problem, so they fixed it—and then let their customers know that the problem had been solved.

Mark Hoplamazian, CEO of Hyatt, has earned a reputation for being passionate about customer satisfaction. As I write this, Hyatt recently announced @HyattConcierge, a global, 24/7 dedicated concierge service on Twitter. On the Hyatt Twitter page, you can watch the Hyatt customer service people in action, interacting with customers, any time of the day or night. The customer service people are obviously intent on doing a good job, and the customers are impressed—which makes them want to stay at a Hyatt hotel.

How close are you to this ideal? Would you even dare to let your customer service people work with your customers in public?

POLICIES: PROMISE-KEEPING TOOL #5

As the leader of your company, you set the tone for everything associated with your company. Your policies are your formal way of providing the guidelines people need so they keep your promise and make customer-pleasing decisions.

Policies and mission statements can be stuffy and boring. Policies written in legalese won't be remembered or followed. The best policies are customer-centric, written in plain language, and simple to understand.

Once again, Zappos comes to mind. Its policies, which they call their core values, are:

1. Deliver WOW through service
2. Embrace and drive change
3. Create fun and a little weirdness
4. Be adventurous, creative, and open-minded
5. Pursue growth and learning
6. Build open and honest relationships with communication
7. Build a positive team and family spirit
8. Do more with less
9. Be passionate and determined
10. Be humble

The CEO of Zappos, Tony Hsieh, says that his main job is customer service. His goal is for every customer and every employee to be happy. It's no wonder they have done so well.

Other policies that will affect your employees and customers include:

- Privacy

- Dress code

- Returns

- Hiring and termination

- Benefits

- Partners

Creating successful policies is a huge subject, one that could fill yet another book. My goal here is to remind you that your policies are a key promise-keeping resource. If you attempt to set your company moving in a new, customer-pleasing direction without adjusting your policies at the same time, you will have problems. You'll be sending mixed messages to employees, customers, and partners.

What do your policies say now? How customer-centric are they? Do they encourage your employees to give the customer the benefit of the doubt? Do they help employees take good care of customers? Are they clearly written, in simple language? Or, do they contain cleverly worded loopholes that make the customer *think* they're going to be treated fairly, when in reality, they will be disappointed in how they are treated?

BUILDING YOUR COMPANY'S PROMISE

We've just covered the promise-keeping resources and why they're important.

Now let's get back to the Brainstorming and Planning Meeting. You're sitting in the conference room, surrounded by the easel sheets listing your customers' needs and your promise-keeping resources.

It's time to build the promise that your customers *want* you to keep, and that you *can* keep. It should be all about them and how you can best help them.

Start a new easel sheet, and write:

Promises our customers want us to keep

- Processes:

- Products/Services:

- People:

- Passion:

- Policies:

Using input from everyone in the room, and as everyone looks at the customer comments all around them, list all the promises that customers want you to keep in these categories. If you run out of room on the sheet, start a new one. Do this until you've covered all of the main points in each category.

When you're done, step back and see if you can find a common thread. Usually one idea stands out from all the rest, or the comments have a single theme in common.

Start a separate sheet. Use it to list the words and phrases that do the best job of describing either the "key" promise, or the "overriding" promise. Work hard to make every word count. Be as specific as possible. Take this exercise as far as you can with the time and energy you have left in the day.

Don't feel defeated if you didn't end up with the "perfect" promise on this first day. Often solutions occur to meeting participants after the meeting, as they process further. Encourage people to add to the sheet as the second day progresses.

How to brainstorm effectively

On your first day, you will have a brainstorming meeting to come up with the promise that customers want you to make and keep. You will also be brainstorming on Day Two. This is a good time to talk about brainstorming sessions in general.

Running a successful brainstorming meeting involves more than following the rule we all know: "Don't judge any idea that anyone brings up." Even this rule has its nuances, if you want the brainstorming meeting to be successful.

First you will need the right moderator. It could be you, or the person who put together the Executive Summary and Recommendations Report. Whomever you choose should have the customer input in her head and be thoroughly familiar with the company's products/services, capabilities and position in the market.

She must be able to:

- **Keep the meeting moving.** You only have so much time to discuss and come to agreement about all the issues that have to be resolved. It's quite common for one person to dominate the meeting without moving it in a productive direction. The moderator must be able to extract what is useful from each person's contribution, make a note of it, position it properly in the big scheme of things, then keep moving.

  Quite often the person doing the distracting has an axe to grind or a pet peeve. Everyone knows what it is, and everyone knows why the person has that pet peeve. And everyone is bored stiff about it.

  At the same time, the point the peever is making may be valid. The moderator should let the peever vent for a minute or two, then stop the peever and sum it up. "OK, so Bob, your point is that it will be impossible to make this change unless we install that new system, is that correct?" Bob will agree. "All right. Let's write that down over here on a separate page, and we will call it 'Items that must be considered.' Sound good?"

  This will give Bob his just due. If Bob brings up the point again, inappropriately, later on, the moderator must stop the meeting, look Bob in the eye, and say, "Bob, we have that point recorded, and we know it is an issue. Let's get back to that last point, about the customer service process."

  Some people dominate meetings just because of who they are. They are absolutely convinced that the best ideas are the ones coming out of their own heads. Their "enthusiasm" can dominate the meeting and discourage others from speaking up. The moderator should acknowledge their ideas, in the same way described above, but then extract additional ideas from other people. Dominators may insist that their idea is superior. If it is—because it best meets all of the customer and company criteria—fine. If not, the moderator must be able to explain to the dominator where the idea falls short, and then go back to soliciting new ideas.

- **Recognize the good ideas when they come up.** It's true, you don't want to dismiss any ideas. Not so much because the ideas themselves might be good enough, but because a weak idea might lead to a better idea.

When do you stop recording ideas? How do you know you've got the right idea?

As the ideas are generated, the moderator should ask herself how well they satisfy the known requirements. The idea that best meets the requirements is the one that should win.

- **Recognize the stupid or silly ideas.** Yes, all ideas must be considered, but some ideas are really going to be lame. The moderator should be able to quickly and effectively point out why the idea is lame, referring to the customer input. The idea should still be recorded, in case it could lead to a better idea, but it's appropriate to mention why the idea is truly undoable or unacceptable.

  Humorous ideas will occur to people; they are just as likely to lead to the right idea as something serious. Funny ideas should be allowed.

- **Overcome prejudices that will prevent The Shift from taking place.** Your interviews will uncover problems. The problems are occurring because people in your company are doing things that aren't working for your customers. When employees do something that is not customer-pleasing, it's usually because they assume it's the right thing to do, or because they don't think they can do it any differently.

  You can't expect to do the same things you've always done and get a new, revenue-growing result. You have to change. The moderator must be able to detect and drill down on the problem areas until everyone understands what's really going on and why it has led to the problems you've had.

  The people who thought they "had to do it that way" need to know that the process must change—and should be asked to participate in coming up with a more successful alternative.

  During the entire meeting, even though the participants have read the Reports and this book, there will be a natural tendency to engage in company-centered thinking. It should be a conference room sport to point it out when it happens.

  A few people will resist doing things the new way because they are uncertain about their ability to succeed. For some, it will be a matter of self-confidence; for others, a lack of ability. The moderator and managers in the room should sense when these issues are stalling progress, and address them.

  If self-confidence is the problem, the person should be assured that training and resources will be made available. If lack of ability is the problem, the answer will be to find something in the new system that the person can do successfully. In some cases, these issues should be taken "offline," and addressed personally and privately in subsequent meetings with the employee.

- **Know when to stop trying to come up with the final idea.** Sometimes a suitable solution simply won't materialize during the brainstorming meeting. That's OK. In those cases, the moderator should summarize the issue and encourage everyone to think about it overnight. The solution will come out quickly enough—in subsequent conference calls or email discussions.

- **Encourage the quiet ones to speak up.** The quiet people are often the best thinkers, and have their share of the best ideas. It's the moderator's job to capture those ideas. The moderator should be watching everyone in the room. If one of the quiet people shifts forward and lifts his hand off the table a bit, something has occurred to him. The moderator should then stifle the dominator, and say, "OK, Jack, we have gotten your point loud and clear. Now, Jason, it looks like you had a thought. What was it?"

THE END OF THE FIRST DAY

The promise you end up with will drive everything you do for the next year, or even for years to come. Yes, even in today's fast-moving markets. Basic customer expectations don't change that much over time. Don't be rushed about it. In the end, you will want to make sure everyone is comfortable with the final result.

Of course, you'll have to run the promise by some customers after the meeting, and ask them how they feel about it.

This concludes the first day of your Brainstorming and Planning Meeting. Congratulations. You're well on your way.

Review of the Roadmap to Revenue steps in this chapter:

1. Arrange to hold a two-day Brainstorming and Planning Meeting. Participants should include senior managers and those responsible for product management, marketing, sales, websites, systems, operations, and customer service.

2. Make sure all participants read the Conversation Report and the Executive Summary and Recommendations Report prior to the meeting. Quiz them about it to make sure they're reading it prior to the meeting.

3. Day One of the Brainstorming and Planning Meeting:

   - List, prioritize, and discuss the important issues contained in the Conversation Report and Summary and Recommendations Report.

   - Use an easel sheet (or more) for each report category, and for any other categories that surfaced in customer interviews.

   - Put a star next to the issues that were either most important or were evidence of a recurring theme.

   - Put a star next to the issues that are preventing your company from growing as fast as it could.

   - Recognize and acknowledge the promises you are currently making in your marketing and selling tools (including your website).

   - Compare those promises to the information gathered in customer interviews, which revealed the promises that your company is currently *keeping*.

   - List the promises that customers *want* you to keep, that you *could* keep, using these resources:

   - Processes

   - Products/Services

   - People

   - Passion

- Policies

- Identify a common thread. Start building your promise on a separate sheet, one word or phrase at a time. Leave this subject open; more ideas will come to all of you, as you proceed with Day Two.

ROADMAP STEP #3: DEPLOY

5

DOCUMENT YOUR CUSTOMERS' BUYING PROCESS SO YOU CAN SUPPORT THEM EVERY STEP OF THE WAY; BUILD AN ACTION PLAN

DAY TWO OF THE BRAINSTORMING AND PLANNING MEETING

Day One:

Covered in the previous chapter

In the previous chapter, we described the first day of your Brainstorming and Planning Meeting, where you listed all of the issues that are important to customers. You then started to build your promise, using information gathered from the customer interviews.

Now you know what you have to deliver. It is time to decide how you will deliver it.

Day Two:

Covered in this chapter

- **Build your Buying Process Roadmap(s).** You will lay out each step of the customers' buying process, and the accompanying marketing and selling resources you will use to answer their questions at every step.

- **Build your Revenue Growth Action Plan.** This is the plan you will follow to improve your existing marketing and selling tools, create the additional tools that your customers need, and make the changes that are necessary to correct the deficiencies in your organization and its products and services.

Before we jump into the meeting, a little perspective is in order. When my clients first hear what customers are saying about them, they find some of the comments disturbing. A common reaction is, "How do they know that?" Another: "Why do they think that? We've done so much work in that area, and they're talking as if we've done nothing!"

I bring this up now, because sometimes your brain will start racing on the evening of the first day. You may find yourself getting discouraged when you realize how open your kimono has been, or how little appreciation people have for something that you have worked on for months—or years. It may feel as if your customers have fixated on the weakest aspects of your product/service or company, rather than recognizing your strengths. In fact:

PERCEPTION IS REALITY.
MORE SPECIFICALLY,
YOUR CUSTOMERS' PERCEPTION
IS YOUR REALITY.

Your customers felt this way all along. Now you know about it. Knowing it makes progress possible. Now you can fix it—and go back to those customers and tell them you fixed it. Nothing earns the respect of customers faster than seeing a business owner or CEO face reality and take the right action. Customers see that they can depend on you to make good decisions. It inspires confidence and trust. Just this shift alone can lead to new revenue.

It's also important to remember that the customers you interviewed bought your product/service in spite of the weaknesses. Imagine how much more successful you can be, if you remove those barriers to the sale.

I've also found that employees often know more about your company's weaknesses than you or your managers, simply because they are the ones who normally interact directly with customers. They are the ones who must apologize for the policy that customers find irritating, or the product that doesn't work as it should, or the services that are not up to par.

When they hear that you have spent two days in a meeting addressing these issues, those customer-facing employees will be encouraged. They will have hope that something will be done about the problems they face every day.

Employees, on the whole, know when a company is being managed for success—and when it isn't. Morale always goes up when they see things moving in the right direction.

Because you have done the interviews, and developed the promise you can keep, you are well on your way to higher revenue.

Let's continue our journey ... with Day Two of the Brainstorming and Planning Meeting.

MAPPING THE BUYING PROCESS

We're going to talk now about the customers' buying process. As you read, put yourself in the shoes of a buyer. Put aside your role as a seller for now.

When someone sets out to buy a product or service, they bring two antithetical emotions to the process: *desire* and *skepticism*. Desire compels them forward, skepticism yanks them back.

They **desire** certain product/service attributes. They desire a smooth buying process, including friendly, helpful sellers, straightforward and reasonable pricing, and an easy way to examine the product and compare the product to other choices.

Their **skepticism** comes from their past experiences with sellers who promised good products and exceptional service but who delivered a disappointing result. The product or service was substandard. The buying process was uncomfortable, confusing, or difficult. Customer service didn't help them.

Reading copy on websites, you'd think that 1) buyers have no desires and 2) buyers are not skeptical. For some reason, marketers and website copywriters completely ignore these two realities. The copy treats the customer as if he had to be *encouraged* to spend money—when, in fact, most people spend every penny they can. People are *always* thinking about the next thing they're going to buy, what it's going to cost them, and how soon they can get it.

Buyer desire, of course, works in your favor. In our Google-driven world of commerce, people usually decide they want something before they go looking for it. So the desire is present when they start their search.

I need some new clothes.

I need a new house.

I need to refinance my current house.

I need a vacation.

I need a new pair of earrings for the party on Saturday night.

I need a car seat for my baby.

I need a new pair of shoes.

This car is on its last legs. I need a new one.

Our service fleet needs new equipment to service emerging technologies.

We need to upgrade the materials handling system in our warehouse.

We need to redecorate our restaurant.

We need someone to handle our overseas shipments for us.

I need a good search engine optimization vendor who will actually get my listing to the top of the results page.

The list goes on and on. Millions of times a day, someone decides he needs something, and he begins his buying process.

Desire is what starts the person on his buying process. However, as soon as he begins the buying process, his skepticism kicks in. The more expensive and complex the purchase, the greater the *scrutiny* that the customer will apply to the purchase.

Desire brings the customer to your website. Once there, he doesn't need anyone to stoke the fires of his desire. *He needs the website to allay his skepticism.* He needs your website (or a salesperson) to answer his questions, so he can decide if the product or service is going to solve his problem.

The answers the customer seeks must be easily accessible on the website. And, if the buying process proceeds to the next stages, the company representative must be available—and able—to answer the customer's questions.

All companies, small and large, in every industry, don't get this right. They behave as if they want your business, but when you come to them, eager to buy, they behave as if your business doesn't matter to them. They don't help you take the next step.

For example, small, local companies who want business tend to advertise in local papers, on the radio, and make sure their listings show up in Google Maps, complete with the name of the proprietor and the phone number. You would think, given all the places they advertise, that they were eager for business.

However, *most* of the time—as much as 90% of the time—when you call the number displayed in the ad for a local business, no one calls you back. Those who do call back set up an appointment to come out for the first job or to create an estimate. Then they often arrive late—or don't show up at all. They always have a great excuse. But, that's their problem—not their customer's problem.

Big companies also fail to support the latter stages of the buying process. One of the largest companies in the world runs clever commercials showing people getting their business problems solved by the large company. But when a customer actually decides that the large company might be able to meet his need, he goes to the company's website—and his buying process is stopped dead in its tracks. He can't figure out where to start.

There is no relationship between those clever commercials and the products and messages shown on the company's website. There is no easy way to figure out whom to contact. The company spends literally hundreds of millions of dollars to encourage customers to come to the company's website at the beginning of the buying process, and yet does nothing to support the customer's subsequent steps in that buying process.

A sale is what happens at the very end of the customers' buying process. Marketers typically focus all of their efforts on the beginning of the buying process. They think that what happens at the later stages of the buying process, and after the sale, is someone else's responsibility.

We have all set out to buy something and have soon became discouraged from doing so. Our skepticism—and or our inability to find exactly what we wanted—forced us to abandon the effort. At first, our desire overcame the obstacles we encountered. But then, our skepticism uncovered issues that convinced us that our desire would not be satisfied.

This is one of the reasons it is so important to map out the *entire* buying process for your product or service, from the initial desire all the way through the purchase, and beyond, including customer support. From the customer's perspective, all phases of the buying process are important. Customers are just as likely to ditch the process near the end as they were at the beginning. If you're the seller, that's not good news for you. It means that you've invested heavily in that buyer, and now he has left you—empty-handed. In fact, *both* of you are empty-handed.

To address that problem, one of the things you will be doing with your Buying Process Roadmap is analyzing where most of your sales fall apart. This is where you will find important barriers to the sale. You will be able to remove those barriers, and close more sales as a result.

THE FOUR LEVELS OF BUYER SCRUTINY

As customers go through their buying process, their skepticism causes them to *scrutinize* the product or service along with the company that sells it. However, not all products and services are scrutinized to the same extent.

I'm sure all of us have spent more time than we'd like to admit, poring over product specs for a particular item as we were investigating a purchase. We looked at vendor sites, product reviews, and the comments made in discussion groups.

We have also test-driven cars, tried on clothing, and walked through dozens of houses. We have gone through contracts with a fine-toothed comb, making sure we agree with all the terms in the contract, and to ensure that we won't regret our decision. The larger the price, the more we are concerned about avoiding "buyer's remorse."

On the other hand, there are products and services that we hardly scrutinize at all. We're standing at the checkout counter and we see a candy bar. We don't have a whole lot of questions about that candy bar. We're not going to be talking to any salespeople or signing any contracts. We may even ask ourselves only one question: "Can I afford this [both in terms of money and my waistline]?" If we desire it, and decide we can afford it, we simply pick up that candy bar and add it to the rest of our grocery items.

In fact, all of the products and services in the world fall into one of four levels of scrutiny. They scrutiny levels are: Light Scrutiny, Medium Scrutiny, Heavy Scrutiny, and Intense Scrutiny. They comprise the Scrutiny Spectrum.

Your product or service will fall into one of the four Scrutiny categories. You will know immediately where you are on the Scrutiny Spectrum. All business managers who have seen these four scrutiny categories have immediately known where their product or service falls on the Scrutiny Spectrum.

A candy bar is a Light Scrutiny product. The decision is made in seconds. A car or a house is a Heavy Scrutiny product—a big-ticket, high-risk purchase that requires a great deal of thought. The buyer will be living with the consequences of the decision for a long time.

Companies waste billions of dollars marketing Light Scrutiny, candy-bar types of products as if they are Heavy Scrutiny, big-ticket types of products, and vice-versa. Such methods are completely out of sync with the customers' buying process.

Once you see where you are on the Scrutiny Spectrum, you will start to realize which parts of your selling process need changing. Knowing where your product or service is on the Scrutiny Spectrum will prevent you from wasting precious resources promoting your product/service inappropriately.

Here is a summary of the four levels of the Scrutiny Spectrum.

THE SCRUTINY SPECTRUM: LIGHT, MEDIUM, HEAVY & INTENSE

■ Light Scrutiny Products & Services ■

- Many millions buy Light Scrutiny products and services.

- Buyers only ask a couple of questions.

- Prices typically run from one dollar to tens of dollars.

- The buying process takes seconds or minutes; the need is immediate.

- Examples: Food, souvenirs, trinkets, freeware, batteries, simple hand tools, extension cords, grooming items, craft items, and small-commitment services such as dry cleaning.

▪ Medium Scrutiny Products & Services ▪

▪ Although millions of people buy Medium Scrutiny products and services, they cost enough to give those buyers pause. The purchase is not an impulse purchase. These purchases are made less frequently and with more scrutiny than Light Scrutiny products and services.

▪ The buyer asks 5 to 20 questions.

▪ The price typically runs from tens to hundreds of dollars.

▪ The buying process takes minutes or hours. However, while the buyer wants to solve the problem, she can easily put off the purchase if she is not happy with what she has found so far. She may go on several hunting expeditions until she finds what she wants.

▪ Examples: Clothing, appliances, inexpensive software, stationary power tools, components for manufacturing, office equipment, lawn mowers, and services such as hair cutting, jewelry repair, and cleaning services.

▪ Heavy Scrutiny Products & Services ▪

▪ Even fewer people buy Heavy Scrutiny products and services. It is a very serious purchase, not easy to pay for, and rarely carried out In the person's lifetime. The purchase is a big event. There is usually more than one person involved in the buying decision.

▪ Multiple buyers ask 25 to 50+ questions.

▪ The price typically runs from thousands to millions of dollars.

▪ The buying process takes weeks or months, and usually involves a sales-person and a signature document (contract, agreement, or estimate).

- Examples: Cars, houses, complex business systems, recreational boats/ yachts/vehicles, private jets, and expensive/complex medical services.

■ Intense Scrutiny Products & Services ■

- Very few buyers are interested in Intense Scrutiny products and services.

- Multiple approvers are involved in the buying decision, and each asks dozens of questions. The lead buyer, or champion, is taking a big risk. If the decision turns out to be a mistake, his reputation will be stained.

- The price typically runs from thousands to millions (or even billions) of dollars. It is a significant amount of money.

- The buying process takes weeks, months, or even years. A salesperson is involved and a contract is signed. The buying process is ongoing, as further add-ons and services are considered. The buyer decides, as services are performed, if he wants to purchase additional or ongoing services from the vendor—or not.

- Examples: All professional consulting services, large-scale development projects, very expensive custom products, nursing home facilities, and ongoing medical services.

Some companies sell a product, and an additional service associated with that product. For example, it's common for software companies to sell a Medium Scrutiny software product, plus Intense Scrutiny consulting services. A common mistake is to use the same techniques to sell the Medium Scrutiny product and the Intense Scrutiny service.

I will devote a chapter to each Scrutiny category later in the book (see Chapters 8–11). In this chapter devoted to Day 2 of the Brainstorming and Planning Meeting, it's appropriate to simply provide a quick overview of each Scrutiny category.

If you are selling a Light Scrutiny product or service, the bulk of your marketing budget and selling activities should be devoted to attracting as much attention as possible. Your product or promotional items for your service need to be where the buyers are—checkout counters, online Web retailers, and so on. You only need to answer a couple of questions. Your revenue will come from a high volume of small-expense purchases.

You don't need to develop a deep relationship with your customers. They don't want a deep relationship with you. As long as your product lives up to its promises—the candy bar *inside* the wrapper had better look like the candy bar photo on the outside, for example—you will be able to grow revenues by focusing on getting the attention of as many buyers as possible.

I should note that companies selling Light Scrutiny products and services, because their model is set up for a low-relationship sale, can be blind-sided by a crisis. If someone finds a piece of glass in the candy bar, the candy bar manufacturer has a public relations nightmare on its hands. In that situation, the goals are to 1) immediately face the problem, 2) fix the problem, and 3) get the word out to as many people as possible, as fast as possible.

When you're selling Light Scrutiny products or services, you must react very quickly to market trends.

If you are selling a Medium Scrutiny product or service, your customers have a series of questions that must be answered. Don't assume that putting up a "frequently asked questions" (FAQ) section on your website is sufficient. As I pointed out earlier, if you create the questions and answers without customer input, your customer will not find the answers she seeks.

You absolutely must know the real questions that customers have as they attempt to buy and use your products and services. These are the questions—and answers—that should appear on your website. Your in-house or retail salespeople should have those answers at their fingertips in a searchable database, and on the tips of their tongues for as many of those questions as their mental capacities can retain.

Someone in marketing should be in charge of keeping the questions and answers up to date, by searching discussion forums and interviewing customers. This person should report findings to top managers, and product/service development and product management folks, so that everyone knows the issues that customers are struggling with and can incorporate the knowledge into their product improvement projects.

If you are selling a Heavy Scrutiny product or service, your customers will have a great many questions and there will be multiple people involved in the buying decision. There is usually a demo or trial period involved, and a contract of some sort. All of these aspects of the buying process should proceed smoothly. When the customer is ready to move to the next phase, it should be effortless to do so.

Heavy Scrutiny sales almost always involve a salesperson. Once the customer has gotten most of his questions answered on the website, and makes contact with the company, the salesperson should be right there on the phone, answering the customer's specific questions. No voicemail, no "our customers are very important to us," no "all our salespeople are busy helping other customers," no "press one for this and two for that."

The salesperson should be able to answer those remaining questions. When the customer is ready to look at a detailed estimate or contract, the salesperson should be able to produce it quickly. Contract templates should be used, so the salesperson only has to tweak the template a bit to make it ready for the customer.

The customer may already be personally sold at this stage, but may want the salesperson to present to additional approvers. The salesperson should use pre-fabricated sales presentations that can be easily custom-tailored for the prospect. No salesperson should be scrambling to create a presentation or a contract at this stage in the buying process.

Unfortunately, most salespeople are trained to push, rather than educate. Their pushiness becomes a barrier to the sale rather than enabling it to proceed. It puts the prospective customer in a defensive, even *more* skeptical mode.

The *best* salespeople *assume* that the buyer is bringing plenty of desire to the purchasing activity, and, additionally, that the buyer's skepticism level is high.

Rather than push the buyer to a decision, the successful Heavy Scrutiny salesperson focuses on building trust by being able to answer all questions to the buyer's satisfaction. He also *asks* intelligent questions, and listens to the answers, to best determine how his company can help the customer. The successful salesperson responds *immediately* to customer queries, provides the information, then makes sure that the customer is satisfied. He calmly, methodically, and honestly alleviates the customer's skepticism. "I understand why you're concerned about that. Most products like ours don't do that right. Ours does. Let me show you how."

If you are selling an Intense Scrutiny product or service, you are entering into a working relationship with your customer. All of the buying process steps are the same as with a Heavy Scrutiny product or service, but now you're also "getting married."

Customers buying these types of services pay a great deal of attention to the people running the company. Because they are "getting married," they want to know whom they're going to be living with. What is their character? What drives them?

If you're selling consulting services, your customers will want to know a lot about you before they even contact you the first time. Make sure you're generating useful new content every week.

Anyone buying your Intense Scrutiny product or service will want to get to know you through your content. So while it's not that important for the president of a candy bar company to publish a blog or write articles, it's incredibly important for the president of a consulting company to publish a blog and write articles.

This is all you need to know—for now—about the Scrutiny Spectrum. It's time to focus on the remainder of the Brainstorming and Planning Meeting.

BUILDING A BUYING PROCESS ROADMAP

Once you've determined which scrutiny category your product/service belongs to, it's time to build your Buying Process Roadmap.

Your finished Buying Process Roadmap will show the actions customers take in the course of their buying process, and the actions you should take to make it easy for them to take the next step.

Chapters 8–11 contain the Buying Process Roadmaps for each scrutiny category (Light, Medium, Heavy, and Intense). Take a quick look at the Roadmap for your Scrutiny Spectrum category.

The buying process stages shown in the Roadmaps have proven accurate for hundreds of products and services we have worked on over the years. However, if you find that your product or service doesn't fit the stages, please contact me. I'll be happy to help.

I have made templates of these maps available for you to download at http://www.RoadmapToRevenue.com/Resources

In your two-day Brainstorming and Planning Meeting, you will be building your own Buying Process Roadmap for your product(s) and service(s). The downloaded Roadmap that is closest to your situation should be displayed on the conference room screen. Your own data should replace the data currently in the template, and be entered on the controlling laptop. (Use a speedy typist, because when the ideas are flowing and people get excited, only a fast typist will be able to keep up.)

The customer and company activities will certainly be distinctive to your product/service and market, your customer's buying situation, and your own marketing and selling activities and tools.

Be conscientious and ruthlessly honest about each of the customer steps. This is the discipline that will make your marketing efforts and selling tools apropos and effective. Your selling success depends on getting this right.

Make sure your best salespeople are in the room during this Buying Process Roadmapping session. At first, they will say that there is no such thing as a standard buying process—that they just "make it happen," themselves, personally, with their sales techniques. They will squirm in their seats, roll their eyes, and keep trying to check their smart phones and PDAs under the conference table. Ask them to hang in there. Tell them that they are the experts in the room on this process, that you need their input, and that they might even like the end result.

As you build the Map, they will agree on the discrete steps. After about fifteen minutes, they will also start to realize that this is an exercise they can significantly contribute to, and that the results of the exercise will help their selling efforts. As this reality sinks in, their enthusiasm will rise.

Build one Buying Process Roadmap for each product or service; don't try to intermingle them.

Once you have built your Buying Process Roadmap(s), it's time to identify the problem areas. Ask these questions, and attempt to answer them using the results of the customer survey and the experience of the people in the room:

- Where does the buying process get stalled? At what point does our company disappoint, frustrate, and then lose the customer, either online or through the course of a normal selling process?

- Where should we be investing more resources to better support the customers' buying process?

- If we need to increase our investment in one area, how can we safely reduce our investment in the areas where we currently invest more than necessary?

- What could we do to reduce the amount of scrutiny that the customer feels is necessary? How could we establish credibility and build trust earlier in the buyer's process?

STREAMLINING THE BUYING PROCESS

One of your goals should be to shift your product/service away from the higher end of the Scrutiny Spectrum towards the lower end.

In other words, if you sell a Heavy Scrutiny product or service, you will considerably lower your cost of goods sold if the customers' buying process is primarily satisfied by your website content, rather than by a salesperson. Answer their questions before they ask them, with content that you make readily available. The buyer will think, *These people really know what they're doing. The product's probably good, too.*

In my own consulting business, by the time someone contacts me, I don't have to answer dozens of questions, even though I am selling an Intense Scrutiny service. All but three questions have been answered by the content that I make available to potential clients. This means I spend much less time in the first phone call answering questions. The person already knows who I am, what I stand for, and what I can do for him. Because of the content I generate, he already knows he can trust me.

His three questions are:

- "Would you be interested in working with us?"

- "When could you start?"

- "How much do you charge?"

These questions are best answered in a phone conversation. Answering them takes a few seconds. Then we start working on solving the client's problem.

There are many ways for a buyer to learn more about you when they are searching for your kind of solution online. If you use their favored channels correctly, you will decrease the amount of time and effort required to close a sale. We'll discuss how to use channels and methods in the following chapters.

As an aside, I'm using the word "channels" throughout *Roadmap to Revenue* to represent any platform on which you can place a marketing message or any platform through which customers are talking to each other—or interacting with you. The word more commonly used for this used to be "marketing vehicles," which tended to refer to one-way, broadcast marketing platforms. However, in today's environment, dominated by customer conversations, platforms/sites such as Facebook, Twitter, LinkedIn and YouTube are most commonly referred to as "channels,"—as in, "channels of communication" as well as "channels for reaching consumers." Since online marketing has become more dominant than offline marketing, it's appropriate to use "channels" rather than "vehicles." It does have the potential to be confusing—since there are "distribution channels" and "TV channels," but the context in which these phrases occur should provide sufficient clarification.

Remember: As far as the customer is concerned, your marketing and selling efforts are working when his questions are answered, to his satisfaction. Every channel and tool you use should be designed to answer the questions asked by customers, in a way that causes them to nod and take another step toward the purchase.

What is the most important question that ANY seller must answer?

No matter what you're selling, there is one question that must always be answered in all of your customer-facing copy. That question is:

"What's going to happen to me after I buy?"

People don't buy "products" or "services." They buy *experiences.* They imagine themselves using the product or service. Experiencing it.

You need to be able to explain to them what it will be like using your product or service. Put them in the driver's seat. Make the copy active. Start sentences with a verb. "Plug in the device. Press the silver button." Don't make the customer read through a lot of "useless" words to find the meat.

And, you need to make it easy for them to know how it will be to interact with your company, including how you protect the personal information they give you, how you process returns, and how you handle problems that might arise.

BUILDING YOUR REVENUE GROWTH ACTION PLAN

So far, in your Brainstorming and Planning Meeting, you have:

- Analyzed, prioritized, and summarized the comments made by your customers. You know what is important to them. Their key issues are right there, in the room with you.

- Started to formulate your real promise, the promise your customers want you to make, and that you can keep—with your products/services, processes, people, passion, and policies.

- Built your Buying Process Roadmap(s).

Now it's time to pull all this together into your Revenue Growth Action Plan.

Revenue Growth Action Plan

	Issue	Solution	Steps	Owner	Due Date	Current Status
Barriers to the sale						
Product/ Service changes						
Process changes						
People changes						
Policy changes						

Here's a spreadsheet template that will help you. Note that there may be multiple "barriers to the sale" or "product/service changes," or any other item in the first column. You may also come up with your own categories.

On a screen displayed in the conference room, fill out this template. Make sure the plan is complete, with appropriate and realistic items. When you think you're done, look it over again, making sure you haven't left anything out and that your goals and deadlines are realistic.

Also make sure that the product/service changes category includes the necessary improvements in documentation and education.

BEFORE YOU FILL THE TABLE WITH YOUR DATA, IT'S IMPORTANT TO TELL YOU ONE OF THE SECRETS OF THE ROADMAP TO REVENUE METHOD: START WHERE THE CUSTOMER WANTS YOU TO BE AND WORK BACKWARDS.

Each solution you list in the Solution column should be the *customer's ultimate desired result*—rather than small, incremental changes that are comfortable for you. If you inch towards the desired result, you *may* arrive someday—or not at all. When you're trying to move your company in a new, customer-driven direction, it's tempting to cling to your own traditional ways of doing things, or to have your efforts constrained by other internal limitations, including how you think of yourselves.

Remember that a new company entering your market won't have any such inhibitions or restrictions. If you don't deliver the customer's ultimate desired result, you are creating a golden opportunity for an aggressive, customer-centric competitor. You will be making a promise that you are not keeping, which is one of the ways that a market need is created.

Customers will go first to the company that makes an attractive promise, but if the company doesn't deliver, customers will still have the need—and will now believe that it can be satisfied. They will have imagined how nice it will be to have that problem finally solved. They will be even *more* determined to have that need met by *someone*. They will search determinedly for someone who will actually meet their need. You will no longer be part of that search.

To avoid this fate, describe the customer's perfect solution in the solutions column. Then ask yourself: How can we deliver that solution as quickly as possible? How would another company do it, if they didn't have our constraints? What fundamental shift could we make in our products/services, people, processes, or policies?

You'll be far more prepared to solve the problem using this method than you would if you started "where you are" and took small steps toward the ultimate goal.

A few other notes about the Revenue Growth Action Plan:

- After the spreadsheet is created, it should be stored in a shared location so owners can update the status column as they make progress.

- As I mentioned, there may be more than one barrier to the sale (quite common), more than one product/service change, and so on. Just add new rows as needed.

- Note that the Product/Service category should also include changes you need to make to anything associated with the product or service—including service modules, product packaging, pricing, documentation, and education.

- Every solution needs an owner so that someone is held accountable and the issue is actually resolved.

- Set realistic, but aggressive timelines.

- There should be a way to track the progress of all projects.

- There are several ways to validate that the change has been successful. It may be a multi-step process, including:

  - Simple verification of the completion of the task, by someone other than the owner

  - Tracking lead acquisition and conversion rates, using tools designed for the purpose

  - Conducting usability studies or interviews to make sure that the barriers have been removed and customers are no longer confused or obstructed in their buying process

  - Measuring your top-line and bottom-line results

The Revenue Growth Action Plan table may seem simple, but it is a powerful tool, especially when you start with the customer's desired end result and work backwards.

More than likely, all departments in your company will be affected in some way—including marketing, sales, product development, product management, distribution/fulfillment, finance, production/manufacturing, and IT.

Financial policies or back-end website processes often create revenue-inhibiting barriers to the sale. For example, a barrier to the sale could be the way you charge for shipping, or the way your website shopping cart is designed. Don't let the bean counters tell you that it will cost too much to remedy the deficiencies. Ask them, "What is it costing us because we are *not* correcting those deficiencies?" This is the real question that must be asked (and answered). This is the right way to approach the problem.

As you discuss the back-end infrastructure, if you find yourself arguing with IT people, the best way to settle the arguments and come to agreement is to diagram whatever it is you are discussing. I can't tell you how many times an IT person has crossed her arms and said, "Can't be done." My answer: "That may be true. But just for kicks, let's diagram this and see where we end up." By the time the diagram is complete, it has *always* become obvious that there *is* a way to solve the problem. That it can, in fact, be done. You have to have enough knowledge of systems and technology to see the possibilities as you diagram, but if you do, you'll be able to move beyond the impasse.

ONCE YOU ARE DONE CREATING THE REVENUE GROWTH ACTION PLAN, IT'S TIME TO WRAP UP THE BRAINSTORMING AND PLANNING MEETING

- Do what you can to finalize your promise now. If it still hasn't quite come together yet, schedule a meeting a day or two later. The goal will be to revisit the subject after everyone has had a chance to mull it over—then finalize the promise.

- Discuss how you will continue to interview customers. If each executive in the room were to contact one customer per week, by the end of any given month you would have gathered sufficient data to know if you were still on track—and if new issues have surfaced.

- Make sure you have a "listener/responder" charged with monitoring online customer conversations, and set up a reporting and response structure for those activities.

- Discuss the idea of having customer service people ask customers *one* research question each time they are on the phone with a customer. Keep track of who is questioned, so that any one customer isn't repeatedly asked the same question every time they call. Their answers will help you determine how well you are staying in sync with your customers.

Your customer service people should ask the same question for one month straight, and then switch to another question. You can return to the first question after a couple of months have passed.

Questions asked by customer service people should be more specific than those asked in the telephone interviews. When someone calls in for service, they don't want to spend a lot of time educating you. Instruct the customer service people to ask the question only after (and only if) the customer's problem has been resolved. They should introduce the question by asking for permission to ask the question ("If it's okay with you, we are asking one question at the end of our calls today. The question I would like to ask you is ...").

Examples of appropriate questions include:

- On a scale of 1—10, how do you feel about our product/service?

- On a scale of 1—10, how do you feel about our documentation?

- On a scale of 1—10, how do you feel about our website?

- Is there anything we could do to improve the product/service?

- What could we have explained better or handled better during your buying process?

- What was the main reason that you bought our product/service?

- What was the problem you were trying to solve when you bought our product/service?

- How did you find our company and product/service?

- If you used a search engine to find us, do you remember what you first typed in?

At the end of the meeting, make sure that all the easel sheets are collected and someone is put in charge of converting them into digital format. Send the digital report around to everyone once this is complete.

Congratulations. You have just created the framework for your own custom Roadmap to Revenue. In the next chapter, we'll dig into the tools and materials you will be using to acquire more leads and close more sales.

Review of the Roadmap to Revenue steps in this chapter:

Day Two of the Brainstorming and Planning Meeting

1. Decide which type of product or service your company sells: Light Scrutiny, Medium Scrutiny, Heavy Scrutiny, or Intense Scrutiny. You might be selling more than one type of product or service.

2. Build a Buying Process Roadmap for each type of product or service. Visit www.RoadmapToRevenue.com/Resources for the appropriate Roadmap file. Agree on the discrete steps followed by customers as they purchase your product/service. List what customers expect to happen at each step, and what you need to do to answer customer questions and help the customer make a decision.

3. Identify the problem areas—where the customer drops out of the process, or where the customer becomes frustrated or confused.

4. Identify areas where you should be investing more resources to better support the customers' buying process. Identify the areas where you could be spending less.

5. Discuss how you could answer questions more efficiently, shifting your product or service to a lower position on the Scrutiny Spectrum. The goal is for your website and other content to answer as many customer questions as possible, as early as possible in their buying process. Pay particular attention to the Critical Characteristic.

6. Build your Revenue Growth Action Plan. Fill in the table with your own action items, listing the barriers to the sale, and the changes you need to make to your products/services, processes, people, and policies. In each category, list the issues, solutions, steps, owners, due dates, and current status. Decide how you will confirm that the issue has been solved.

7. Wrap up the meeting:

   - Finalize your promise, or agree to meet again to finalize it.

   - Agree to the number of customers you will contact on a regular basis in the future, and set up a monthly meeting to discuss your findings.

- Set up the "listener/responder" system to monitor and report on online customer conversations.

- Discuss having your customer service people ask one question each month, to continue to keep tabs on customer issues.

- Make sure the easel sheets are collected at the end of the meeting and someone is in charge of documenting them in digital format, and then distributing them to all meeting attendees.

HOW TO SUPPORT YOUR CUSTOMERS' BUYING PROCESS

6

AN EXAMPLE OF A CUSTOMER'S BUYING PROCESS

So far, we've described how you will interview customers, create the reports, and what you will do in your two-day meeting, including building your promise and your Buying Process Roadmap.

When you interview your customers, they will tell you what they think you need to know, what their problem is, and what they want. They will also tell you how you're missing the mark. They may make a suggestion or two about how to fix it. However, they believe it is *your* responsibility to fill in the details, and do your part. What they say will point you in the right direction.

Then it is up to you to figure out the best way to solve their problems and meet their needs. Your customers are hoping you will do a first-class, professional job.

This chapter will help you do your part properly. It will also serve as an overview of buyer behavior. In the subsequent chapters, we will look more closely at the buying process for each level of scrutiny. Having this information in your head will result in more successful customer interviews—and a more effective Brainstorming and Planning meeting.

All successful purchases follow this basic structure:

1. **Need:** Joe has a need.

2. **Search:** Joe goes searching for a solution.

3. **Arrival:** Joe comes to you.

4. **Answers:** You answer all of his questions, to his satisfaction.

5. **Purchase:** He buys from you and experiences your company and its products/services.

6. **Rating:** He tells others about his experience.

Let's look at these steps in detail.

1: NEED—JOE HAS A NEED

Your first job is to know all about Joe's need.

Joe's need could be **immediate**. He just realized, as he was pouring his cereal into a bowl, that he was out of milk.

Joe's need could be **unhurried**. He and his wife, Julie, have decided that they want to remodel their kitchen. Or, Julie, who is an IT manager at a large company, has decided to find another ISP (Internet Service Provider).

Joe's need could be **ongoing**. He is an avid gardener, and he's always looking for better garden tools and seeds. Julie is always looking for a pair of jeans that fit just right.

If you convince yourself you know all about Joe's need, without asking Joe, you will be marketing to a caricature of Joe, not the "real" Joe. In other words, you can easily deceive *yourself* about Joe, which is what most company leaders do, because it's the easiest thing to do. But *Joe* will not be fooled.

Joe is completely familiar with his need, and will know—immediately and assuredly—if you understand his need or not. That's why attempting to fake it is guaranteed to cause your sales to limp along. If Joe's need is great enough, and your competition is just as clueless and careless, you'll make *some* sales. But if Joe has other, better options, you'll never sell enough to grow your business, and your company may not survive.

To relate successfully to Joe, you need to understand all aspects of his need:

- His current situation

- The urgency of his need (his timing)

- The seriousness of his need (and his willingness to accept a sub-optimal solution, such as a cheaper version of your product or service that a competitor sells)

- His knowledge of current solutions—his buyer sophistication. Don't underestimate this!

- What he has done already in an attempt to meet his need

- The experiences of others who have tried to solve a similar problem

- The promises others have made to him—then kept or broken

- Any resistance he has to meeting his need (in other words, he may not want to spend as much as you're charging, or to put up with the shortcomings of your partial solution)

- What he is willing to pay (or give up) to meet his need

- What would make it easier for Joe to accept your solution

This list shows how far you should be going in your understanding of his problem. "The gardener needs a shovel" is only the tip of the iceberg.

It's quite common for sellers to be off the mark in some of these areas. An over-eager seller will want Joe to be desperate, despite the fact that Joe feels no such urgency. Conversely, Joe may be in a big hurry, but the seller may behave as if Joe has all the time and patience in the world. Sellers may assume that Joe is more than willing to pay a particular price, when in fact Joe has decided he'd rather do nothing about his need than to pay that much.

Most sellers misjudge the intensity of the buyer's need—one way or the other. That means that *all* of their marketing and selling messages are consequently off-target. It's a terrible, sad waste of marketing and selling resources.

Worse, there are marketing gurus who take advantage of this ignorance. They prey on the urgent need of the entrepreneur to bring in revenue, and create campaigns that assume the same intensity of need on the part of the entrepreneur's customer. The entrepreneur, who thinks that the urgency is dead-on, bets the ranch on a campaign that doesn't resonate with customers.

The marketing guru moves on to the next client, richer, while the entrepreneur struggles to survive the cash drain and lost opportunity.

I am quite familiar with these sad situations, because I am often called in after the predatory guru has moved on. Frankly, it makes my blood boil, and it's one of the reasons I'm writing this book.

Another common mistake is over-generalizing the need. For example, customer interviews we conducted for a weight-loss food manufacturer revealed several categories of need. Some customers wanted to replace meals with a high-protein shake. Others wanted snacks they could "afford" to eat between meals. Some were trying to lose massive amounts of weight. Others were only about 15 pounds overweight. And still others were at their desired weight, but needed help maintaining.

A message that simply says, "Use these foods to lose weight," would not appeal to any of these specific needs. We would be asking the *customer* to do the work—to figure out if the product or service will help her with her specific type of need. Instead, each type of person should be able to find herself when she comes to the website.

If you interview your customers, you will learn what their *specific* needs are. You will understand the details and nuances of their needs. This knowledge will inform your decisions. This will also help you talk to them in your marketing and selling materials, using the words that they use. They won't have to translate your internal jargon into their vernacular. They will know exactly what you mean.

Customer terminology should also be incorporated into the design of your product or service. If you sell software, for example, your programmers should be using the words that customers use, rather than forcing customers to figure out the meaning of a term that the programmer used. Using the product will feel natural. The instructions will be easy to follow, and the adoption process will seem easy.

Your customers will know immediately if you understand their needs. They will recognize themselves. That's the first step in any successful sale. The customer will begin to trust that you have a solution, because you obviously understand their problem.

2: SEARCH—JOE GOES SEARCHING FOR A SOLUTION

Joe may not be actively searching yet. He may simply decide that he has a problem and start thinking about the possible solutions. Or, the work he does—or activities he engages in—may make him an active candidate for your type of solution.

However, until he is actively searching, no amount of advertising, PR, direct mail, or other outgoing campaign messages will have much effect on him, which is why response rates for these traditional marketing efforts typically run in the 1% to 2% range.

Once Joe decides he is going to take action on his need, everything changes. The convenience and the immediacy of the Internet make it easy for Joe to click over to Google and type in a search phrase.

Obviously this is where Search Engine Optimization (SEO) and Search Engine Marketing (SEM) come into play. As you probably know, SEO focuses on placement in the non-paid search engine results, and SEM refers to the paid ads appearing on the search results page.

The best way to make sure you appear when Joe goes searching is to know the phrases and words that Joe enters into Google—the first time he searches.

I should note here that this first search phrase may never show up on your own website tracking logs. The terms you see in your logs often reflect Joe's third or fourth attempt.

As buyers, we've all had the experience of typing in a phrase and getting the wrong kinds of results. We then modify our search terms until the results become relevant. This tweaked term is the term that will lead the buyer to your site. This is the term that will show up on your Website tracking logs.

It would be better to know what Joe typed in for his *first* search attempt. Imagine that your company or product/service appears on the top of the first results screen, along with other results which are not as relevant. Instead of being surrounded by your competition, you'd be standing out as the only relevant search result. Yours would be the link that Joe would click on.

This is why you ask, in the interviews: "If you were looking for this type of product/service again, and you didn't know about our solution, what would you type into Google?"

Ask enough customers this question, and you will have some excellent guidance for your search engine optimization and search engine marketing efforts. You will be there when Joe goes looking for you—the first time.

Note that Joe's phrase will probably *not* be the generic, "expensive" phrase that you might assume it will be. In my experience, the right phrase is something that Joe—and other buyers like him—think of naturally, but that you and your competitors haven't thought of at all.

Social media comes into play at this stage now as well. Joe will look to his own communities—online and offline—and ask them what they have done to solve this problem. He may also look for solutions via online retail sites, find your product, and read the reviews that others have written about your product. Most online buyers are bypassing the "formal" marketing copy provided by product sellers now, and going straight for the reviews.

If Joe thinks he will find a solution in a physical store, he will look there.

3: ARRIVAL—JOE COMES TO YOU

Now Joe has arrived at your website—or is standing in front of your product at a store. Or, he has called you, or emailed you, to ask you about your product or service.

What happens next will determine if Joe continues "following the scent," as usability expert Jakob Nielsen[4] says, or if he will lose interest, back out, and look for a better way to solve his problem.

- **When he comes to your website, does Joe immediately feel that he has come to the right place?** Does he recognize himself and his need? Or, does a fancy animation get in his way? Does the navigation work the way he expects it to, or is it confusing? Are your products or services hidden behind some "big idea" campaign that has little to do with Joe's problem? Is it obvious to him what he should do next—to successfully purchase your product or service?

- **When he sends you an email—either directly or using a Web form—does he get an *immediate* response from a real person?** That's the best outcome, of course—to have an email come back to him from a real person. Or, does he get an automated response saying someone will get back to him within 48 hours? Does someone actually get back to him within 48 hours? Or, does Joe wait for days and days? Or, does he never hear back from you at all? This last situation is the most common.

  Very sad, when you consider that Joe wants to buy from you, *now,* and even sadder when you consider how much trouble and expense you invested to make sure Joe showed up at your website.

  Quite often, by the time Joe gets one of these too-late responses, he's already made his purchase. That sale is gone forever. If Joe will be making repeat purchases, you will have lost those sales as well.

- **When he calls, does a real, live human being answer the phone and help him?** Or, does he land in voicemail directory hell, which is really convenient for you, but, in truth just another frustrating barrier to the sale?

You may think that what you are doing is "good enough." You may think you can't give up your voicemail system. Think again.

To a customer, a good receptionist is just a joy—and worth every penny. The phone is answered by someone with a pleasant voice, who is helpful. The customer tells the receptionist what he needs, and she actually takes care of it. She connects him to the person he needs, or gives him the answer he wants. Whatever needs to happen, to make the customer happy, she makes happen.

If you want, don't call this priceless person a receptionist. Call her a "primary customer interface." Call her "the voice of the company." Whatever you call her, don't think of it as a menial task. It should be considered a high-level job. And yes, it could be a woman or a man. It could also be a team of customer service people who take all the incoming calls.

The point is, there is a real person there, who solves the problem. The customer has hope, as soon as he starts talking with the person, that the problem is going to be solved.

Perhaps you think you are saving money using voicemail. But if one out of every two buyers drops out because they are encountering too many barriers, and are met—from the beginning—with a cold, automated, frustrating experience, you've just sacrificed half of your potential revenue.

It's stupid to make the customer hunt for someone who can help. Voicemail is the difference between being customer-driven—and driving the customer away.

Companies *always* make it too difficult for buyers to do business with them. There are only a few exceptions. Amazon.com consistently comes to mind. But even Amazon.com can make it tough to find what you're looking for. For example, it took Amazon.com a long time to include a "Did you mean" function in its search engine. At this writing, Google's "Did you mean" function is still more reliable and relevant. Often, on Amazon.com, if you mistype, the results are meaningless or non-existent.

In larger physical stores, there is often a greeter at the door. But a few minutes later, when you're in the aisles and actually need some help, there is no one around.

If the options on your website are presented in a cluttered, disorganized way, it will be difficult for visitors to figure out how to find and do what they want on your site. If their patience is strained, they won't stick around to figure it out. They'll just click away.

So often, it is the determination of the buyer, and the intensity of the buyer's need, that completes the sale, rather than any assistance the seller offers.

4: ANSWERS—YOU ANSWER ALL OF HIS QUESTIONS, TO HIS SATISFACTION

Let's say that Joe sees himself when he comes to your website. He is able to "follow the scent." He thinks you might have a solution for him.

He is now reading (or, more likely, *scanning*) what you've written about your solution. He's looking for the answers to his questions. Not the questions you *think* Joe is asking, or that you have the answers to, but the *real* questions that Joe has.

Joe scans the copy written about the product and zooms in on the photos, but his question just isn't answered. He's likely to then leave your site and go back to Google, refining his search phrase until he finds the answer he seeks.

If he's buying that DVD player for his entertainment hutch, and wants to know how far the cords stick out the back, he has to type something very specific into Google, such as "Sony DVD DVPSR200P/B picture of the back of the unit"—and then search through the images for a review that actually shows the cords sticking out the back of the unit. He'll be lucky if he finds it.

Or, let's say Joe wants to rent a villa in the Caribbean for a week. He has already decided he wants to go to St. Barts. He types "St. Barts" into Google, and the first item on the list is a villa rental company. He clicks on their link, and is happy to see that he is taken directly to the St. Barts section of the company's website—so he doesn't have to re-enter his desired location. The company provides an advanced search engine. Joe can select the number of bedrooms he needs and his desired arrival and departure dates. So far, so good.

He is then presented with a number of villas. Many of them have pools and a view of the water. Suddenly his questions are much more specific. He wishes he could narrow his results in a way that addresses his new concerns. How close is the villa to the town? Will they be able to see the sunsets from the main view area? Is the kitchen range gas or electric? How close are the neighbors? How private is the pool area? How recent are the pictures? Sometimes these questions are answered in the villa description, sometimes not.

This brings us to another serious deficiency in almost all product-selling websites: the ability to do an apples-to-apples comparison between products, in a way that is meaningful to the customer. In spite of billions of dollars being spent on websites every year, eBags.com is still one of the few sites that will let you build a comparison table. Physical stores offer this ability naturally; you just stand in front of the products and compare one against the other. You can't do this online unless the vendor makes it possible—and few vendors do.

eBags.com will also let you search for a bag or briefcase based on what you're going to put into it. For example, they will tell you if your specific laptop will fit into a particular backpack. But even on eBags.com, while you can find the backpacks that fit your laptop, you cannot then narrow down those results to, say, backpacks that are also waterproof.

Target.com offers more relevant ways to narrow down your search than most. If you search for "drapes" in Target.com, you can narrow down by general categories (Home, Bed + Bath, Kids, etc.), then by more specific categories (Curtains + Blinds, Decorative Hardware, etc.), by price, color, or brand. But you can't select several of these categories and see which items meet all of your criteria (Home/Curtains/Multicolored), and they don't offer other selections—such as the type of curtain or fabric.

Zappos.com is another site that attempts to give customers relevant choices, and has taken it farther than most. Within any given category you can quickly narrow down your choices, using categories that are often surprisingly appropriate. Of course, Zappos.com is fanatical about staying close to customers, so you can guess where their categories have come from.

A fully functional product or services site would use the following tools to answer Joe's questions:

- Straightforward, customer-relevant navigation, designed so that Joe can quickly see which options are available, and select the one most likely to lead to what he's looking for

- Search box to begin the search

- The ability to filter the results—using a mixture of customer-relevant criteria, including looking for a word or phrase in the descriptions—such as gender, size, weight, colors, brands, and special characteristics

- Thumbnail pictures of the product, shown with the listing, along with pertinent information such as price, customer rating, when it would arrive, manufacturer name

- A way to view ALL products on one "page," not just a certain number at a time

- A complete product or service description—including characteristics, size, proper use, examples of use, accessories, etc.

- Pictures of each item—from all angles, with zoom ability—and size comparisons (such as a coin or a ruler)

- Customer reviews of products/services
- Customer ratings for products/services
- A support discussion forum, moderated and responded to by a knowledgeable support person
- A way to compare products or services before purchasing ("add to comparison")
- Previously viewed items
- "More like this"
- The ability to visit the shopping cart at any time (or see it off to the side)—and for the cart to fill up without taking the buyer to the cart every single time a product or service is added to the cart
- The ability of the site to retain the items in the shopping cart forever—and for the buyer to move items to a "save for later" section of the shopping cart
- A wish list
- An "on sale" section
- The ability to register, sign in, and update customer account data
- A way to send gift certificates to others
- A help function
- A chat-with-a-representative window, plus an easy way to contact customer support
- The ability to provide feedback to the site owner, or ask questions
- A way to view products or services previously ordered—and easily reorder, with a single click (Staples.com does this well, as does VitaminShoppe.com)
- An "about" section that reveals the people behind the business—and their passion for the business
- The street address of the company, with directions, and the phone number for the company
- Testimonials and case studies
- Professional videos showing how the product is used or service is provided

- Downloadable product or service documentation in PDF form, for current and discontinued products/services

Given these tools, Joe will find the products/services and the data he needs to make a buying decision. He won't have to leave your site to get his questions answered (or find the solution somewhere else).

If Joe is shopping in a physical store, all of his questions should be answered on the packaging or display. He shouldn't have to call over a sales representative to answer a question that should have been answered on the packaging. The package should clearly show the product and provide detailed information about what is inside the box and how the product works. Providing one item, outside the box, which Joe can "test" or "try on" before buying, will help to answer many of his questions.

If Joe is buying a complex product or service through a salesperson, that salesperson should either have the answers to all of Joe's questions, or have that information at her fingertips, printed or on her computer. Too often, the salesperson doesn't know what Joe's real concerns are. So when Joe brings them up, the salesperson either fakes it, avoids the question, or says, "I'll get back to you." Joe decides (to himself) that he will take his business elsewhere. (You will find more about salespeople and their role in the buying process in Chapter 10.)

You will be able to answer all of Joe's questions because you will have conducted interviews with real customers and made the necessary changes to facilitate his buying process. You will know what Joe is looking for, and where he is looking for it. You will make it easy for him to buy.

5: PURCHASE—HE BUYS FROM YOU AND EXPERIENCES YOUR COMPANY AND YOUR PRODUCTS AND SERVICES

Joe has gotten his questions answered, made his decisions, filled his cart, and then makes his purchase. As he does so, he should be able to:

- Select the arrival day, carrier, and shipping cost—*before* he enters his payment information

- Check "same as shipping address" so he doesn't have to fill out the address info twice

- Manage his credit card info as he prefers—either filling in his credit card information each time he buys from you, or agreeing to let you store his credit card details for the next purchase

- Opt-in to receive additional promotional information—if he wants it. (Don't pre-check the box! If you're a customer-driven company, you won't have to trick people into finding out about your products.) Hint: If you want more people to check the box, tell them how *often* you'll be sending messages to them, and what those messages will contain. "We will send you notices of product discounts, every two weeks."

- Go "back" in the online buying process while filling out the information, without having to re-enter the information he already entered

- Receive a confirmation on the final screen, and a detailed receipt that he can save to his computer or print out

- Click on a "continue shopping" button

- Receive an email confirmation of his order

- Track his order after he places it

If Joe is in a physical store, he should be able to check out easily, without waiting in line for more than a few minutes. If Joe is the only person stepping up to the checkout counter, the checkout clerks should cease any conversations they're having with each other, and a clerk should immediately take care of Joe.

If Joe is working with a salesperson, and there is a contract of some sort involved, the salesperson should be ready to pull the contract out of his briefcase or computer and give it/send it to Joe, as soon as Joe is ready for it. It should be written in plain language, as simply as possible—even the lawyerly sections. It should be very clear what will be delivered, how and when it will be delivered, who will be expected to set it up and get it working properly, and what role Joe is expected to play after the contract is signed.

Once Joe starts using the product or starts to work with your company on a project, he experiences and evaluates:

- How well your product is designed, manufactured, and documented, or how well your service is designed and delivered

- How closely the actual product or service matches your description

- How available you are and how quickly you respond when he needs help

- How knowledgeable, pleasant, and helpful you are while assisting him

- Your willingness to make changes, so that his needs are met, and to resolve any issue that has arisen as he's tried to use the product or service

- Your willingness to issue a refund if the product or service fails to work as promised (and the ease with which he can return the product and obtain a refund)

- The strength (or weakness) of your processes and systems—such as tech support and documentation

- The overall culture of your company—and the behavior of the people you've hired and trained

6: RATING—HE TELLS OTHERS ABOUT HIS EXPERIENCE

Your buyers have a number of ways to enthuse about their good experiences and rant about the bad ones to other potential buyers—in the form of "tweets" on Twitter, comments and pictures on Facebook, reviews in e-commerce sites, emails sent to friends and family, blogs, and, of course, plain old word of mouth.

We are living in an age where dozens, hundreds, or even thousands of people can find out how you treated Joe—within seconds of him feeling he was either mistreated or treated well.

Revenue has always been tied to reputation, and reputation has always been tied to behavior. What's changed is that the buffer between your behavior and your reputation has vanished. It used to be that customers could only express their disappointment to a small circle of friends. Now every customer comes with a megaphone—and the ability to influence others immediately. More importantly, one customer's negative review can—and often does—show up when the next customer is about to make a purchase. The review that appears on your product/service page will have a direct effect on the new customer's decision to buy from you, or not.

You don't have control over these customer activities; you really don't even have control over your reputation. But you can—and should—control your own *behavior,* which then determines your reputation.

As manager, you exert control over the behavior of your people. The best managers successfully guide their teams with a combination of:

- "Big picture" concepts

- An obsession for building a customer-focused company

- Regular, consistent, and clear communication

- Continual efforts to make processes and systems more efficient

- Regularly diving down through the layers of management to see what's going on for themselves. While reports from middle managers can make their workload more manageable, successful top managers know they can't depend on those reports unless they regularly and randomly check up on things. They walk the halls.

The best managers split their time between customers, managers, partners, and non-managerial employees. It is the "lowest" people in the corporate hierarchy who actually come in daily contact with customers. They should be thoroughly and regularly trained, monitored, and rewarded for taking good care of customers.

In order for a sale to be made, your buyer must either trust your brand (the content/story associated with your brand) or the recommendation of someone they trust. Remember that helpfulness and trust are joined at the hip.

You don't have control over people trusting you—that's their side of the equation—but you do have complete control over how helpful and trustworthy you are. Whatever you do, as you promote your product or service, make sure you provide helpful content in addition to the sales pitch. People trust people who help them.

Review of the Roadmap to Revenue steps in this chapter:

All successful purchases include 6 basic steps:

1. Need

   - If you guess about the buyer's need, you will lose sales—because you will guess incorrectly. Joe is intimately familiar with his need. You can't fool him. He will know if you understand his need or not.

   - You must know the buyer's situation: How urgent his need is; how serious he is about finding a solution; his knowledge about what others have done to solve his type of problem; what he has already done in an attempt to meet his need; the experiences of others who have solved the problem; the promises made to him; any resistance he has to meeting his need; what he is willing to pay; and what would make it easier for him to accept your solution.

- If you guess, over-generalize, or assume your customers feel or buy the same way you do, you will be wrong about many aspects of the buyer's situation.

2. Search

- His interest may only be passive; he might be thinking about a solution, but he hasn't begun to search in earnest.

- Until he is searching in earnest, your messages will make only a minimal impression on him.

- Once he decides to search, your search engine marketing and search engine optimization come into play.

- You must know and use the words and phrases customers use to describe their problems and solutions. Guessing will prevent you from making sales.

- The most powerful, revenue-producing search terms are those a customer types in at the *beginning* of his search, not the refined phrases he uses to finally find you. You want to turn up as early as possible in his search process, increasing your chances of him continuing with you instead of a competitor.

3. Arrival

- A customer comes to your website. He should immediately think, *Good. Just what I was looking for.* If not, he won't keep rummaging around on your website. He will leave.

- When a customer sends you an email, if he doesn't get an immediate response from a real person, you're already on your way to losing the sale, because a competitor may respond immediately.

- A customer calls. Does he get dumped into voicemail hell, or does a real, live person answer the phone and help him?

- Most companies put up *several* barriers at the Arrival stage.

4. Answers

- A customer comes to your website, and starts scanning your content, looking for answers to his questions. If you answer his questions to his satisfaction, he will stick with you. If not, he will leave your site and likely revise his Google search so that he is more likely to find the answer to his questions. He won't be visiting you again.

- Most sites lack helpful content, such as "apples-to-apples" comparisons and useful filtering and sorting criteria.

- The "search within results" function should be part of your on-site search function, especially if you sell a large number of products or services.

- Sites that answer questions successfully include everything listed on pages 141–143.

- The salesperson should either know the correct answer to a question, or be able to find it immediately. Salespeople who try to avoid the question or fake it will lose the trust of the customer—and the sale.

5. Purchase

- As the customer makes the purchase on your website, the process should be as convenient as possible. He shouldn't have to enter data twice. He should be able to choose his shipping and credit card preferences with ease. Terms and conditions should be clearly written and presented at the right time in the buying process. He should be able to print out a receipt and track his order after he has placed it.

- If he is buying in a physical store, he should be able to check out quickly, without waiting more than a minute or two.

- If he is buying from a salesperson, the contract should be ready as soon as the customer is ready.

- When the buyer makes the purchase, and as he receives your product or starts to use your service, he will be noting the quality of your product/service and the helpfulness of your people, processes, and policies.

6. Rating

- The buyer will remember his experiences with your product or service, people, policies, and processes. He will take note of how well you kept your promises.

- He will relate his experiences to others, verbally or virtually. Virtual reviews are far more long-lasting and visible to anyone who is thinking of buying your product or service. They can and should appear right on your product/service description page. Numerous studies have found that customers are more likely to buy from the company that displays ratings and reviews on its website. There are companies that offer rating and review modules, and other "customer conversation" functions, which you can incorporate into your website. One company that offers this service, Bazaarvoice, has found that, on average, about 80% of ratings and reviews are positive.

- You can't control your reputation. You *can* control your behavior and you do have management control over your people, products and services, policies, processes, passion, and promises.

- The best managers guide their teams with a combination of a big-picture vision and careful attention to customer-driven product/service development, efficient processes, and employee activities and training. Good managers communicate regularly.

- People buy from companies they trust. The more helpful you are, the more you will be trusted.

AN OVERVIEW OF THE FOUR LEVELS OF BUYER SCRUTINY

7

... AND THE TRUTH ABOUT MARKETING METHODS AND CHANNELS

Now that we've looked at the customers' buying process from a big picture perspective, it's time to address each level of Scrutiny: Light, Medium, Heavy, and Intense. Each level is covered in its own chapter. I will be describing what works best for each, right after we cover two quick topics in this chapter:

- Why you need to read all the Scrutiny chapters

- Universal truths about marketing and selling channels (any medium that can carry your message). This is an important topic, because most company owners and managers get taken advantage of by media channel sellers. By understanding how your customers want to buy from you, you will be able to avoid costly mistakes.

Here's why you need to read *all* of the Scrutiny chapters, not just the Scrutiny chapter that pertains to your current product or service:

- If a channel would be used in more than one Scrutiny category, I will only discuss it in the earliest category's chapter, to avoid unnecessary repetition. If you only read a later section relevant to your particular product or service, you will miss valuable channel advice.

- **You may be selling more than one type of product/service, or your Scrutiny level may change.** As we shall see in the Light Scrutiny section, sometimes you must enter into an Intense Scrutiny relationship with a distributor or outside sales force in order to sell a lower-scrutiny product/service. Or you may end up selling an Intense Scrutiny service (such as consulting services) along with your Medium Scrutiny product (such as a business software program). Or you may decide to expand your product line, and the new product fits into a different category. It's important to know what is required to sell each type of product/service.

- **You will learn from the information in other categories.** Every Medium Scrutiny seller can learn from Light Scrutiny techniques. Every Heavy Scrutiny seller can learn from Medium Scrutiny techniques, and so on. For example, I talk about a product's buzz and reputation in the Light Scrutiny section. Every type of product/service needs a strong buzz and reputation. Plus, a method that we mention in an earlier section might trigger a powerful idea for you, even though your product or service belongs in a different category.

- **Moving your product/service down the Scrutiny Spectrum will lower the cost of supporting the purchase—and make your business more profitable.** As you become more adept at supporting your customers' buying process, you will be able to ease your product/service downwards on the Scrutiny Spectrum. You will be answering the potential client's questions more efficiently. Your salespeople will spend less time answering questions and more time taking orders. That's nice for them and great for your business.

UNIVERSAL TRUTHS ABOUT MARKETING AND SELLING CHANNELS

All four Scrutiny Levels have one thing in common: you will be using marketing and selling channels to reach your customer and/or answer your customer's questions. In order for your marketing and selling efforts to be affordable and successful, you need to use these channels effectively.

New channels come (and often go) faster than ever now. The "traditional" or "broadcast" marketing mix, consisting of advertising (print, TV, radio), PR, direct mail, tradeshows and events, was elbowed aside by websites, email, and search-engine marketing. Those "new" Web-based channels then became the older, established channels, and they are now being displaced by customer-created content channels, including social media, discussion groups, streaming video, and blogging. As these shifts occur, the older media fade away, but never completely disappear.

Don't be swept up by the hype perpetuated by people who are selling the latest tools or methods. The only time you should go near one of those salespeople is *after* you have interviewed your customers and they've told you how *they* expect to find out about your product/service.

Don't think that just because someone is using a method successfully for one type of product or service that it will work for yours. This is one of the most common mistakes in marketing—and the one most often exploited by consultants who specialize in a particular marketing channel.

The people who sell channels and advertising on channels make it their business to come up with exciting new suggestions designed to harvest your marketing budget. Every media salesperson will assure you that their method will work best for you.

Whom should you trust? None of them, really. There are only two reliable sources of guidance.

THE CHANNELS YOU DECIDE TO USE SHOULD BE GUIDED BY TWO RELIABLE SOURCES: YOUR CUSTOMERS' BUYING PROCESS AND TESTING.

Your customers' buying process will provide basic guidance regarding the best channels to use. When customers describe their buying process to you, they will be telling you where they go to find you, how they search for you, and what they are hoping to find.

Once you have gathered the vital knowledge from customers on the best channels to use, you'll need to develop the messages that will appeal to them. Again, the insights you gain from customer research will make this easier; you'll know what is important to them and what appeals to them.

Once you have created your messages, you'll need to refine them by testing them. Testing has become a hot topic in marketing circles, in part because it is much easier than it used to be to set up an apples-to-apples message comparison (and quickly see the results) using tools such as Google AdWords.

The media mix landscape changes quickly. My goal in this chapter is to help you evaluate and use whatever channels are available to you now.

I do cover the latest channel trends in my revenue-growth blog, the Revenue Journal,[5] so check there for updates on the subject.

HERE ARE SOME BASIC PRINCIPLES TO HELP YOU MAKE BETTER-INFORMED DECISIONS ABOUT CHANNELS

1. **Traditional broadcast marketing is still with us.** You still have the traditional, one-way, broadcasting media at your disposal: TV, radio, direct mail, events, billboards, advertising, product placements in movies, event sponsorships, and go-through-the-journalists PR. However, broadcast marketing is falling out of favor, for a number of reasons.

   - There are too many commercial messages. People are exposed to thousands of advertising messages a day and have learned to tune them out. Advertising messages are really only interesting to customers when they're actually starting their own buying process.

   - The message seldom reaches the buyer when he is in the process of making a purchase.

   - You have to broadcast to a lot of eyeballs in the hopes of getting one person to respond. Response rates are really low—and continue to decrease.

   These are all valid points, but what really matters is the buying process your customers follow—and the role that any type of channel plays in their buying process. For example, direct mail is still a great way to reach someone if you're promoting a local event. Some companies that have tested a variety of methods—even in business-to-business markets—have been surprised to see that direct mail still out-pulls email.

   The success of your use of broadcast media depends on what you're selling, how customers want to receive information from you, and how easy it is for them to act on your messages. But broadcasting is usually an expensive way to acquire leads.

[5] www.RevenueJournal.com

2. **Don't be rudely intrusive.** Interactive media have the potential to be much more intrusive than passive media. Mind your manners. For example, computers and the Internet now make it possible for any software vendor to interrupt what you are doing on your computer, force you to update your software, and reboot your computer. This is very irritating.

There is a line between using and misusing any type of channel. The more interactive the channel, the more necessary it is for you to respect the line. If you're not sure where the line is, ask your customers what they'd like you to do.

For example, as a customer, if *you* get an email that you didn't ask for, and you don't want to get more like it, you will want to tell the sender to take you off their list. You should be able to do this by hitting "reply" and typing "unsubscribe" in the subject line, or by clicking on a link and then seeing a screen that shows you your address and says you've been unsubscribed.

These "opt-out" methods are currently required by the CAN-SPAM Act[6] in the U.S Anything more cumbersome will be a major irritation to your customer. Make it as easy as possible for your customer to stop receiving your messages.

Another example of crossing the line is the self-promoter whose Twitter tweets consist entirely of pushy sales messages that are not helpful in any way. In the short term, these methods might make a few extra pennies here and there, but in the long term, the single-message tweeter will simply be encouraging people to avoid him in the future—and tell their friends to do the same.

If you cross over the line, your own actions will erode the trust you've built. It's much harder (if not impossible) to regain trust that you have lost than it is to earn it from scratch.

Customers don't want to buy things from people who are ill-mannered and irritate them by intruding into their space.

3. **Your first responsibility is to those who are already searching for what you sell.** Marketing is more of an inbound exercise now. Inbound marketing consultants are springing up like weeds on the guru landscape. They're right—buyers who want something typically start at Google. They come *looking for you.* How you handle those inbound customers

---

[6] http://www.ftc.gov/bcp/edu/pubs/business/ecommerce/bus61.shtm

will have more of an effect on your revenue—positive or negative—than all the outbound marketing you might do. These inbound customers are already standing in the doorway of your store, money in hand. Roll out the red carpet. Ignoring them is stupid. Making sure they have a great experience is very, very smart—and starts to create revenue momentum. You and your salespeople should be all over those inbound leads, like white on rice, as the saying goes. Too often, that's not what happens at all. Interested buyers are commonly ignored.

4. **Whatever you do, be truthful.** I don't care where you're promoting yourself, or what channel you are using to promote yourself. If you're not honest about who you are, what you can do for people, and what you sell, you are sacrificing future earnings for short-term gain. You are, in short, blowing it. You will be found out, and your dishonesty will become your brand.

Bait-and-switch behavior will lead to you being outed and vilified on public forums—often the exact places where your buyers are congregating.

If I am unsure about the veracity of a seller's offer, I go to Google and type in the name of the person or the offer, and the word "problem" or the word "scam." If there is a problem with that person or the offer they're making, this type of search will almost always reveal it.

Don't even think about hiring people to write fake reviews and rave about your product or service in online discussion groups. It's a terrible practice—and one that will get you into all kinds of trouble. Plus, one negative review that was obviously written by a real customer will counteract all the rosy reviews that everyone believes have been planted by the seller.

These methods can immediately and perhaps permanently dry up your revenue stream.

5. **Tell a story.** The most beloved products, services and companies have strong stories associated with them. Types of stories that appeal include "David and Goliath," "poor person makes good," "person persists until the world recognizes and rewards his approach," and "person finds a unique way to solve a problem."

Most companies have interesting stories to tell, but they are reluctant to tell them. It's important to remember, however, that the best stories are those where the customer is the star. At the very least, the CEO of the company should be an avid customer advocate (Amazon.com, Zappos, and Southwest Airlines come to mind). The customers of these companies *know* the CEO is dedicated to their satisfaction and delight. That's a story in itself.

6. **Knowing the channels and messages that your customers will pay attention to—and respond to—will allow you to focus exclusively on the channels that will work.** The choices you must make about *which* channels you use should be driven by your customer's preferences and buying process. Don't guess or assume you know. It's a guaranteed way to waste money. For example, your most profitable buyers may not be watching TV or reading newspapers.

7. **Assume that news travels fast (especially bad news) and that your reaction to any bad news must be almost immediate.** Make sure you have a process in place to resolve these issues. Apologize. Be humble. Explain what you're going to do to fix the problem. Be specific. After the problem is fixed, return to the place or person where the complaint first appeared, and tell them what has been done to fix the problem.

8. **Regardless of the channel, people's word-of-mouth activity remains the same: Saying what they know, and asking others what they know.** New technology and methods may make it easier for these activities to take place, and word of mouth stories spread faster, but the basic activity hasn't changed.

    People like saying what they know about something. People also like to find out what their friends know about something. And their "friends" can now include other buyers of a product/service who have described their experience in the form of a review, a "tweet," a comment, or a blog entry.

    You will have to stay up to date on the latest platforms people use to communicate, but the basic principles remain the same: Be helpful. Be interesting. Tell the truth.

Now it's time to look at the channels available to you, and the best ways to use them, for each type of product or service: Light Scrutiny, Medium Scrutiny, Heavy Scrutiny, and Intense Scrutiny.

HOW TO SUPPORT
THE LIGHT SCRUTINY
BUYING PROCESS

Characteristics of Light Scrutiny
Products and Services

- Many millions buy Light Scrutiny products and services.

- Buyers only ask a couple of questions.

- Prices typically run from one dollar to tens of dollars.

- The buying process takes seconds or minutes; the need is immediate.

- Examples: Food, souvenirs, trinkets, freeware, batteries, simple hand tools, extension cords, grooming items, craft items, and small-commitment services—such as dry cleaning.

Following is the Buying Process Roadmap guide—which can serve as a template for your own Light Scrutiny Buying Process Roadmap. At each step, you will want to answer these questions:

- **Customer Actions:** Who is the buyer at this stage, and what are that buyer's concerns and questions?

- **Company Tasks:** Where is the buyer expecting to find these messages at this stage in his/her buying process? What messages and tools must we create to address the buyer's concerns and answer his or her questions?

LIGHT
SCRUTINY

? ?
$

BUYING PROCESS
ROADMAP

CUSTOMER ACTIONS	COMPANY TASKS
SEES IT, OFTEN WHILE BUYING OTHER THINGS	**CREATE A GREAT PRODUCT OR SERVICE & PUT IT WHERE IT WILL BE SEEN**

CUSTOMER ACTIONS

The customer sees your product, usually while shopping for other items in a retail store, often at the checkout counter with other Light Scrutiny products.

Or, he is about to check out while making an online purchase, and the product is offered while he is checking out. The product or service catches his eye—and addresses a need he has.

If you are selling a simple service, the customer will see it when he passes by, or he may have searched for it online, looking for your type of service in a local online directory.

Light Scrutiny products are often referred to as "impulse" purchases, which places them at the low end of the Scrutiny Spectrum.

COMPANY TASKS

- Interview buyers so you know what they want in your type of product or service, where they expect to find it, and the words and phrases they use to describe it. Identify the Critical Characteristic.

- Build buyer personas and the Buyer Scenario for the buyer.

- Understand how well your competition is meeting the customers' needs and where they fall short.

- Design the product or the service so it meets buyer needs. Don't try to push them into buying something that isn't good for them.

- Identify and articulate the promise that customers want you to keep— and that you *can* keep—with your product, people, processes, policies, and passion.

- Place the product or locate the service where it will be seen. Take advantage of any "piggybacking" opportunities available to you.

- Build an *Intense* Scrutiny Roadmap for any selling partners, to make it easy for them to decide to carry your product.

- Build buzz for your product or service so that partners are more likely to carry and promote it, and customers will "recognize" it when they see it. Regularly "rebuzz" your product, to keep it on buyer radar.

- If you are selling a local service, make sure your signage says what you sell and why it's special. Signs should be readable while driving by.

CUSTOMER ACTIONS

COMPANY TASKS

2

ASKS A FEW QUESTIONS

ANSWER THEIR QUESTIONS

If he hasn't purchased it before, he will pick it up and read the package, (or click on the link) to make sure there aren't any "show stoppers," such as an undesirable ingredient or function.

If he has purchased it before, he has only three basic questions: Do I want this now? How was it last time? Can I afford it? "Affordability" doesn't just apply to the cost. Can his waistline afford it? Will he have time to use it?

If you are selling a Light-Scrutiny service, the person will look for important information in your shop window or on your website.

- State specifically what is inside the package, in clear, simple language. ("Offset crank action screwdriver with two interchangeable Phillips tips and two interchangeable slotted tips.")

- Show a high-quality close-up picture of the product, or provide a see-through window to the product.

- List all of the ingredients—and things that you purposefully left out ("No high-fructose corn syrup.").

- Display the Critical Characteristic prominently on the package.

- Include your basic promises in all of your copy—product packaging, listings, or store windows.

CUSTOMER ACTIONS   COMPANY TASKS

BUYS IT	**3**	MAKE IT EASY FOR THEM TO BUY

If the customer is at the checkout counter, he will pay for the item using cash, credit card, or debit card.

If he is shopping online, he will add the item to his cart, and enter all the data required to check out.

- Retail stores: The barcode on your packaging should be easily scanned.

- Online: Make it one-click easy to buy. The fewer the screens, the better. Don't make them enter data more than once as they are filling out the forms. If they have to go "back," retain the data they've entered so they don't have to enter it again.

USES IT, LIKES IT, REVIEWS IT, & PURCHASES IT AGAIN	**4**	KEEP YOUR PROMISES & MAKE IT EASY TO PURCHASE AGAIN

Was it as good as expected? Did it do what the packaging or signage said it would do? If so, he will be more likely to buy your product again.

He may also write about it somewhere, although he is less likely to do this for a Light Scrutiny product or service than any of the heavier-scrutiny products or services.

- Make sure your product keeps all the promises you make.

- The customer should be able to open the package easily, but should also be able to tell if it has been tampered with.

- Give customers a URL where they can post their reviews.

- Encourage them to purchase again— with a coupon or other incentive.

CUSTOMER ACTIONS   **COMPANY TASKS**

OR CUSTOMER RETURNS IT   **5**   **MAKE IT EASY TO CONTACT YOU; TAKE ACTION AS NEEDED**

If the product disappoints, the person will want to return it.

He may write about his negative experience online ("This program slowed my computer to a crawl!").

Monitor online mentions of your company and product names, so you can see negative reviews when they pop up, and respond to them in the same venue where the review appeared. Be courteous, informative, and helpful.

Note that buyers who are "on the fence" about whether they should buy or not will read these reviews — and your response. If the prospective customer sees how nice you were to the previous customer, the new customer will be much more likely to buy.

- Make it easy for customers to return the product. It should also be easy to contact you — via a toll-free number listed on your package, and/or a special URL or email address — all of which should be handled by real human beings who respond immediately.

- Resolve the issue quickly and courteously. Listen and take action. Talk to the person. Solve the problem.

- Keep track of return issues and make any changes necessary — to your product, services, processes, packaging, promises, or policies.

HOW THEY FIND YOU

We all know that more people are using Google when it's time to buy something. This is absolutely true for Medium, Heavy, and Intense products and services.

But what if you're selling a Light Scrutiny product or service that customers aren't necessarily searching online for? Something very affordable that they would normally buy on impulse, when they are already in a physical or online store?

You have two strategies you must implement, in parallel:

YOU NEED TO BUILD YOUR PRODUCT'S "BUZZ," AND YOU NEED TO GET YOUR PRODUCT PLACED WHERE THE BUYERS ALREADY ARE.

BUILDING YOUR PRODUCT'S BUZZ

When you're selling a Light Scrutiny product, you need the word to spread. What causes ideas to spread? People talk about things they find interesting or useful.

Interesting and useful things fall into several categories:

- Something new

- Something outrageous—a spectacle

- Something entertaining

- Something connected to a celebrity

- Something that could make them money—or something they could win

- Something that could help them—or help others whom they care about

Here's your assignment: Work for several days on a list where you come up with ways to associate your product or service with these "word-spreading" tools. We'll call this your Buzz List. You'll want your Buzz List to be as long as possible, because each of the ideas will lose their effectiveness over time. Once the interest dies down, it's time to ramp up the next idea.

As you create this list, engage the assistance of potential customers, current customers, and trusted advisors. During this phase, write down anything— even if it seems crazy or impractical. Then, test the Buzz List with your trusted advisors and customers, and ask them to comment.

Whatever you decide to do should somehow relate to the benefit of the product/service. Keep asking yourself, "Is this going to help the person remember and buy my product/service? Will this actually lead to a sale?"

Your final, fully refined Buzz List should contain things that are newsworthy, interesting, or useful about your company, product, or service.

Some aspects of your buzz will be more apt to spread than other aspects. In order to keep your sales going over time, you may as well test all of the concepts that you can afford to test, one at a time.

Prioritize the items according to how easily, affordably, and quickly you can implement them. The items at the top of the list—using these criteria— should be the ones you test first.

The nature of an item on your Buzz List will determine what you do with it. For example, if you have an outrageous use for your product or service, make a video showing that outrageous use. Then do everything you can to expose the link to the video. Use all of the channels that can include a link—Tweets, Facebook and other social media entries, and your own blog. Approach bloggers who might be interested. Include a link to your video in your comments on their blogs. Be helpful and don't pitch in the comment, but at the end of the comment, include your name and the link to your video right under your name. Email everyone you know (without spamming, of course).

You can also post a press release on a service such as PRWeb.com. I should note that press release distribution services are not as effective as they used to be; citizens of the Internet get most of their news from bloggers, news aggregation sites, and discussion groups. Journalists—the main target for press releases—play less of a role in the news business now.

Here are some examples of "buzz" ideas:

- **Invite others to share their outrageous ideas**—so you end up with "101 ways people use [our product/service]." You will be expanding your product or service's buzz as you interact with customers who are talking about and using your product/service.

- **Show the product/service being used.** If you are selling an item that can be used to create something else (such as a food ingredient), you'll want to show the product being used. Ina Paarman, a very successful spice and sauce producer based in South Africa, does this beautifully. Check out her website[7] and take a look at some of her videos.

- **Keep a lookout for current events onto which you can piggyback.** Be ready to take advantage of a new trend or news story that relates to your product or service. Never stop looking for ways to enlarge your buzz. Pick carefully; there's a fine line between outrageous and gross, a line that too many marketers have been more than willing to cross, to their detriment.

- **Associate your product or service with a good cause.** Newman's Own has donated $265 million to charity since 1982, and sent over 135,000 children to the Hole in the Wall camps for children with life-threatening illnesses. Doing something similar (most likely on a smaller scale) will help people feel good about buying your products or services, and will also give you new opportunities for publicity.

- **Associate your product/service with a celebrity.** Endorsements are quite common in the Light Scrutiny category, but they require a big budget. I wouldn't even think of doing it if the celebrity doesn't have a natural connection with a product/service—such as associating swimming trunks with an Olympic swimming champion. There is also the danger that the celebrity will do something stupid and your brand will then be tainted by association. We've all seen this happen.

  Anyone can become a celebrity now, thanks to YouTube. Consider ways to make your customers the celebrities.

- **Create a mascot that you can associate with your brand.** Cereal companies have done this for years. Again, it must be appropriate for your audience.

- **Make the CEO the celebrity.** This should *only* be done if the CEO will make an exceptionally good spokesperson for the company. If the CEO is a friendly, knowledgeable person, making him the star of your promotional efforts could help you humanize the company. Of course, the CEO is not the person who should decide if this approach is appropriate or not. He is not in the position to make an unbiased decision

---

[7] InaPaarman.co.za

about this. And, unfortunately, the people who advocate this approach are almost always doing it because it's easy to sell the CEO on the idea—not because it's the right thing for the company or the customers. In fact, the CEOs who are naturally inclined to play this role are usually doing it already—starting the day they founded the company.

There are dozens of channels for your buzz messages:

- Free but resource-consuming channels such as social media, community sites, and video sites. Use social media to start a conversation with your customers. Begin by listening, then start responding in a relevant and helpful way.

- Bloggers. Contact them directly or write a relevant, non-spammy comment that includes your link. Whatever you do, don't set up a robot to include a nonsensical comment and your link in a zillion blog comment sections.

- Free or relatively inexpensive press release distribution sites.

- Paid advertising—search engine ads, content-related ads, banner ads, print ads, radio, and TV ads. Always start small, always test, always include a way for customers to contact you—and give them a good reason for doing so.

- Direct mail or email, offering something free for responding (coupon for your product/service, an e-book or guide, etc.). Don't forget about plain old letters in a plain old hand-addressed white envelope with a plain old stamp. Tests have shown these to be one of the most effective methods, for certain types of products or services. People get much less mail than they used to, as marketers have turned their attention to other channels. This can also be a great way to test a concept, in a small, inexpensive way.

GETTING YOUR LIGHT SCRUTINY PRODUCT PLACED WHERE BUYERS ARE ALREADY CONGREGATING.

Light Scrutiny products often fall into the category of an impulse purchase, where someone picks up the item while shopping for other items. Obviously, the more places your product appears, the more likely it will be that your product is purchased. If you're selling a Light Scrutiny service, especially a local one, try to get your flyers (or, even better, coupons) displayed on the counters of other local establishments.

Distribution. For Light Scrutiny products, distribution is key. The product has to be present in the physical and online retail locations where similar or related products are sold. In order to sell to the consumer in retail locations, you have to convince a distributor or retailer to carry your product. You'll want to choose a distributor who is already selling your type of product or complementary products.

Selling through distributors will complicate your sales process. Even though you are selling a Light Scrutiny product, establishing a relationship with a distributor or retailer will involve an Intense Scrutiny buying process on the part of the distributor or retailer. If they decide to carry your product, they will be entering into a long-term relationship with you, so there are many factors they must consider before they will take you on. Look for a way to earn their trust faster, by associating yourself with an organization or company that specializes in introducing new products and services to appropriate distributors.

Distributors and retailers are only going to carry products that are proven sellers. Their big question: "Will it sell?" (This is *their* Critical Characteristic.) The most convincing way to answer this question is with a proven track record. You need to be able to prove that you have been successfully selling the product in other retail environments or on your own website.

The key here is to start local or start small, focusing on one retail store or your own website. Another option open to you is a program such as the Amazon Marketplace, where you can sell your products on Amazon.com. The Amazon Marketplace fee is minimal. Amazon.com will handle the credit card processing for you.

Use your "buzz" activities to make as many sales as you can. Keep track of sales growth data and build nice-looking charts that tell the success story. You'll want to use that information when you pitch the distributor or retailer.

You probably won't be able to interview the distributor before your pitch (you can try, but assume you will only be able to ask a few questions). Instead, you can learn a lot about the distributor ahead of time by going to the distributor's website. You can also learn more about the distributors in your industry by talking to people in your industry's trade association. They may also be able to tell you how much others in your industry pay distributors (usually based on a percentage of the retail price), what kinds of perks other companies offer (such as extra cases when a certain number of cases have been ordered), and so on.

Establishing the first distribution relationship will be the most challenging. Once you've had some success with the first one, it will be easier to secure additional relationships with non-competing distributors who cover other geographic territories or who specialize in specific industries or markets.

Again, the buying process for a distributor who is thinking about carrying a new product is an Intense Scrutiny purchase. You will need to answer a lot of questions. Pay close attention to the Heavy and Intense Scrutiny chapters. Answer their questions on a special page or section of your website, as well as in a PDF document that you can email or hand to the distributor. Include plenty of information about your target consumer and their need or desire for your type of product. Include testimonials. Use all of this to back up your proven sales numbers.

Piggybacking. Your product or service may be a perfect candidate for a piggyback approach. Is it the type of product that someone would buy when they are at the virtual or real-world checkout counter? Is it something that "goes with" another product/service? If so, work on convincing sellers of those other products/services to place yours in proximity to theirs.

I bring this up because entrepreneurs frequently fail to recognize these obvious opportunities. They create a product/service and then assume that the only way they can sell it is to go it alone.

Make a list of all the products and services that are in any way related to yours, and think about how you could approach those businesses in a way that will benefit both of you.

Packaging. Packaging plays a significant role in Light Scrutiny products, regardless of where they're sold. Don't skimp on your packaging. A well-designed, easy-to-recognize, easy-to-stock, informative package will get you more attention and more customers, making it more likely that distributors and retailers will carry your product.

Find a designer who has designed packaging for similar products and has experience with the all-important bar codes, ingredient lists, and legal information. A good package will make you look successful even when you are just starting out.

During the process of designing your package, take the mockups to a real retail environment, and place each mockup next to the other products in your category (get permission from the store owner or manager—and use this as an excuse to introduce him to the product!).

Seeing your product packaging in context is one of the best ways to determine how well your product will fare on a crowded retail shelf. Does the product name stand out clearly? Does the packaging look like it belongs there, as professional as the brands next to it? Is it obvious what's inside? Is the key customer benefit big enough for someone to see at first glance? Take pictures of the packaging in the store context, and use those pictures to discuss the packaging with potential customers, partners, and your designer.

On your packaging, make sure you:

- Make it very clear what the package contains—and how the product addresses the customer's Critical Characteristic

- Show a picture of the product in use, in addition to showing the product itself (unless you have transparent packaging)

- List all of the ingredients or contents, including weight and/or volume information

- Include the necessary legal, barcode, and warning information

- Provide directions for use. Make sure they are clearly written and test them on real people before finalizing the copy.

- Do everything you can to answer the question, "What's going to happen to me, after I buy?"

- Make it easy to open the package when the customer gets home, and easy to reseal it, if appropriate

- Make the price obvious, if the price is to be shown on the packaging

- Make sure your brand—the promise you can keep—is on the package

Product Web pages. On the Web page associated with your product, make sure you do the following:

- Clearly state what the product is and what it is used for. Describe how the product addresses the customer's Critical Characteristic

- Show very crisp, expandable pictures of the product, from several angles

- Show the item next to a size reference

- If it performs a function, show it in action. Include a video if it would help people understand how they would use the product.

- Show the price right next to the item. Don't make your buyer hunt. If people don't see the price, they assume the item is overpriced.

- Include testimonials, ratings, reviews, and case studies. Keep this content up to date.

- Include the "buzz" stories and videos

- Ask for the order frequently on your product page. The "buy now" button or the "add to shopping cart" button should be easily available to the buyer, no matter where they are in their process—or on your site. Once they've decided to go ahead, they will want to press the "buy now" button without searching for it.

- Present the product information with a minimum of navigation. If it all fits on one Web page, great. Don't make the shopper mouse around. This is especially important for Light Scrutiny products, because the buyer wants to make a quick decision. It's better to make them scroll than it is to send them to another page to get a question answered. Every click is yet another barrier.

- Don't inflate the shipping costs—that's a tip-off that you're a chiseler, and it can easily cost you the sale

If you've done everything you can to make it easy to buy, your buyer should be able to complete the transaction in a couple of minutes.

ONCE YOU HAVE GOTTEN THE ATTENTION OF THE LIGHT SCRUTINY BUYER, YOU WILL NEED TO ANSWER HIS QUESTIONS— EVEN THOUGH HE WILL ONLY HAVE A FEW.

In the physical world, the Light Scrutiny product is usually displayed on a shelf. If the actual product is visible, it can speak for itself to a certain extent. If not, the packaging will have to tell the story and make the promise.

If the person has bought the product before—that oh-so-tempting candy bar comes to mind—the customer will immediately recognize the packaging, and make their buying decision by asking only a couple of questions: "Do I want this? Can my waistline afford it?"

A lot of food falls into the Light Scrutiny category. People tend to go to the same grocery store (or stores) every week. They pass by thousands of items on the shelf. They become familiar with what the store sells—the various items and their associated brands. Mostly they buy the products they have come to trust and enjoy, but they will also buy new items, if their budget allows it.

One of the reasons it is possible for them to shop easily in a supermarket is because groceries are displayed in categories. All the bread is in one place. The eggs are in another. And so on. Too many website designers fail to make proper use of categories. Sales suffer as a result.

Categorization is one of the most powerful tools available to anyone presenting products/services to customers, especially when the customer is in a hurry. Customers are always in a hurry when buying Light Scrutiny products and services. They just want to see it, then buy it. They want the information to be displayed where they expect it to be displayed, the way they expect it to be displayed (for example, the way ingredients and nutritional information is displayed on food packaging).

Find out how your customers categorize your products/services in their own minds, then use those categories on your website, and in your promotional and partner material.

Budget allocation for the Light Scrutiny product or service

The bulk of your marketing and sales budget should be devoted to making customers familiar with your Light Scrutiny product/service.

Most of the remainder goes to your packaging, distribution, point-of-purchase materials (promotional materials that sit on a shelf or a counter), and your website. And finally, every campaign must have tracking built into it, so you know what is working best for you.

The percentages below represent the non-employee costs. If you have someone in-house who would be good at carrying out part of the buying process support plan, the actual budget allocation for that item may be somewhat less.

I recommend the following budget allocation for Light Scrutiny Products and Services.

45% on establishing familiarity (social media, PR, ads, contests, videos, email, mail, product placements, events)

40% on distribution support and point-of-purchase (packaging, displays, product/service flyers, etc.)

10% on your website, assuming it is mostly used for information, rather than for e-commerce (for an e-commerce site, see below)

5% on monitoring and tracking your efforts

If you sell your Light Scrutiny product/service exclusively on your website, your budget allocation would be:

45% on establishing familiarity

10% on packaging

35% on your website

10% on monitoring and tracking your efforts

At the end of each Scrutiny chapter, you will find budget allocation recommendations as you see here. These are guidelines to ensure that everything gets its due and no phase of the process is neglected. They should not be treated as a straightjacket, but as a general guide. As you allocate budget amounts to your buying process support plan, if something departs substantially from these guidelines, you should re-examine that portion of the plan. Something is probably out of whack.

HOW TO SUPPORT THE MEDIUM SCRUTINY BUYING PROCESS

THEY SEE IT,
ASK FIVE TO TWENTY QUESTIONS,
THEN BUY IT

Characteristics of Medium Scrutiny Products and Services

- Although millions of people buy Medium Scrutiny products and services, they cost enough to give those buyers pause. The purchase is not an impulse purchase. These purchases are made less frequently and with more scrutiny than Light Scrutiny products and services.

- Buyers ask 5 to 20 questions.

- The price typically runs from tens to hundreds of dollars.

- The buying process takes minutes or hours; the buyer wants to solve the problem, but she can put it off if she is not happy with what she has found so far. She may go on several hunting expeditions.

- Examples: Clothing, appliances, inexpensive software, stationary power tools, components for manufacturing, office equipment, lawn mowers, and services such as hair cutting, jewelry repair, and cleaning services.

Following is the Buying Process Roadmap guide—which can serve as a template for your own Medium Scrutiny Buying Process Roadmap. At each step, you will want to answer these questions:

- **Customer Actions:** Who is the buyer at this stage, and what are that buyer's concerns and questions?

- **Company Tasks:** Where is the buyer expecting to find these messages at this stage in his/her buying process? What messages and tools must we create to address the buyer's concerns and answer his/her questions?

MEDIUM SCRUTINY

BUYING PROCESS
ROADMAP

CUSTOMER ACTIONS

COMPANY TASKS

SEARCHES FOR IT, OR SEES IT

1

CREATE A GREAT PRODUCT OR SERVICE & MAKE IT EASY TO FIND

The customer goes looking for your type of product. She will most likely use a search engine first, to find out if what she's looking for exists—and then she will choose between buying it online or in a physical store.

She may also run across your product while shopping for something else. This is likely to happen while she's in a physical store, but it can happen online as well.

- Interview buyers so you know what they want in your type of product or service, where they expect to find it, and the words/phrases they use to describe it. Identify the Critical Characteristic.

- Find out if any other person will influence the buying decision. Understand who they are and what they care about. Build buyer personas and buyer scenarios for each type of buyer.

- Understand how well your competition is meeting customer needs and where they fall short.

- Design the product or the service so it meets buyer needs. Don't try to push them into buying something that isn't good for them.

- Identify and articulate the promise that customers want you to keep— and that you *can* keep—with your product, people, processes, policies, and passion.

- Make it easy to find your product. Know the search terms they use when they *first* start searching online. Know the attributes they're looking for while shopping in a store.

- Build an *Intense* Scrutiny Roadmap for any selling partners, to make it easy for them to decide to carry your product.

- Create buzz for your product or service so partners are more likely to carry and promote it, and customers will "recognize" it when they see it.

CUSTOMER ACTIONS

ASKS 5 TO 20+ QUESTIONS

2

COMPANY TASKS

ANSWER THEIR QUESTIONS

Examples of questions customers will ask:

- Will this actually solve my problem?
- What does it look like? Do I like the style or design?
- How much does it cost?
- How well will it fit or work?
- Will it work with or in my [whatever]?
- What's it made of?
- Does it come in other colors or models?
- How durable is it?
- How will I use it?
- How will I feel while using it?
- Are there instructions? Can I see them? Are they well-written?
- What has been done to make it work better/best?
- Is it in stock? If not, when will it be?
- When will it arrive?
- How easy will it be to return it?
- What have others thought of it? Do I care about what they care about?
- How does it compare to similar items?
- What's included in the services provided—and what's not?
- Do I really need this? Can I get by without it? Can I make or do it myself?

The customer wants to "experience" the product, and compare it to other items. If you make it easy, she will make her decision more quickly.

- Know all the questions that customers ask when they're buying your product or service.
- Build a database where you store and continually update/improve your answers to those questions.
- Answer their questions everywhere – your packaging, landing pages, websites, videos, diagrams, catalogs, emails, printed pieces, and social media sites. Offer an abundance of photos and illustrations, with the ability to zoom in, showing the product in use from various angles.
- Describe and show how your product or service satisfies the Critical Characteristic, and keeps your brand promise.
- Give customers all the information they need to make a decision, including sizing guides, videos, comparison tables, information about materials and manufacturing processes, how to use the product, how services are offered, etc.
- Include product ratings and reviews on your website.
- Make it easy for them to talk to a real human being—online or by phone. Respond immediately to questions asked via email or web forms.
- Train sales reps so they can answer the common questions, and equip them with tools that make it easy for them to find answers to rarely asked questions.
- Tell potential customers of relevant new products and services.

CUSTOMER ACTIONS

TRIES IT ON OR TRIES IT OUT

3

COMPANY TASKS

MAKE IT EASY TO TEST

The customer has decided that she's interested. Now she wants to be sure that she really wants this item, and that she won't regret the purchase.

In a physical store, she will try the item on or hold the item in her hand and think about how it will be to use it. She will read directions and the information on the label. If someone is with her, she may involve that person in the buying decision. However, most Medium-Scrutiny purchases are made independently.

In the online environment, she will look carefully at the photos and read the descriptions and reviews until she is convinced that it is safe to make a purchase.

If it is software, she will download a trial version. It should be a full, working version that expires in a given time period. Give your busy buyer at least two weeks to test the product.

If it is a physical item, prior to ordering the item she will make sure she can easily return it if she is not satisfied.

If it is a service, she will decide to try it once, or on something "safe." For example, she may send an inexpensive jewelry item in for repair before she will trust the company with an expensive and cherished item.

- Make it easy for the buyer to try it on or try it out. Packaging should make it easy for the customer to imagine using it.

- On your packaging and website, show how the product or service will look or work. Show it in action.

- On your website, display your return policy prominently, so the customer can buy with confidence. Zappos, a company that has set the standard for creating rabidly happy customers, pays for shipping "both ways," and lets customers return an item for 365 days after purchase.

- Include ratings and reviews on your site. If your product is well-designed and manufactured, only about 1 out of 5 reviews will be negative, on average (source: Bazaarvoice). If one product gets a high number of negative reviews, make changes. It's better to fix products than lose sales—and your reputation.

- If you offer a trial version, test it (and the method of downloading and obtaining it) to make sure there are no barriers to the sale.

- Contact the person soon after they have bought the product to make sure they're getting full use out of it. This is especially important if they're using a trial version.

CUSTOMER ACTIONS		COMPANY TASKS
BUYS IT	**4**	**MAKE IT EASY FOR THEM TO BUY**

If the customer is at the checkout counter, she will pay for the item using her debit card, credit card, or cash.

If she is shopping online, she will add the item to her cart. Some companies pick this moment to tell her that the item she has chosen is not in stock. Big mistake—it feels like bait and switch. Display the "in stock" and "out of stock" status (with future expectations) on the *product* page, not the checkout page.

This is the time to give her the incentive to add more items to her shopping cart, with methods such as "You are $15.05 away from free shipping" or "customers who bought this also bought ...."

She will enter all of the billing and shipping data required to check out. The less data she is required to enter, the better.

If you ask for data that is "none of your business," such as the year she was born or her gender, she may abandon the entire shopping cart and buy the item elsewhere.

Most company managers are unaware of the "show stoppers" embedded in their checkout procedure. For example, a company selling dried food (for survival, camping, etc.), offers the ability to try six meals for free. One would think that the box containing these free meals would weigh very little. Yet the "you only pay shipping" cost is $14.95, which feels like a rip-off. The customer decides, at that moment, that she doesn't want the free meals, and that she doesn't want to do business with this sneaky company.

- Make the process smooth and fast. Eliminate steps. Once the customer has chosen her items, she will want to buy it quickly and get on with the rest of her day.
- Online, don't make her enter data more than once. Retain any data she's already entered, even if she has to go "back" during her shopping process.
- If she enters an item into her cart, put the item into the cart—but don't take her to the cart until she is ready. If you take her to the cart every time she buys an item, she will get irritated and stop shopping.
- Make the process logical; first have the person confirm the items and shipping options, then enter their shipping and billing information.
- Make it easy to update quantities, delete items, or save items for later.
- After she has hit "submit" and sent her payment data, the easy-to-print confirmation and thank-you screen should show all items purchased, an order number, and a one-click way to track her purchase. The receipt should include return information.
- Give the customer options: Create an account or just check out; retain her credit card information or ask her to enter it each time; and sign up for a newsletter (or not). Do not pre-check the boxes for her.

CUSTOMER ACTIONS

USES IT, LIKES IT, REVIEWS IT, & PURCHASES IT AGAIN

5

COMPANY TASKS

KEEP YOUR PROMISES & MAKE IT EASY TO PURCHASE AGAIN

The customer takes it back to her home or office, or receives it via delivery. She opens up the packaging and starts to use the item.

If she is pleased, she may write a positive review of some sort, especially if you encourage her to do so via an easy-to-respond-to email you have sent her, soon after she makes the purchase.

She may want to purchase the product again, and will appreciate being able to go back to your site, click on her previous orders to see a list of products she's ordered, and buy the item with one click.

If she is not pleased, she may write a critical review, and then return the item (or just live with the inadequacy). She will be impressed if you respond to the negative review in a helpful and humble way.

- Items should be packed for shipping so they do not get damaged in transit. Too many companies do this poorly, especially office supply companies. Have someone randomly check boxes ready to ship, and hire secret shoppers to find out how well retailers are packing products for shipping.

- Solicit, check, and publish reviews on your website, so they appear next to the associated product. Reviews must be moderated, since they become part of your site's official (and legal) content. Publish negative reviews (you will lose all credibility if you don't). If you sell many products, hire a review platform company that provides moderation services.

- On your website, make it easy to reorder products purchased—not by date, but by item. The customer should be able to click on the item from a list and add it to her cart.

- If she writes a negative review, respond to her—in the reviews section. Take action, if it is something you can fix. At the very least, apologize and tell her you're working on making it better (and then do that, of course).

CUSTOMER ACTIONS

| COMPANY TASKS

OR CUSTOMER RETURNS IT

6

MAKE IT EASY TO CONTACT YOU; TAKE ACTION AS NEEDED

If the customer is not pleased, she will want to return the item. If she ordered online, she will want to be able to put it back into the original packaging, affix a pre-printed label to the package, and mail it. She'd prefer not to pay shipping charges when returning the item.

If she bought it at a store, she will want to be able to walk right into the store and know immediately where to go to return the item.

- Even if you are a one-person operation, your packaging should include a return slip to make it easy for the person to return the item, with a copy of the receipt and a place to write why they are returning it.

- You can have them fill out a "reason for return" code, which will help you, but if the person's real reason is not listed, you will never know, specifically, why the product was returned—and you may miss important clues about the product. It's better to ask them to describe exactly why they are returning it. If the sleeves are too long, and the only option you give the customer is "too large," you'll never know that the sleeves are the problem—not the overall size of the garment.

- If the customer has given you her email address, use her email address to let her know when that similar item is on sale or if a new, similar item has been added to your inventory. These offers should be relevant, based on purchase history, and she should be able to opt out easily at any time.

HOW THEY FIND YOU

If you're selling a Medium Scrutiny product/service, your customer will come looking for you. She will have a problem she must solve, or a need she wants to fill. She will use Google, most likely, or the search function in an online store, online directory, or social media platform. She may also have driven to the mall. We'll address that situation also, but first let's stick with the online purchase.

You need to show up in the search results when she goes looking for you. In order to do that, you need to:

- Know the *problem* she's trying to solve, and the words she uses to describe it

- Know the *solution* she's looking for, and the words she uses to describe it

- Know the *Critical Characteristic*—the characteristic that *must* be present for the sale to be made

Most marketers decide which search terms to include in their website code and online ads by using search term tools such as the Google AdWords Keyword tool or WordTracker. That's fine, but as I mentioned earlier, you must also interview your customers to find out what they typed into Google when they were *first* looking for you, and what they would type now if they were looking again, and didn't know you existed. These are the words and phrases that will bring in the largest number of buyers, and ace out your competition in the search results.

While many existing customers will understand industry jargon, new potential customers probably won't. Make sure you use the words that *they* come up with in search terms and on your landing pages. Also, while some customers will be deeply interested in the technical aspects, others will only care that the product works, and they won't even use the technical terms.

You can also look at what your competition is doing. There are a number of competitive tools that will tell you the keywords your competitors are using and how much they're spending on those keywords in their Google AdWords campaign.

Remember, though, that your competitors might be *wrong*. Doing what they're doing will only ensure that your ad appears when their ad appears. But your competitor's ad may not be appearing when your customer is typing in the first search phrase that occurs to her. Nail that phrase and you might make yourself appear to be the sole supplier.

Another place to look for keywords or phrases is in the reviews done by customers for your type of product or service on online retail sites. Here's an example: "I was looking for a camera with fast click-to-snap speed, image stabilization, and decent zoom." Not the precise technical terms, but this is how people say it—and search for it.

Whether you use an outside consultant to do your search engine work or do it in-house, you'll want to make sure you also scan the virtual world for keywords and phrases. Social media sites such as Twitter, because of their search function, can help you understand how people are talking about your type of product/service, and what is important to them.

I'm afraid that this is an endless job. There is always room for improvement in your search results ranking and your online ad click-throughs and conversion. Also, search phrases are influenced by current events, including new concepts introduced to the market by your competitors.

Catchy new ways of referring to things associated with your product or service can emerge out of nowhere—and spread like wildfire—to the point where they become the normal way that people refer to the subject, seemingly overnight. It's your responsibility to monitor these trends and adopt those terms.

It's easier than ever to track trends, using search tools and social media sites, but it does take discipline and you must devote resources to it.

Selling locally: If you're selling products in a physical store, check into local advertising offered by Google (Local Listing Ads).

If your area has a truly local newspaper, which is actually read by local residents, advertising there might work for you.

And if your type of buyer is listening to a particular type of radio station, consider local radio advertising. Ask each customer who comes in if they listen to the radio, and if so, which station/programs. This will help you decide where to advertise.

Here are some rules that will help you get the biggest bang for your local advertising buck:

- **Make sure that your ad always appears in the same place** in the publications you run in, so people can find you easily when they decide to contact you.

- **Don't just say you're there. Give people a reason to come to you.** In other words, make an offer that will put you on their "to-do" list. Something that will encourage the buyer to take that first step:

  - Have a sale

  - Offer a "two for one" deal

  - Offer a discount if they bring in the old item

  - Offer a discount for their first purchase

  - Have an event where they can receive an additional service—such as an appraisal, meeting a celebrity or expert, or receiving instruction

- **When they come into your store, ask them one question:** "What type of product do you wish we carried that we're not carrying now?" If enough people tell you the same thing, start carrying that product and then make that fact—that you now carry that product—the focus of your next ad. "You asked for it—we have it!"

- **Inject urgency into the promotion.** "All garden tools and seeds are 15% off this Saturday."

- **Include your customers in your ads.** Next time someone comes into your store and buys something, ask if you can take their picture (or, better yet, video them). Interview them, asking: "What did you come here to find?" "What did you get? How are you going to use it?" The photos and the copy can be posted on your Facebook page, Twitter site, website, and printed ad, as long as you obtain permission from the person (have them sign a simple model release form—you can find an example on Google by typing "example of model release"). Obviously, the video can be posted everywhere except your print ads. These interviews will spread. The customer will point her friends and family to it, at the very least. You will be showing your prospective customers a satisfied customer. Don't try to make these too professional, or they will just fade into the advertising background noise.

- **Focus on educating your buyer with every message,** and your buyer will come to trust you—and think of you next time she is looking for your type of product or service. You know a lot about your products and services, the companies that make or provide them, and how to use them most effectively. You may think that these bits of knowledge aren't very useful to anyone, but you'd be surprised. Someone who is interested in your type of product/service will appreciate any advice you can give. A store selling outdoor clothing could talk about the properties of different types of fabric. A store selling hardware could talk about the best way to clean your barbeque, or why they carry a certain type of hammer. If your educational and helpful ad appears on the same page with ads that simply say, "Here we are," the comparison can only help you. The customer will be more likely to trust the company that is already helping her.

Always be thinking of ways you can engage your customer, rather than just saying, "We're here."

Medium Scrutiny products/services, just like Light Scrutiny products and services, will sell better if they have buzz and are distributed to as many retail outlets as possible. Make sure you follow the advice in the Light Scrutiny chapter on how to create buzz for your product/service; how to make it newsworthy; how to help the word spread; and how to make it easy for distributors to do business with you.

Keep in mind that customers may also discover you via referral. A friend or family member may refer them. Your job is to make it easy for existing customers to refer others to you. Give discounts for referrals, or offer some other incentive. If it's appropriate, send an email to the customer after she makes a purchase. Ask her to rate her experience and give her an easy way to refer others to you.

Ease of referral is most affected by the name of your company or product/service. If the name of your product/service is obviously associated with what it is, what it does, or the problem it solves, you will get more referrals. If the name is nonsensical or requires some kind of tagline to tie it to the product/service or its function, you won't get as many referrals. This can drastically inhibit your ability to generate revenue.

Just the other day I was trying to remember the name of a stock photo website I had used only once. It wasn't an easy name to remember (such as StockPhoto.com). I tried to find it via Google. It was, as it turns out, "Veer."

It wasn't in the top 25 search results, and the name was so odd that it would have been easy to click on any other odd name, hoping it was the site I was looking for.

Veer will have to spend more money promoting itself than StockPhoto.com, simply because its name has nothing to do with the product being sold. A lot of entrepreneurs, who are unfortunately in love with the name they created, fail to realize how much their inappropriate name is killing sales.

StockPhoto.com has an advantage over Veer, right out of the gate. StockPhoto.com sounds like a big company with lots of pictures to choose from. Veer sounds like a boutique that may or may not have the pictures you're looking for. Veer sounds like you made a wrong turn or is something to avoid.

If you have a name like Veer, come up with a new name that is memorable and descriptive. Start by writing down every single word that pertains to your business and what customers are hoping to achieve by buying from you. The longer the list, the better.

Brainstorm and check the URLs available until you have one that really, truly works. The best name is always a clear winner, once you find it.

Test the new name by asking customers what they think. Give customers a choice between five names, including the one you are hoping they'll choose. Ask them which one they would be most likely to associate with your products and services, and which name would be easiest to remember.

You'll still need to be confident that the new name will lead to increased website traffic and conversions. One way to create an apples-to-apples website comparison is to select one of your products or services and build two landing pages for it—one using the old name and one using the new name. In the About Us section of your new test page, say that the company is a division of [your current company name]. You'll have to give the sites some time to gain traction—several months at least—to provide useful comparative data, in part because of the longevity factor in Google's algorithms.

One of our clients was struggling with an inappropriate name. We developed a replacement name that everyone—including customers—agreed was better, but the client didn't have the funds to make the transition right away. As we helped him secure financing, the investors all responded very positively to the prospect of business growth with the improved name. The funding was secured, the name was changed, and the client's sales increased dramatically. As usual.

Make sure the name of your product/service or company helps the buyer remember what you sell. Make it a priority. Even if you have been in business a while, your chances of making more sales are greater if you bite the bullet and go through a rebranding process than if you cling to a name that is not naturally associated with your product or service. It's always difficult to let go of the familiar name, but once you've made the change, you'll wish you had done it sooner.

ONCE YOU HAVE GOTTEN THE ATTENTION OF THE MEDIUM SCRUTINY BUYER, YOU WILL NEED TO ANSWER HER QUESTIONS— EFFICIENTLY AND COMPLETELY.

Once the customer finds you, she will expect you to answer her questions. She will want you to do it quickly. She'd rather spend minutes—not hours or days—on her Medium Scrutiny purchase. She may have already visited your competitors' sites, and is comparing you to them. She wants your product or services page to contain all the information needed to make a buying decision. She also wants to feel confident she's found the best solution, and that it will satisfy all of her requirements.

Answering questions in your store. If you're selling products in a store, customers may need some assistance from store personnel. Salespeople should know the questions that customers will ask and should be prepared to answer them. This seems ridiculously obvious, but how many times have you walked into an office supply store and asked a clerk a question he couldn't answer?

Other than "Where's the [whatever]?" I honestly can't recall a single time I have asked a clerk a question that he *could* answer. Usually, what happens is that you haven't been able to find the answer to a question on the product package. So you ask a clerk for help. He takes the box from your hands, and reads, lips moving, looking for the answer that you already know isn't there.

Staff training is non-existent in most retail establishments. If I were a store owner, I would test my salespeople weekly—asking them to answer certain questions (new ones each week). I would also ask them to tell me the kinds of questions they had been asked during the week. I would incorporate those new questions into their pop quizzes.

Answering questions in your product/service descriptions. In the Light Scrutiny section, I talked about what a good description should include, on pages 172–173. For Medium Scrutiny products, you will also want to add:

- Sizing charts, including examples of how to measure for the correct fit

- Directions on the best way to use the product or service (such as examples of how to tie a scarf or how to make sure your new tool doesn't get rusty)

- Relevant information about how much it can contain or how strong it is ("This bucket weighs 19 pounds when it is filled with water")

- A link called "More like this"

- A link called "Customers who bought this also bought"

- Goes with: "The shoes that go with this scarf are on sale" or "This product works well with X"

If you're selling a downloadable software product, make sure you include large-as-life screen shots. Allow your buyer to download the product and use a fully functional version of it for an appropriate time period—15 days for a simple program and 30 to 60 days for a more complex program. Make sure you contact the customer after they've downloaded—within 48 hours—to ask if you can answer any questions or help them.

Make it easy for the Medium Scrutiny customer, during her initial search, to contact you with a question. Respond immediately (via chat) or almost immediately (via email). If you move fast enough, you will catch her while she is still in the midst of her buying process. If not, she will be done by the time you contact her.

Answering questions in your ads. If you're selling a service, and you're advertising in the local paper, your ad should answer as many questions as possible. The more questions you answer, the more likely it is that the person will contact you in the first place—and ultimately buy from you.

- Have others been happy with your work? (Include a testimonial.)

- What do you specialize in?

- What separates you from the others in your business?

- Do you guarantee your work?

- What makes clients glad they chose you?

- What are your hours?
- Can you provide a free estimate?
- How quickly will you respond?

Make sure you know the problems your buyers have had in the past with similar services, and address those issues in your ad. For example, promise that you'll call back in 20 minutes, and then keep that promise.

No matter what you're selling, the goal is to be an "Answer Machine." Keep a constant lookout for new questions customers may be asking, and answer those questions everywhere—on your website, in your ads and releases, and in your social media messages.

The more questions you answer, the more likely it will be that you make the sale, because you will be making it easy for the customer to make a buying decision. She won't have to go hunting. She won't have to wonder. She won't shake her head and go back to Google, or ask her friends. She will stay with you, get her questions answered, and decide to buy from you.

Answering questions in the materials you send to influencers. Some Medium Scrutiny products and services are sold or reviewed by others. These folks are your ambassadors. Make sure that they have all the answers to their questions as well.

For years, the standard method for approaching influencers has been a press release. This is changing. Now it's more effective to send a personal email with the basic pitch in the first few sentences and factual bullets that the writer can use to create a story. This can work for anyone who could reach your audience, including bloggers, reporters, partners, and customers.

- Bloggers and other influencers should be given a product sample or a way to try the service so they can write about it. Make sure that you answer all of their questions as well. Create a simple document that goes with the product/service (electronically or physically) that answers all their questions. Be ready to respond immediately to any messages they send you. Keep in mind that bloggers are now being held to a strict standard of disclosure. If you have provided the product for free for them to review (or any other form of compensation), they should say so in the review.

- Your customers can be ambassadors for you. Think of ways to make it easy for them to help you answer customer questions. "Send us a picture of you in our clothing, and you could win $500!" Use the pictures on your website, then hold a drawing and announce the winner with an email, a story about the person, and a picture. Make sure you get their permission—in writing—to display their testimonial.

■ Reporters don't matter as much as they used to, but they do still matter. Create a standard press release for them, but pitch them individually and personally with the press release embedded in the email, or attached to it.

Repeat sales of Medium Scrutiny Products and Services. Once someone has purchased a Medium Scrutiny product/service from you, chances are good that they will return to purchase more. Email can be a very effective channel for ongoing sales of your Medium Scrutiny products/services. Here are some tips:

■ It won't be that difficult to obtain the person's email address; the best time to ask them for it is during the checkout phase of the purchase.

■ When you ask for her email address, ask if she would like to be notified when you are having a sale. Do not pre-check the box for her; this is stepping over the line. Instead, just have one box, and ask her to check it. Since she's already justified her current purchase in her own mind, she will be interested in saving money next time, and she will probably check the box. Tell her how often she will be receiving emails from you.

■ Clothing manufacturers such as Land's End (LandsEnd.com) and Monterey Bay (ShopTheBay.com) are becoming quite adept at sending out an email that offers certain items for sale. Setting a deadline and putting it in the subject line—"Sale ends at 12 midnight"—will encourage your buyer to open the email.

■ Don't over-clutter her email box. Your emailing schedule should be appropriate for the industry, the product/service, and the frequency of purchase. Of course, the email should include the normal opt-out conventions (unsubscribe via reply email, or via an "unsubscribe" Web page).

All of the shopping cart advice given in Chapter 6, starting on pages 143–144, applies to both Light and Medium Scrutiny products/services.

Remember to let the shopper stay on the page she's on, when she's just added something to her shopping cart. She can view the shopping cart any time, as long as you've put the button where she expects to find it (usually up in the top right-hand corner of every page, or in the right navigation panel). She may want to buy that blouse in three different colors. If you take her to the shopping cart every time she adds an item to it, you will be forcing her to take unneeded steps to make those additional purchases. In other words, you will irritate her, discouraging her from adding more items to her cart.

Budget allocation for the Medium Scrutiny product or service

If you sell your product both online and through distributors, I recommend:

40% on establishing your product and service's existence (social media, PR, ads, contests, videos, email, mail, product placements, events)
20% on answering questions—on your website, on partner websites, and in online or printed catalogs
10% on supporting selling partners
25% on your website
5% on monitoring and tracking your efforts

If you sell your Medium Scrutiny product/service exclusively on your website, your allocation would be:

40% on establishing your product or service's existence
25% on answering questions—on your website
30% on your website (the back-end infrastructure)
5% on monitoring and tracking your efforts

HOW TO SUPPORT THE HEAVY SCRUTINY BUYING PROCESS

10

THEY SEE IT, ASK DOZENS OF QUESTIONS, GET OTHER BUYERS INVOLVED, TALK TO A SALESPERSON MORE THAN ONCE, TRY IT OUT, DECIDE TO BUY IT, SIGN A CONTRACT, THEN START TO EXPERIENCE IT.

Characteristics of Heavy Scrutiny Products and Services

- Even fewer people buy Heavy Scrutiny products and services. It is a very serious purchase, not easy to pay for, and rarely carried out In the person's lifetime. The purchase is a big event. There is usually more than one person involved in the buying decision.

- Multiple buyers ask 25 to 50+ questions.

- The price typically runs from thousands to millions of dollars.

- The buying process takes weeks or months, and usually involves a salesperson and a signature on a document (contract, agreement, or estimate).

- Examples: Cars, houses, complex business systems, recreational boats/ yachts/vehicles, private jets, and expensive/complex medical services.

Following is the Buying Process Roadmap guide—which can serve as a template for your own Heavy Scrutiny Buying Process Roadmap. At each step, you will want to answer these questions:

- **Customer Actions:** Who are the buyers at this stage, and what are their concerns and questions?

- **Company Tasks:** Where are the buyers expecting to find these messages at this stage in their buying process? What messages and tools must we create to address their concerns and answer their questions?

You may already know all of the phases involved in the "sales process" for your product or service. The question you must ask yourself—and your customers—is how well you are actually supporting those phases. Are you making it *easy* for the buyer to complete each step, and move from one step to the next?

HEAVY
SCRUTINY

BUYING PROCESS
ROADMAP

CUSTOMER ACTIONS

SEARCHES & RESEARCHES

1

COMPANY TASKS

CREATE A GREAT PRODUCT OR SERVICE & MAKE IT EASY TO FIND

This is a serious purchase. It's expensive and complex. He wants to avoid buyer's remorse, and not just because it's an expensive item that he can only afford to purchase a few times in a lifetime. Once he's committed, it's almost impossible to "undo" the purchase. Agreements will have been signed, and the old house or car sold.

Or, in the case of business-to-business (B2B) products, data and processes are switched to the new system. This is an expensive and disruptive process that is doubly painful to reverse. The success of the buyer's career depends on making the right decision.

For all these reasons, he spends quite a bit of time online, educating himself about your type of product or service, and poring over content—on websites, blogs, discussion groups, dealer sites, online magazine sites, and so on. He also solicits recommendations from others. He will be open to downloading detailed product documents or white papers that you produce.

- Interview buyers so you know what they want in your type of product or service, where they expect to find it, and the words/phrases they use to describe it and search for it. Identify the Critical Characteristic.

- There is almost always another person involved in a Heavy Scrutiny decision. Understand who these people are and what they care about. Build buyer personas and buyer scenarios for each of the buyers and approvers involved.

- Understand how well your competition is meeting customer needs and where they fall short.

- Design the product or the service so it meets buyer needs. Don't try to push them into buying something that isn't good for them.

- Identify and articulate the promise that customers want you to keep—and that you *can* keep—with your product, people, processes, policies, and passion.

- Make it easy to find in-depth information about your solution. Reading a comprehensive document is an early step in their buying process. Don't sell. Educate.

- If you sell through selling partners, build an *Intense* Scrutiny Buying Process Roadmap.

- Create buzz for your product or service. Provide helpful materials and facts. Again, don't pitch; educate.

CUSTOMER ACTIONS

ASKS QUESTIONS & ANALYZES OPTIONS

2

COMPANY TASKS

ANSWER QUESTIONS & HELP CUSTOMER WEIGH OPTIONS

The customer's questions will fall into two main categories: "Which product/service do I want to buy?" and "Who do I want to buy it from?"

Which product/service:

- How well does this meet my needs—especially my most pressing need?
- Am I taking the right approach? What other options do I have?
- How much does it cost—to buy and maintain? Are there hidden costs?
- Will it "fit" my lifestyle or our business? Will it work with or in my [whatever]?
- How does it work? How durable is it? How are others using it?
- Are there accessible and clear instructions?
- Is it available now?
- How easy is it to buy, install, and use?
- Will the other influencers like it? Will users like it?

Which company:

- What do others think of the company?
- Are they being helpful?
- Is the salesperson "hearing" me?
- What will happen when something goes wrong?
- Is it easy to test before I buy?
- What's included in the services provided—and what's not?
- Is the contract straightforward, or slippery?

- Know all the questions that customers ask when they're buying your product or service, and build a database where you store and continually update/improve your answers to those questions.
- Answer their questions everywhere – your packaging, landing pages, websites, videos, diagrams, catalogs, emails, printed pieces, case studies, testimonials, white papers, webinars and seminars, speeches, blogs, and social media sites. Provide comparison tables. Show the cost-effectiveness of your product over time and the time savings possible due to your product or service.
- Describe and show how your product or service meets the Critical Characteristic, and keeps your promise.
- Provide the main buyer (the "champion") with materials he can use to convince others.
- It should be easy to contact a salesperson. Salespeople should respond immediately. Train them *constantly* so they can answer general and specific customer questions. If they don't know an answer, they should find out what the answer is—fast.
- Send new educational information about the product or service to potential customers regularly, via emails that contain the content or link to it.

CUSTOMER ACTIONS

DISCUSSES WITH OTHERS

3

COMPANY TASKS

ASSIST DISCUSSIONS

The buyer has now narrowed down the possibilities to you and several of your competitors.

In B2B situations, he invites each vendor to present to the entire decision-making team, usually via web conference calls.

The "perfect scenario" in the buyer's mind includes a salesperson who listens until he has truly understood the situation, then makes intelligent and appropriate recommendations. He will help the customer see options that the customer might not have considered. He does not attempt to manipulate the customer in any way.

The principal buyer—the "champion"— will ask many questions during the pitch, as will the others on the buying team. After all of the companies have presented, the champion may create a document recommending one vendor over another, and/or the team will have a discussion.

In B2C (business-to-consumer) situations, where the consumer is buying a car or house, the buyers— often a couple—will discuss their options and all the tradeoffs.

The Critical Characteristic will play a large role in these discussions. Each approver will have his or her own. The goal will be to achieve a balance between each person's Critical Characteristic

Business to business:

Before the meeting, the salesperson should learn all he can about the buyers: Their positions in the company, their political clout, their history with this type of product, their preferences and key concerns. He also needs to know:

- Why does the customer need this particular solution?

- How did they try to solve this problem previously? How did it work out for them?

- What do they already know and/or believe about the solution? Have they been misinformed by other salespeople?

- What's their budget? Timing?

- Have they been burned by other vendors in the past?

He will need sales presentations that are modular, so they can be customized to be relevant—which will only happen if the creator interviews customers regularly.

Business to consumer:

The salesperson must be able to "read" the buyer. That won't happen if he does all the talking. He should ask questions, listen, then help the customer analyze options. If the customer hesitates, the salesperson should slow down, and go with the customer to that thoughtful place, to help the customer weigh the tradeoffs.

CUSTOMER ACTIONS

TESTS IT

4

COMPANY TASKS

DEMOS & TRIALS

It's time for a final test before signing on the dotted line.

Business to business:

- The buyer wants the vendor to make it easy to test the product or service. Perhaps a small project, or a proof of performance using a portion of data supplied by the customer, or a limited version of the product could be tested. This phase in the process should be highly structured—all details worked out ahead of time—and smooth.

Business to consumer:

- The consumer will take that car out for a test drive. Or, he will go back to the house and spend some quality time there, walking through, thinking about his daily life and how well the house will meet his requirements.

- The best thing that can happen for the buyer at this point—and the seller, too—is for the buyer to "bond" with what is being sold. Some aspect of the test will make up his mind for him; suddenly the most important Critical Characteristic will be how he feels while mentally trying on, or trying out, that large-ticket item. These emotional tipping points usually come when the salesperson is NOT talking, but is instead letting the customer bond with the product.

- The salesperson must continue to answer questions, and check in with the customer to ask how he can help.

- When interviewing current customers, find out how they felt about each stage of the buying process, including the testing/trial stage. Most companies fall short at this stage. If you make it easy, you'll be more likely to close the sale.

- Support your salesforce and monitor their progress with a strong Customer Relationship Management system. Have a daily, short meeting with the team to find out "what's working and what's stuck." Get those stuck things unstuck as fast as you can.

- Have weekly meetings where salespeople discuss what they've learned over the last week. Also use these meetings to teach salespeople more about the product and how customers use the product, and the problems that your services solve. The best salespeople are educators; they can't educate if they haven't been educated.

- Experts should be available to answer the deeply technical and customer-specific questions.

- After the trial, the salesperson should summarize the results in a report. The champion can then pass the report to other influencers.

CUSTOMER ACTIONS		COMPANY TASKS
SIGNS CONTRACT, PAYS PORTION OR FULL PRICE	**5**	**GUIDE THE CUSTOMER THROUGH THE CONTRACT PROCESS**

The customer has made his decision. Now it's time to get the contract signed and all the legal details out of the way.

Business to business

- The customer will want a plain-language contract that clearly spells out exactly what is being delivered, what the vendor will do, what the customer is expected to do, any limits on the product or service, and what will happen when something goes wrong.

- The customer will expect the contract to clearly state what the company will deliver and when, the amount of each payment and the due dates for those payments. It should include penalties for non-delivery or non-payment. Payments may include a "starting fee," which should also be clearly stated.

Business to consumer

- There will often be financing involved, and other third-party vendors such as lawyers, appraisers, insurance agents, title companies, and service suppliers. Since the customer only makes this type of purchase a few times in his lifetime, he will want the seller to explain what will happen with these vendors.

- He will appreciate helpful tools such as a checklist that lists all the vendors involved and a couple of sentences about what each will do, and when.

- Make the contract modular and customizable, so the salesperson can quickly create an appropriate contract for each customer.

- Create a checklist that spells out everything that must be done to complete the sale, including things that the customer, you, and any other vendors will do. For example, if you were selling the customer a house, there would be appraisers, attorneys, inspectors, and financial institutions involved. The salesperson should discuss those steps with the customer, before the customer signs the contract.

- The customer will read through the contract and ask questions; the salesperson must be able to answer them.

- Keep the momentum and energy, even if the sale is "almost" closed. The customer can still back out.

- At the same time, the salesperson must continue to answer the customer's questions carefully and manage expectations, even though he can smell the commission.

- In B2B situations, the implementation team takes over after the contract is signed. They should be ready to jump in. The salesperson should stay involved after the contract is signed. This is often done poorly. Be the company that does it well.

- Provide references that the customer can call.

CUSTOMER ACTIONS

THE PRODUCT IS INSTALLED OR THE SERVICE BEGINS

6

COMPANY TASKS

GET THE CUSTOMER STARTED & KEEP THE CUSTOMER HAPPY

Business to business

The contract is signed. Now the real work begins. The customer has been promised a smooth implementation process by the salesperson, and has read through the implementation checklist. Any activities that don't match those promises or that checklist will be a red flag to the customer.

This is more serious than one would assume. At this stage, the customer could still decide to pull out of the deal, even if there is some kind of financial penalty involved.

Further, even after the product or service is implemented, competitive salespeople are going to continue to pitch the customer, and if you aren't keeping your promises, that customer will become more and more interested in the competitive options. This is especially true if your solution doesn't solve all of the customer's problems or solve them as elegantly or cost-efficiently as you promised.

Business to consumer

As with the B2B customer, the B2C customer will be paying attention to how you treat him after he has signed the contract. When he has a problem, how easy is it to get help? How helpful are the people he talks to? Does he get a thank you from the salesperson? Is he offered any special incentives to come back to you for service? Does he feel you are working as hard to satisfy him as you were when you were selling to him?

- Never forget that you are still selling (in fact, *always* selling), even after they sign. Your competitors never stop trying to steal customers from you.

- Stay in touch. The B2B salesperson should call 2 weeks, 2 months, then 3 months after the contract is signed. The customer will let the salesperson know if there is a problem, or may offer an opportunity for another sale. Put the customer on a low-key email program, filled with tips, and always including contact information.

- Once the customer is up and running successfully, the marketing people should interview the customer about his buying process, and also see if he'd be willing to provide a testimonial (this should not be asked until the interview is finished).

- Work hard on your customer service. It is actually as influential—or more influential—than your salespeople. Constantly check in with customers, to see how your customer service is treating them. Monitor social sites to quickly discover any disgruntled customers. If you get a reputation for "great products but terrible service," your sales will suffer significantly. Be as aggressive about great customer services as you are about selling.

HOW THEY FIND YOU

Most buyers start their Heavy Scrutiny purchase with research—using Google. The search engine advice given in the Medium Scrutiny chapter (page 186) applies to Heavy Scrutiny products and services as well.

Again, your customers are always your best source of search engine terms.

Also make sure that when they arrive at your site, their search path will continue seamlessly.

Here are some of the things that complicate a Heavy Scrutiny sale:

- **You may be selling the same thing that other people are selling—such as a brand of car or pleasure boat.** The source of your differentiation can't be the product, since it's the same product that your competitor is selling. It has to be something else that you offer, something that is valuable to the buyer and relevant to the product being sold.

- **Your customer is not just buying a product or service.** He could be buying peace of mind or a status symbol. Obviously, you need to know what he is really after. The content and the services you offer need to address how the buyer's inner needs (status, comfort, etc.) can be met.

- **He may be buying the product/service because of what he expects to do with it.** Your messages should focus on functions, not features. Help him imagine himself using the product or service.

- **Your customer is likely to have a whole laundry list of needs.** The car has to be big enough for the large family, yet not a gas-guzzler; reliable; slightly sporty-looking; and so on. The customer will have to weigh a number of tradeoffs.

  You need to understand which issues are most important. You need to know the customer's Critical Characteristic. A car salesperson who stresses safety with a buyer who actually wants a more sporty-looking SUV will cause the buyer to shut down—and leave.

  This is probably the most common mistake made at car dealerships. The salesperson launches into the standard spin on a given car, before (or without) asking the customer what is really important to him. People buy a certain car for different reasons. This is where personas can be helpful—if they are based on the needs and preferences of real, live customers. People are unique. The most successful salespeople listen more than they talk.

- There will be more than one buyer or influencer involved in the buying decision. Each person will have their own set of needs, experiences, and preferences—and even a different buying process. You must address the needs of all the buyers, in ways that are relevant to them individually. You also need to make it easy for these folks to share information with each other. A classic example is writing a white paper aimed at top managers, which is given to a "champion" who can pass the paper up to the top. Another example is creating a comparison table that a husband and wife can use to discuss the tradeoffs.

- The decision is high-risk. Once the person has made the Heavy Scrutiny decision, it's almost impossible to go back. Her old car will have been sold. She can't just return the new car for a refund, because she will have already made other changes in her life that force her to live with the decision—even if it turns out to be a decision she regrets. If she's sold her old car, and the new car is a lemon, she'll have to try to get the new car to work. She knows all this before she begins her search, so she is very cautious during her buying process. Her skepticism level is very high.

- Trust plays a major role in the buying decision. He's not just buying a product or service. He's buying a product that must work after it's sold, or a service that must deliver the proper results over time. He is expecting the seller to make things right if things go wrong. He's buying your honesty, experience, and professionalism. He's buying your reputation. He's buying your ability to solve his problem—and your successful track record solving problems just like his.

- The buying process takes time and effort. It's a big investment of her time and attention. Once the buyer has made the decision, she doesn't want to have to go through that process again. She wants to be sure, she wants to close the deal, and she wants to move on to all the other things on her to-do list that were neglected while she was busy with her long search and purchasing process.

- The buyer might not be very good at making these kinds of decisions— or helping the other influencers make up their minds. The buyer, in fact, might be *unselling* the other influencers involved in the buying process. For the couple buying a house, the wife wants a sunset view, but the husband wants a big garage and a small lawn. If the wife is not including her husband's desires in the decision (or vice-versa), the buying process will be sabotaged by hidden agendas. As the seller, you will have to make sure that both buyers are able to state their preferences, and then work with each buyer to reach a mutually acceptable decision.

- **There will be a contract involved, and perhaps lawyers.** The contract may be poorly written or may contain clauses that raise new suspicions in the customer's mind.

- **The customer may have heard horror stories from others about the type of product or service you're selling.** They may or may not share these concerns with you during their buying process (chances are good that they won't). You'll need to know what those horror stories are, so you can sense that the concern exists—and address it—even though the customer hasn't actually verbalized the concern. Social media sites can be useful in this regard. Type the name of your product and the word "problem" after it, then go through the content in discussion groups. See what people are saying. However, your current customers—interviewed by phone—are your best source of this information.

- **The customer may abandon the buying process at any time, for a variety of reasons.** The customer buying a Heavy Scrutiny product or service is constantly weighing one bit of information against another. For example, the customer may think the price is reasonable until he learns more about what is *not* included in that price. Or, he may be concerned about your ability to help him when things go wrong. He will find a way to answer that question sometime during the buying process. Everything may be flowing along smoothly, from your perspective, but then the process will be terminated suddenly by the customer. What you don't know—and what he will not tell your salesperson—is that he finally talked to someone who wasn't on your official "references" list, and his concerns about poor service were confirmed. Only a "lost sale" interview, done by someone other than the salesperson, will reveal the actual reason the buying process was abandoned. Because they put so much effort into the purchase, Heavy Scrutiny buyers who didn't buy your product or service will often consent to an interview.

- **Everyone in your industry makes the same basic promises** about what the product or service will do for the customer, how they will be treated, how much they care, and so on. By the time the customer has come to you, he's heard it all before—and no longer believes any of it. This only increases the amount of scrutiny that the customer applies to the buying process. You must be able to *prove* that you are different, by your actions, the information and help you provide from the outset, and the recommendations and testimonials of others who have purchased your product/service.

Helping your champions sell for you

If you are selling a Heavy Scrutiny product or service to a business, there is usually a "champion"—someone who is technical, or a specialist. The decision is on his head. Depending on how it turns out, he ends up a hero or a zero.

We'll use a business-to-business Heavy Scrutiny software purchase as an example. In this purchase, others involved in the purchase include the champion's direct manager and higher managers; people who will be using the software in their daily work; and IT people who must install and maintain the software after it is purchased. All of these people have a say in the buying process.

Here's how to avoid the most common mistakes:

- **Focus on the champion first, and most thoroughly.** This person must be convinced before he can convince anyone else. This person must be ready to answer any questions when you are not present. You must educate and equip him with the selling tools he needs to educate the other approvers involved.

- **Don't make the mistake of kissing up to the champion's boss at the expense of your relationship with the champion.** Many salespeople love to rub elbows with the CEO, while snubbing the champion—and they lose the sale as the result. In the end, the CEO will value his employee's opinion more than the opinion of any salesperson. If you set yourself up as an adversary of the champion, the champion will win, at your expense. Do everything you can to empower the champion— and make it easy for the champion to sell the CEO on your behalf.

- **Make sure you explain how the new program will affect users and their work.** During the installation process, as well as after, they will want to know if they will be able to retain and use the work they have already created using the older programs. Include detailed testimonials and step-by-step descriptions to show what will happen to their current work, and how they will use the new program.

- **Make it easy for the champion to explain how the product will be rolled out within the organization.** If the implementation is complex, create a "rollout kit" or "adoption kit," which gives the champion all the tools he needs to make it easy for others in the organization to accept and start using your product.

- **Focus on education.** Hold webinars and seminars. Create videos and product demos that show people exactly how they will use the new product to achieve their goals.

- **Use case studies to establish immediate credibility and rapport.** The best case studies are industry-specific. They tell the story from the beginning, including a short description of the customer's problem, why they picked you, and what happened after they purchased your product. Effective case studies also include as many statistics as possible, such as time or money saved.

- **Always be helpful, and the champion will come to trust you.** Trust must be established before you can make a Heavy Scrutiny sale. Don't rush the buyer, but be constantly at the ready to answer the next question, or present to the next influencer.

- **In every conversation, ask the champion what he needs next to move things along.** Too many salespeople just call to "check in," and fail to ask this all-important question. The champion becomes increasingly frustrated because he wants to make the purchase, but he can't without help from the seller. What happens in these situations is a competitor's salesperson comes along who is more helpful, and that competitor makes the sale.

- **Learn how to ask questions that the champion will actually answer.** "Is there anything I can help you with?" won't get you very far. "What are your specific concerns at this point?" works better. Asking the question in a way that assumes there are concerns, and letting the champion tell you what they are, is more effective than just asking how you can help. It's up to you to decide how you can help, after you understand what the issues are.

The Heavy Scrutiny purchase occurs in a series of steps. It's tempting to try to rush the customer through his steps, but it's always a mistake. Instead, it is far more profitable to thoroughly understand and support these steps.

For example, one of the most successful methods for selling a Heavy Scrutiny product or service is to offer content as the first step, in the form of a white paper, tips piece, video, or guide—something that the customer can download and/or easily pass on to others. Rather than simply offering your product or service for sale in the search engine results, use content to attract the customer to your site and to learn more about your solution.

Content consultants will tell you to make it entertaining or educational, but I have found that customers—even those buying consumer products—prefer education over entertainment. The customer making a Heavy Scrutiny purchase is putting a lot on the line. A piece that is predominantly entertaining will make your customer feel as if you don't appreciate the seriousness of the purchase in his or her mind.

Someone buying a new home is not going to be entertained by a video with a "Money Pit" theme. Someone scrapping their still-working-but-old business system for a new, untested system is not going to be amused by a video showing frustrated employees and clueless managers. What works on TV will not work in this situation. You wouldn't think I have to say this, but, unfortunately, too many consultants have convinced CEOs and marketers that it's cool to be entertaining. Ad agencies are notorious for this. It backfires, especially in Heavy and Intense Scrutiny situations.

When a prospective customer downloads your educational piece, ask for the minimum of information. You don't need to have them answer 10 questions. You'll lose a lot of people that way. It's better to have a salesperson contact them after they've had a chance to read the educational piece, so you can learn more about their specific need.

You can also try this alternative method: Invite the customer to download your first-step educational piece *without registering,* and then display a thank you screen after the download that asks for their contact information. Marketing guru Mac McIntosh[8] created and tested this method. He found that he got a 40% download rate when he didn't ask customers to register to download a guide he was offering, and then an astounding 80% of those who downloaded the material provided their contact information after downloading the guide—on the "thank you for downloading" screen.

---

[8] www.SalesLeadExperts.com

The point is, Mac gave them something they valued (the guide) before he asked them to give him something he valued (their contact information). He made a promise and kept it, by delivering the guide without requiring them to register, then asked them to return the favor. This very wise strategy should permeate your Heavy Scrutiny buying process support program. Always be willing to help buyers by providing something useful before asking them to take another step that will help you.

The smartest Heavy Scrutiny marketers continue to generate new content and offer it to their buyers via search engine advertising and unpaid results. The content doesn't have to be a guide; it can be a blog or a video.

Subjects can include:

- How to install the product or start using the service

- How to use the product or service

- How to maintain the product after purchase

- How to get maximum results from the product or service

- Why the product/service was designed the way it was designed (in other words, how customer needs drove the design)

- How the product is made—the care and attention paid to the creation of the product—or how the service is carried out, and why

- How people are using the product/service

- What's included in the product/service and why

- Problems that the product/service solves (without being a sales pitch)

You can use social media sites to let people know that your content is available, as long as you are up front about who you are and you don't over-pitch it. In other words, if your "tweets" are 100% promotional, or even 30% promotional, people will tend to "unfollow" you.

Of course, you shouldn't even bother with Twitter if your customers aren't expecting to find you there—or they aren't congregating there to make buying decisions. An IT manager who uses Facebook to share new pictures of her family would consider it an intrusion if you became her "friend" and started pitching your wares to her because of her job. On the other hand, contacting her via LinkedIn, or running ads on LinkedIn, would be entirely appropriate—assuming she was paying attention to LinkedIn messages. Understanding who uses each social media platform and why they use it will help you focus your efforts where they will do the most good.

If you have a company blog, have several people in the company contribute to it, so the content stays fresh and varied.

Your customer may be referred to you via a link from another site. This is most likely to happen if you have helpful information posted out on the Web, and you have told potential buyers, bloggers, partners, and journalists that the content is available. You can also use a Web-based press release distribution service to let people know about the content, and you should mention the content in your company's blog—giving the search engines yet another way to lead people to your solution. You can also advertise the content in search engine advertising, and with ads on related websites. Make sure you have a specific landing page for these efforts, so you can test different landing pages and track the amount of traffic coming in and sales you make on each page.

As I mentioned earlier, don't automatically dismiss the use of traditional channels to sell your Heavy Scrutiny product/service. The trick is to offer your customer something free and educational first, using whatever method is appropriate. If you are able to target your audience using postal mail, offer your guide or sample in a mailing that includes a postage-paid, already-filled-out postcard. This method can bring in a healthy stream of leads, as marketing consultant Mac McIntosh has proven—through years of testing—for all sorts of Heavy Scrutiny products and services. Our experience has confirmed this method can work—but only if the content you're offering is truly educational and of interest to your buyer. Test different content and headlines on a small scale before you invest heavily in the approach.

Your salespeople play a major role in the Heavy Scrutiny buying process, often at the earliest stages, especially if you are using your sales force to make outbound cold calls. Again, use your content to create the first "yes" interaction between your salesperson and the potential customer.

A salesperson who calls to ask for permission to send a guide or other useful material is going to hear "yes" the majority of the time. After he sends the guide (email is best—it's immediate), he can follow up with a phone call to ask the customer to describe the problems he's trying to solve. The customer will be much more likely to engage at this point, after he has received the guide and had a chance to glance at it, scan it, or read it. One client of mine had great success having salespeople call the customer 15 minutes after the download, asking if there were "any questions we could answer." The customers didn't consider it an intrusion, surprisingly, and the sale proceeded to unfold.

On the other hand, the nature of your customer and product might be so technical or deep that the customer needs time to absorb the guide. The only way to find out is to make the calls using different time periods, and see how customers respond. The appropriate interval could be anywhere from 15 minutes to 15 days.

Anything you send to the customer should have full contact information on it—giving the customer a way to contact you via email, phone, and even instant messaging.

Salespeople need to be constantly trained so they keep up with changes in how customers want to buy, and in the details of your products and services.

- Your salespeople should understand everything about your product/service and your business

- They should know how the product is made or how the service is provided

- They should understand how it is used

- If they're selling a technical product/service, they should never say to the customer, "I'm not technical." They *must* be technical—they're selling something technical!

- They should understand the other choices that your customers have

- They should know how and why your product/service can solve the customer's problem

- They should be very, very familiar with the customer's problems, but should refrain from jumping to conclusions in a conversation because they think they already know what the customer is going to say

- They should be taught that their job is to help the customer solve his problem, even if the best solution isn't your solution. This is the kind of attitude that causes customers to want to do business with your company, and refer others to you, even if they don't buy from you this time around.

Everyone in your company should be aware that buyers are not obligated to tell sellers the truth, and they often don't. That's why it is *not* a good idea to rely on what customers tell salespeople for your market intelligence. It's fine to talk about the selling process as you create your buying process maps, and you always want to keep track of what salespeople are hearing. Just keep in mind that it's not the whole picture. Many critical aspects of the customer's buying process will be missing; the information that can help you is best uncovered in customer interviews.

During a conversation with the buyer, the salesperson might say something—maybe even an offhand comment—that stops the sale in its tracks. Perhaps the salesperson said something that made the buyer distrust the company or its products/services, such as revealing incompetent or uncaring management or a lax attitude regarding quality. The buyer will decide that he doesn't want to buy from that company, no matter how much he desires the product or service.

The buyer won't let on that his feelings have changed, however. If the buyer is sitting across a table from the salesperson, the buyer's facial expression will not change. The salesperson will have lost the sale without realizing it. He will never know when or how he blew it.

The buyer will pretend that he is still interested—because if he let the salesperson know what blew the sale, the salesperson would just relentlessly counter the objection, as all salespeople are taught to do. The buyer would never be able to get rid of him.

Too many top managers assume that all of their salespeople are selling. In truth, some have an attitude problem—and spend most of their time *unselling*. In well-run organizations, usually there is one salesperson in ten who falls into this category. In poorly run organizations, the number can be as high as three or even five in ten.

Even if the customer is ready to buy, he is dissuaded from doing so by the comments or behavior of the salesperson.

The only way to make sure this isn't happening is to have a manager routinely monitor the interactions between salespeople and customers. Management of a sales force must be very hands-on. Rude, thoughtless, inaccurate, or unprofessional behavior needs to be discovered and eliminated. If the person can't be turned around, that salesperson needs to be replaced with someone better.

This may seem harsh, but why would you pay someone to convince customers that they shouldn't do business with your company?

You may be hesitant to let negative salespeople go, because of their industry and product/service knowledge. I see this quite frequently. However, once you've put rigorous training programs in place, no one employee will be more knowledgeable than any other. Long-time employees will have to be as courteous and helpful as the newbies because they will know that they are just as replaceable.

When a customer is buying a Heavy Scrutiny product/service, the buying process takes time. Too many salespeople give up before the customer is ready to buy, and too many also forget the importance of being top of mind—so when the customer is ready, that salesperson is the one who gets the call or the email. There is a sweet spot—just the right amount of contact without being intrusive. In your interviews, ask your customers how often they would want to hear from you and how long it typically takes to make this kind of decision.

BEST PRACTICES OF HEAVY SCRUTINY SALESPEOPLE

Here's what the best Heavy Scrutiny salespeople do to make sure they convert the highest number of leads into closed sales.

- **Set up a "reader"** (such as Google Reader) so they receive articles that might be of interest to their client—such as news about a competitor or trends in the client's industry. They scan their reader every day, and when they see something they think a client might find interesting, they send it along. A sales administrator can also do the "reading" for the sales force—so the sales force doesn't spend a lot of time on it—forwarding articles of interest to the salespeople for distribution to their prospects. Obviously, sending press releases and case studies is also an excellent way to keep in touch with a prospective customer, as long as the messages are not sent too frequently and they *always* contain something that the customer will find useful.

- **Include a formal, full-contact-info email signature** in every single email they send out. All of us use our email system as a way to keep track of people and projects. When it's time for the customer to call the salesperson, she will sort her incoming email by person, find the salesperson's email, and open it—hoping to find the salesperson's direct line. It should be there.

  Some companies include an image of a business card. That's nice, but for some reason graphic designers tend to make essential information so small that it is literally unreadable. This practice is irritating when it's on a printed card, but it is even worse on the computer screen, where a "6" looks like an "8" or a "9." Don't make the customer squint. Make sure you always use 10-point or even 12-point type to display phone numbers. You may think this is incredibly insignificant, but anything your salesperson does that slows down the customer is literally slowing down the sale. It could even be the last straw.

- **Understand the product or service thoroughly**—and never stop learning. Too many salespeople think they can take a Light Scrutiny approach to selling a Heavy Scrutiny product/service. The customer isn't fooled. It speaks so poorly of the company that the sale is automatically put in jeopardy.

- **Can answer very specific questions.** What often happens in the Heavy Scrutiny process is the customer does her research on the Web, visits many websites, and possibly even configures her desired purchase online, using tools available there. By the time she contacts a salesperson, many of her general questions have been answered. Now, before she goes any further, she needs the salesperson to answer a very specific question. The constantly learning salesperson (or the one who is properly equipped with an easily searchable database of answers) will be able to answer that question—or will be able to get the information with a few clicks. The best salespeople are aggressive learners. They are constantly going to the development, product, and training experts in their companies, asking questions, and accessing other educational sources to increase their understanding of their product/service and how customers use it.

ONCE YOU HAVE GOTTEN THE ATTENTION OF THE HEAVY SCRUTINY BUYER, YOU WILL NEED TO START ANSWERING HIS MANY QUESTIONS.

The Heavy Scrutiny buyer asks a *lot* of questions. These questions will be answered in a variety of ways—your website, your salespeople, guides, booklets, videos, webinars, seminars, brochures, mailers, advertising, PR, blogs, social media, pricing documents, case studies, testimonials, discussion groups, product manuals, and your contract.

It's helpful to realize that the customer's questions—when buying a Heavy Scrutiny product or service—fall into one of two categories:

1. Which product/service do I want to buy?

2. Who do I want to buy it from?

If your site, content, or salesperson helps the customer answer the first question, your chances of making the final sale are better than they would be if you came into the process late in the game.

Helping the customer make the "which product/service" decision will help you earn the buyer's trust. He will assume you will help him with the rest of his buying decision, and that you will be helpful after he has bought the product or service. This is where your educational content will be the most useful.

Granted, there are many selling experts who will tell you that customers can trap you into becoming a "free consultant," where you give customers all the information they need, then they buy from someone else—someone who didn't have to work as hard for the sale.

This certainly does happen. However, it almost always happens because the "first" vendor didn't make it easy for the customer to carry the buying process to its conclusion (including working out a price that made sense to the customer). It's easier for the customer to stick with the vendor he started with, than it is to buy from another vendor, especially when he's buying a Heavy Scrutiny product/service. Going to another vendor in the middle or towards the end of his buying process means he will have to do a lot of duplicate work, poring over the fine print in the contract, making sure there are no "gotchas," calling references, and so on.

If you really are making it easy for him to buy from you, you will be making it easy at *every phase* of his buying process, from start to finish.

Once he has decided on the model or type of product/service he wants to buy, the next question he has is, "Who am I going to buy it from?" This is where referrals—and familiarity with a vendor—play a major role in building confidence.

The customer buying a Heavy Scrutiny product/service is going to think long and hard before finally making his decision. He's going to look at what you have to say about the product/service, but he is also going to look at what everyone else is saying about the product/service—and about you. He will be much more influenced by comments made by real customers than by anything you write.

That means you must be constantly monitoring what is being said about your products, services, and company in discussion groups, blogs, social media sites, and customer reviews. Companies are hiring listeners for this very reason. The goal is to join the conversation, when it's appropriate. The right approach and tone is critical. The person who responds must be articulate, considerate, and knowledgeable. The person should say, right up front, that they work for the company. Their response should be brief and helpful.

Here are the types of messages that this person will be responding to:

1. **Questions from an individual to a group** asking for a recommendation regarding your type of product/service ("Does anyone know where I can find a product that does X?"). **Response:** Very short, as in: "Hi, I work for [name of company], and we make a product that does X. You can see it at http://www.mycompany.com/productX. Feel free to ask me any questions about it."

2. **Negative comments or reviews** ("This product doesn't do what it's supposed to!"). **Response:** "We are really sorry you are disappointed. We're putting a major effort into fixing this problem, and will come back to this group with our progress next week." Or, "We're so sorry you were disappointed. In fact, the product does do what it's supposed to, but you have to do X to make it happen, and we should have made that more clear. We're changing our product documentation now so others don't have the same problem. Thanks so much for bringing this to our attention."

3. **Positive comments or reviews.** It's best to just let the positive comments speak for themselves. Any public "thank you" to the person who made the comments may embarrass the person who made them—he may feel that it somehow compromises his comments. Of course, you may wish to link to these comments from your website, but make sure you check the site regularly, as negative comments may have cropped up there as well, and you'll need to respond to them.

There will be situations where someone makes a really negative comment that is completely out of left field. Of course you will do everything you can to help the person, starting with responding to the person on the forum where he posted his comments, and offering to help. If the person is just a really grumpy type who can't be satisfied, do the best you can. You will know from your customer interviews that this is an isolated case. They will help you keep all issues in context. We all come in contact with people who are emotionally unbalanced, blowing things all out of proportion.

Your customer interviews, conducted properly, will definitely show you which issues you need to fix and which features/functions/characteristics you should be promoting. You will also know the questions that customers are asking. Answer those questions, everywhere you can.

The more scrutiny the buyer applies to the purchase, the more you have to think like an educator rather than a seller. The buyer of a Heavy Scrutiny product/service wants to make an *informed* decision. Your job is to educate the buyer—and not just in a limited way that leads to your solution.

Being helpful without necessarily gaining from your helpfulness is one of the fastest ways to build trust. And you won't sell a Heavy Scrutiny product or service without building trust. Plus, you may help one person, without expecting any gain, and that person, out of appreciation, will be sure to refer others to you. Referrals are incredibly important if you're selling a Heavy Scrutiny product or service. The potential buyer will consult with a number of other buyers.

There is a karma component to selling successfully; the best salespeople know this and act on it. Even considering the small number of people who might take advantage of your generosity, you will always come out ahead if you are generous with your helpfulness.

PRICE PRESSURE AND THE HEAVY SCRUTINY PURCHASE

Salespeople will often complain that they lost the sale because the price of what they're selling is too high. In my experience—both as a seller and as a buyer—price plays much less of a role than is commonly believed.

It is mostly a convenient excuse for the salesperson, as it puts the onus on others in the company to find a way to lower the price, rather than on the salesperson, who failed to help the customer make the purchase. Managers who overreact to the salesperson's excuse can easily become diverted from fixing the real reasons the sale was lost.

The price of a product or service is either acceptable to the buyer or not. Many factors come into play. The cost of a product/service—especially in the Heavy Scrutiny category—involves more than just the actual price. There's the cost of training, product adoption or service utilization, installation, maintenance, and so on. The buyer also pays close attention to the structure of the pricing. If you make it easy for customers to install and adopt the product, you can justify a higher price by showing them how much they'll save on installation and adoption.

You will want to make sure that your price is not a stumbling block to the buyer. Here's how:

- Interview customers—as I teach in this book—and ask, "What would you consider a fair price for this product/service?" The answer to this question will be consistent across your customer base. There may be small variations in prices mentioned, but you won't see major differences. I have found that the prices mentioned are always within 10 to 20 percent of each other. If your price is in the same ballpark as the prices given by your interviewees, then you won't be losing the sale because of price.

- Call the customer after a sale is lost, as I mentioned earlier. They will usually take the call if it is coming from the CEO. If you ask them what you could have done better/differently, they will most likely tell you. Chances are, the cause will not be the moment when price entered the discussion. Customers usually know roughly what something will cost before they contact your company for the first time. Once you know what caused you to lose the sale, focus on fixing that part of your Buying Process Roadmap.

Budget allocation for the Heavy Scrutiny product or service

The bulk of your budget should be spent on answering questions, because that is the part of the process most important to your buyer.

30% on attracting people to your content, using both broadcast and social media platforms

10% on generating content that customers will find interesting and helpful

25% on answering questions—primarily on your website

20% on tools for salespeople and selling partners (presentations, proposals, webinars, seminars, events, contracts, partner portals)

10% on ongoing customer contact, investigating and pursuing new opportunities in your current customer base

5% on monitoring and tracking your efforts

HOW TO SUPPORT THE INTENSE SCRUTINY BUYING PROCESS

11

THEY SEE IT, ASK DOZENS
OF QUESTIONS, GET OTHER
BUYERS INVOLVED, TALK TO A
SALESPERSON MORE THAN ONCE,
TRY IT OUT, DECIDE TO BUY IT,
SIGN A CONTRACT, AND START
TO EXPERIENCE IT—BUT THEN
THEY ALSO GET MARRIED.
SERVICES ARE ONGOING.

Characteristics of Intense Scrutiny Products and Services

- Very few buyers are interested in Intense Scrutiny products and services.

- Multiple approvers are involved in the buying decision, and each asks dozens of questions. The lead buyer, or champion, is taking a big risk. If the decision turns out to be a mistake, his reputation will be stained.

- The price is significant, running from many thousands to billions of dollars.

- The buying process takes weeks, months, or even years. A salesperson is involved and a contract is signed. The buying process is ongoing. The buyer decides, as services are performed, if he wants to purchase additional or ongoing services from the vendor—or not.

- Examples: All professional consulting services, large-scale development projects, very expensive custom products, nursing home facilities, and ongoing medical services.

Following are the Buying Process Roadmap guides—which can serve as templates for your own Intense Scrutiny Buying Process Roadmap and Intense Scrutiny Buying Process Roadmap for Partners. At each step, you will want to answer these questions:

- **Client Actions:** Who are the buyers at this stage, and what are their concerns and questions?

- **Company Tasks:** Where are the buyers expecting to find these messages at this stage in their buying process? What messages and tools must we create to address their concerns and answer their questions?

Note that I am using the word "client" in this chapter, rather than "customer," because Intense Scrutiny buyers do, in fact, become clients.

INTENSE SCRUTINY

BUYING PROCESS
ROADMAP

CUSTOMER ACTIONS

SEARCHES & RESEARCHES

1

COMPANY TASKS

CREATE A GREAT PRODUCT OR SERVICE & MAKE IT EASY TO FIND IT

The Intense Scrutiny purchase includes everything involved in a Heavy Scrutiny Purchase, but with one important addition: the buyer and the seller "get married." The seller provides ongoing services to a client, in the form of consulting or care services, or in the course of custom-building a very expensive product.

A lot is at stake, so the buyer has many concerns and questions. She can't afford for the project to fail, so she must choose very carefully.

At this stage in her buying process, she spends a great deal of time searching for—and researching—all possible options. She studies articles, blogs, white papers, websites, and discussion groups. She asks others, whom she trusts, to make recommendations. She does not rush into this decision.

- Interview buyers so you know what they want in your type of product or service, where they expect to find it, and the words/phrases they use to describe and search for it. Identify the Critical Characteristic.

- There will be more than one person involved in the Intense Scrutiny decision. Understand who these people are and what they care about. Build buyer personas and Buyer Scenarios for each buyer.

- Understand how well your competition is meeting client needs and where they fall short.

- Design the product or the service so it meets buyer needs. Don't try to push them into buying something that isn't good for them.

- Identify and articulate the promise that clients want you to keep—and that you *can* keep—with your product, people, processes, policies and passion.

- Make it easy to find in-depth information about your solution. Reading a comprehensive document is an early step in their buying process. Don't sell. Educate.

- The client won't "marry" you without coming to trust your character. Everything you and your staff do must be worthy of the client's trust. Always behave as if the client is in the room. Anything questionable will drive buyers away. Earn and maintain your reputation for service, leadership, and solid ethics.

CUSTOMER ACTIONS

COMPANY TASKS

2

ASKS QUESTIONS & ANALYZES OPTIONS

ANSWER QUESTIONS & HELP THE POTENTIAL CLIENT WEIGH OPTIONS

The client will ask dozens of questions:

- How well will this meet my needs— especially my most pressing needs?

- How much does it cost—to begin with, and over time? Are there hidden costs? Is it worth it?

- Am I taking the best approach? What other options do I have?

- What have others thought about this product or service—and the company? Can I trust their opinions and experience?

- What will be included?

- Is it available now?

- How easy is it to buy, install, and use?

- Will other buyers and users like it?

- Are they being helpful? Or are they just selling?

- Who are these people? Will I be comfortable working with them?

- What will happen when something goes wrong?

- What's included in the services provided—and what's not?

- Is the contract straightforward, or slippery?

- How will the relationship work? Who will be responsible for what?

- Is it easy to test before I buy?

- What do I find worrisome about this seller? How much will it matter, if my suspicions are borne out?

- Know all the questions that potential clients ask when they're buying your product or service, and build a database where you store and continually update/improve your answers to those questions.

- Answer their questions everywhere— your landing pages, websites, videos, diagrams, catalogs, emails, printed pieces, case studies, testimonials, white papers, webinars and seminars, speeches, blogs, and social media sites. Provide comparison tables. Show the cost-effectiveness of your product over time or time savings possible due to your product or service.

- Describe and show how your product or service satisfies the Critical Characteristic, and keeps your brand promise.

- Provide the main buyer (the "champion") with materials she can use to convince others.

- It should be easy to contact a salesperson. Salespeople should respond immediately. Train them constantly, so they can answer general and specific client questions. If they don't know an answer, they should say so, then find out—fast.

- Send new educational information about the product or service to potential clients regularly, via emails that contain the content or link to it.

- Provide references the client can call.

CUSTOMER ACTIONS

DISCUSSES WITH OTHERS

3

COMPANY TASKS

ASSIST DISCUSSIONS

The buyer has learned everything she can about you, from information provided by you and your salespeople, references, reviews, and other third-party influencers such as bloggers, journalists, prior clients, and analysts.

She has discussed what she's learned with the other buyers, including what they like about your products, services, and company, and things they find less appealing. They've decided to ask you and the other finalists to pitch. They want to know how you propose to solve *their particular problem*.

Personal chemistry plays an important role at this stage in the buying process. The meeting will most likely be face-to-face. Participants—depending on the size of your company and the project—may include you, your salesperson, and the people on your team who will be working with the client day-to-day.

Sometimes, the minute the vendor walks in the door, the client makes her buying decision. She may be surprised and disappointed at the comportment of the people on your team, or feel comfortable immediately.

Small things can make a big difference at this stage. I was helping a CEO select a new PR firm. We visited a half dozen companies in Boston. The firm with the $400 light fixtures was quickly taken off the list, as was the firm where the owner was downright nasty to her own employees.

The goal is to help the client make the right decision. The salesperson should be highly trained, must advocate what will work best, and should never push.

Business to business:

- Before the meeting, the salesperson must learn everything he can about the buyers: their positions in the company, political clout, history with this type of product, preferences, and concerns. He must know what drove the client to seek this solution, how they've tried to solve the problem in the past, and what worked or didn't. He should know their budget and desired timing.

- Create modular presentations. Each customizable module should consist of 1 to 3 slides. Modules: A summary of the client's situation; an overview of the proposed solution; how it will help the client; how others have used it; what will happen after the client says "yes"; and why the company is qualified to provide the solution. Include testimonials.

Business to consumer:

- Clients will be asking many questions about what will happen after they buy. The salesperson should help the clients think through their options, without pushing.

CUSTOMER ACTIONS

STUDIES PROPOSALS & PLANS

4

COMPANY TASKS

CREATE PROPOSAL & PLAN

The client has decided she likes your company, your basic approach, and can live with your proposed budget and timeline.

Sometimes clients ask several firms to submit plans or proposals at this point. However, most often, the client chooses *one* vendor at this stage and asks for plans and/or a proposal.

Some companies charge a minimal amount for these plans; some don't. Standard industry practices (and the amount of detail requested by the client) should dictate whether you charge for these plans or not.

The client will receive your proposal or plans, and study them. She may ask you to make changes before she shows them to others. Once she is satisfied with them, she will discuss them with the other approvers. You will be invited to participate in one or more of these meetings, but not all of them. She will get back to you with new changes.

Once you have made those changes, she might be ready to sign on the dotted line. If so, you would then skip the next stage (#5) and go directly to stage #6.

Then again, she may need to make absolutely sure that she is making the right decision, and will proceed to the testing stage (#5).

- Create a library of plan and proposal modules that you can customize for each client. Make them as straightforward as you can; unnecessary complication only adds more barriers to the sale. Don't weigh down your plans and proposals with pages of legalese.

- Plans and proposals should include a "who does what, when, and how" section, so there is no confusion about roles and responsibilities.

- The salesperson should continue to check back with the client, asking what she needs to proceed. He should send information she might find useful, including case studies.

- The salesperson should "get right on it" when the client comes back with a question or a request. The client should feel that she is very important to the salesperson, and his top priority. This is not the time to leave things hanging. The client can still decide to go back to the other potential vendors and resume the selection process with them.

- The client may have a lingering doubt that she hasn't yet articulated. The best salespeople sense that concern, and ask outright: "Is there anything else that concerns you at this point?"

CUSTOMER ACTIONS

TESTS IT

5

The client is almost ready to commit, but she still needs to experience what it will be like to work with you, and/or experience what it will be like to be the owner and user of whatever you are providing for her. What she wants to do at this stage will depend on what you sell. Here are some examples:

- **Large custom software project.** She will want to hire you to do a small, carefully defined pilot project before committing to a larger project.

- **Custom yachts, vehicles, houses, buildings:** She will want to sail, drive, or spend time with what you have built before, talking to the current owners without you around. She will ask them many questions about what it was like to work with you, while experiencing what you have built for them.

- **Retirement homes and other long-term care facilities:** She will want to spend time in the facility, walking around and interviewing current residents and their families.

At some point during the testing, if she doesn't find any "gotchas," she will decide she is comfortable moving to the next step. She will make an emotional commitment, even though there are many more issues still to be resolved. However, she will certainly be "over the hump" in her buying process.

COMPANY TASKS

DEMOS & TRIALS

The salesperson should arrange testing.

- **Large custom software project:** The client should be able to choose from a menu of "small project" services. It should be easy to get the project started and completed—to the client's satisfaction—on time and on budget.

- **Custom yachts, vehicles, houses, buildings:** The salesperson will arrange for the prospective client to experience existing yachts, vehicles, houses, or buildings. Maintain a list of owners who will be willing to play host to a prospective client. Obviously, if you don't treat your clients well while working for them, this won't be easy. If you never go out of your way to make sure they're happy, many sales will end at this stage.

- **Retirement homes and other long-term care facilities:** If you're hiding something, the client will sense it. There will be telltale signs, no matter how clever you are about hiding them. There is no substitute for doing the right thing all the time.

Experts should be available to answer the deeply technical and customer-specific questions.

After the trial, the salesperson should summarize the results in a report that the champion can pass on to other influencers.

CUSTOMER ACTIONS		COMPANY TASKS
SIGNS CONTRACT, PAYS PORTION OR FULL PRICE	**6**	**GUIDE THE CLIENT THROUGH THE CONTRACT PROCESS**

The client has decided.

Business to business

- The client will want a plain-language contract that clearly spells out what is being delivered, what the vendor will do, what the client is expected to do, any limits on the product or service, and what will happen when something goes wrong.

- The client will expect the contract to clearly state what the company will deliver and when, the amount of each payment and the due dates for those payments. The fee should include penalties for non-delivery or non-payment. Any starting fee should be clearly stated.

Business to consumer

- There may be financing involved, and outside vendors. Since the customer only makes this type of purchase a few times in her lifetime, she will want the seller to explain what will happen with these vendors.

- The client is buying a set of promises she expects you to keep.

- The client will expect the contract to clearly state what the company will deliver and when, the amount of each payment and the due dates for those payments. It should include penalties for non-delivery or non-payment. Any starting fee should be clearly stated.

- The contract should be semi-custom and modular, so the salesperson can quickly create a contract appropriate for each client.

- Create a checklist that spells out everything that must be done to complete the sale, including things that the client, you, and any other vendors will do. The salesperson and the client should discuss these steps, before the client signs the contract.

- The client will read through the contract and ask questions; the salesperson must be able to answer them.

- Keep the momentum and energy high, even if the sale is "almost complete." The client can still back out at this point.

- The salesperson must be very patient at this stage. It's tempting to rush the client because he can "smell the commission." But it is far more important to manage the client's expectations through this process, so there is no disappointment later on.

- In B2B situations, the implementation team takes over after the contract is signed. They should be ready to jump in. The salesperson should stay involved after the contract is signed. This is often done poorly. Be the company that does it well.

CUSTOMER ACTIONS

COMPANY TASKS

7

WORK BEGINS; CLIENT CONTINUES TO EVALUATE

KEEP THE CLIENT HAPPY, LEARN, AND SELL MORE

Business to business

The contract is signed. The client has been promised a smooth implementation process by the salesperson, and has read through the implementation checklist. Anything that doesn't match those promises or that checklist will be a big red flag to the client.

This is more serious than one would assume. At this stage, the client can still decide to pull out of the deal, even if there is some kind of financial penalty involved.

Further, even after the product or service is implemented, competitive salespeople are going to continue to pitch the client, and if you aren't keeping your promises, that client will become more and more interested in the competitive options. This is especially true if your solution didn't solve all of the client's problems or solve them as elegantly or cost-efficiently as you promised.

Business to consumer

As with the B2B client, the B2C client will be paying attention to how you treat her after the sale.

After she has signed the contract, how easy is it to get help? How helpful are the people she talks to? Does she get a thank you from the salesperson? Is she offered any special incentives to come back to you for supplies and service? Does she feel you are working as hard to satisfy her as you were when you were selling to her?

- Never forget that you are still selling (in fact, always selling), even after they sign. Your competitors never stop trying to steal clients from you.

- Stay in touch. The B2B salesperson should call 2 weeks, 2 months, then 4 months after the contract is signed. The client will let the salesperson know if there is a problem, or may reveal an opportunity for another sale.

- Put the client on a low-key email program, filled with tips, and always including contact information.

- Once the client is up and running successfully, the marketing people should interview the client about her buying process, and also see if she'd be willing to provide a testimonial (this should not be asked until the interview is finished).

- Work hard on your client service. It is actually as influential—or more influential—than your salespeople. Check with your clients to make sure they're happy. Monitor social sites to quickly discover any disgruntled clients. If you get a reputation for "great products but terrible service," your sales will suffer significantly.

- Obviously, the more complex the buying process, the more you need a Customer Relationship Management system to keep track of every interaction—before the sale, during the sale, and after the sale. The system you choose should be cross-departmental, so it can record each type of interaction involving marketing, sales, or service.

INTENSE SCRUTINY: PARTNERS

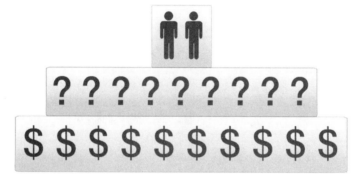

BUYING PROCESS
ROADMAP

PARTNER ACTIONS		YOUR TASKS
EVALUATES PRODUCTS/COMPANIES	**1**	**FIND APPROPRIATE PARTNERS & INTERVIEW THEM**

The less-established partner will go looking for products to represent. The more-established partners will be approached by manufacturers looking for representation.

In both cases, the partner will want to sell products that he has experience with; that customers are requesting; and that have a good reputation for service and partner support.

He will use Google to find products, but he will also get information from customers, from others in his industry and yours, from manufacturer websites, and discussion groups.

- You need to find suitable partners. Ask those you know and respect who they would recommend, and search for appropriate firms on Google. Evaluate their websites.

- Make a spreadsheet. Grade them on criteria such as how long they've been in business; the size of the company (you may want to be a big fish in a small pond, or the opposite); the types of products they carry; the experience and knowledge of their staff; their reputation, and so on.

- Narrow down the possibilities until you have at least five firms that seem well-suited to your situation.

- Interview the potential partners. A little humility at this point will bear a lot of fruit later. Find out:

  - What they want from a company like yours, including the most important characteristic

  - What their challenges are

  - How they envision "the perfect relationship"

  - How they typically structure their relationships

If you have been working with some partners for a while, and you want them to sell more, interview them. Have a knowledgeable third party call them and ask them how they feel about your company and products, what their challenges are, and the trends they see in your market. What you learn will help you all sell more.

PARTNER ACTIONS

IS PITCHED BY THOSE WANTING TO PARTNER WITH THEM

2

YOUR TASKS

PITCH THE PARTNER—ADDRESSING WHAT THE PARTNER CARES ABOUT

The partner gives everybody a chance to pitch him.

The partner's Big Question is similar to the question asked by buyers of complex and expensive products and services: "What's going to happen to me after I sign up?" Partners enter into a relationship needing the other party to deliver as promised.

Of course, your product or service has to "fit" for the potential partner and his clientele.

Here are the other questions prospective partners will be asking:

- What selling methods have you been using so far, and how well have they been working?

- How will you help us sell and service clients?

- Why will it be easier to sell your product, versus a competitive product?

- What are your expectations about our roles and responsibilities?

- Do you have other partners? How's it going? Will they be competing against us?

- Will we be able to make money selling your product or service?

- What are your terms?

- What systems and processes do you have in place to support our efforts?

- Will our investment in your product— time, money, resources, and training—pay off?

- Once you've identified the partners who would be best for your product or service, make an appointment to discuss what you can offer.

- Before going to the meeting, learn about the partner: The products they sell, the ways they prefer to work, their reputation, and what they would expect you to do.

- Don't spend the bulk of your time talking about your product, service, or company. Instead, structure your presentation this way:

  - 10% on the "why"—why you think they'd be a good fit. Why you chose them, in other words.

  - 15% of your time describing the product or service

  - 15% on the success you've had in the market so far, and how you have achieved it

  - 15% on what you will do to make sure they are successful selling your product or service

  - 10% on who you are—the people involved in the company and their backgrounds

  - 15% on terms and conditions— how you'd like to structure the relationship

  - 20% on answering additional questions, ironing out details, and addressing any concerns.

- After the meeting, send a document summarizing all that was discussed and decided.

PARTNER ACTIONS

INTERNAL DISCUSSIONS

3

YOUR TASKS

ASSIST DISCUSSIONS

The partner team members will discuss what you have presented and decide if they want to proceed. It may take them days or weeks to move forward. They will also investigate your firm, products, and services more thoroughly.

They may come back to you with more questions, and will watch to see how quickly and honestly you answer them.

They will also be comparing what you say to what they hear from others as they do their research.

- Answer all of their questions. Be ready to meet again.

- Provide references and further proof of your ability to provide a reliable product and support their efforts on your behalf.

- Send them useful information via periodic emails, not necessarily related to you or created by you, to start to establish your credibility as a helpful business partner. Assume they are very knowledgeable. Don't insult them with "basic" content.

PARTNER ACTIONS

AGREES TO PILOT

4

The partner has decided he is interested. But fully incorporating a new product or service into his offerings requires a lot of work—so he may want to do some kind of test first.

He may want to offer the product on a limited basis:

- To select clients, one at a time, to test their receptiveness to it
- In a specific geographical area
- Via audience-specific, custom websites or landing pages
- Via a mailing or emailing to selected customers
- As part of a larger offering/deal, where your product is a component of that deal
- As a one-time event, where your product or service is offered only for a short time

Sometimes the partner is confident enough to proceed without a pilot test. If so, proceed directly to #5.

YOUR TASKS

PERFORM PILOT

- Put a person in charge of the pilot who is knowledgeable, helpful, and detailed-oriented.
- Give the partner all the marketing and selling tools he needs to sell. These could include:
  - Copy and images he can use in websites, emails, presentations, brochures, blogs, social media sites, datasheets, and other online, downloadable, and printed documents.
  - A pilot agreement template that your internal person customizes, and the partner will sign. Include the goals, commission, fulfillment details, return policies and procedures, etc. This document should spell out exactly what will happen during the pilot. Negotiate any "sticking points" until both parties agree to the pilot process.
- Support the partner during the pilot.
- When the pilot is complete, document the results and discuss next steps.

PARTNER ACTIONS

COMMITS TO THE RELATIONSHIP; STARTS WORK

5

YOUR TASKS

COMMIT TO THE RELATIONSHIP; START WORK

The partner is ready to commit his resources to the partnership.

- You and he will agree to the terms of the relationship, and you will produce a contract.

- He will go over the contract carefully, ask questions and resolve issues. He will want the contract to spell out:

  - What you will do to help him sell, and provide services as needed

  - What he is expected to do

  - What happens if something goes wrong

  - How many units will be involved, how orders will be filled, and the policies and process for returns

  - The timeframe/length of the agreement

  - The conditions under which the agreement can be terminated

  - How funds will be transferred and how often they will be transferred

  - Additional standard contract information, such as the judicial jurisdiction for the contract, how legal fees will be paid in the case of a dispute, etc.

- He will assign a person or people from his company to work directly with you.

- The relationship will begin.

- He will pay close attention to the success of the relationship—how well you work with him, the results of your efforts, and how easy it is to sell and service your solution.

- You will create the contract, which will include details on the marketing, support, and fulfillment efforts you will undertake on his behalf. The contract will also spell out what he is expected to do, and when he is expected to do it. Conditions for termination, financial arrangements, and standard legal information will be included.

- You will iron out the details, until you are both agreed on the content of the contract. You and he will sign it.

- You will announce the partnership to the appropriate press, industry, and client contacts.

- You will assign a person or people to this partner, and begin making the relationship profitable for both companies.

- You will begin marketing and support activities. You will incorporate the new partner into your sales reporting system, and provide access to a web-based partner portal, where you and the partner can exchange information and the partner can access marketing and selling content. Keep it uncluttered and well-organized, so they can find what they want in seconds.

- Interview partners every six months to uncover any information that will make you both more successful.

Charlatans are attracted to the Intense Scrutiny category, because there is big money involved and they can use their pitching ability to sell an intangible product or service. Potential clients are very cautious—not just because of the price, but because they may have been burned by unscrupulous salespeople in the past.

The Intense Scrutiny category shares many of the characteristics of the Heavy Scrutiny category—long buying cycle, multiple buyers, many steps—but in this category, the buyer and the seller get married. This is truly a situation where the buyer and the seller enter into a relationship. However, it's not like a marriage, where (if you're lucky), your spouse sticks with you through thick and thin. Clients always have the option to change horses, even if they have invested a great deal of time, effort, and money to make the Intense Scrutiny product or service work. There's always someone waiting in the wings who will make it as easy as possible for the client to switch.

HOW THEY FIND YOU

The buying process starts with a search. The search terms used by customers of Intense Scrutiny services are different than the types of search terms used by buyers looking for a lower-scrutiny product/service. If a woman wants to buy a Medium Scrutiny cashmere sweater, she simply types "cashmere sweater" into Google; the results will be relevant. She can even type "cashmere sweaters on sale," and get relevant results.

If she's looking for a management consultant—definitely an Intense Scrutiny service—and types "management consultant" into Google, the top results have to do more with a definition of the term than with people and companies who actually provide the services.

Buyers get around this problem by typing in search phrases that are more related to their problem than to the solution. Rather than search for "estate lawyer," they may search for "minimizing estate taxes," which will lead them to articles on the subject written by estate lawyers.

Obviously, it's really important for you to know the search phrases that your customers are typing into Google in an attempt to find you. They will have specific phrases, which may be very different from what you're assuming.

Provide relevant content to prospective buyers that explains how they can solve the problems they are hoping to solve. Every time you create another piece of relevant content, you increase your chances of appearing in their search results. You can also advertise the content in the paid ads that are displayed with search results. Each piece of content provides another pathway for searchers to arrive at your site.

Usually the prospective buyer of an Intense Scrutiny product or service will spend a lot of time with your educational content before making the first contact. Your content can and should include FAQ's, blog entries, articles, case studies, guides, and white papers.

Potential clients will use the content to evaluate how helpful you are; what you believe; how much you respect your clients; how you have solved these kinds of problems in the past; and so on. This is your chance to showcase your experience, expertise, and strategy with well-written content. Here are some of the ways you can get the word out:

Bloggers. Content in the form of newspaper or magazine articles about your firm used to be a well-proven way to attract prospects to you. But, as we all know, buyers have shifted their attention from printed publications to the Web. Now your PR efforts must include bloggers. Very few of them have achieved the status (and subscriber base) of a *Forbes* or *The Wall Street Journal,* but some are incredibly influential within their niche. There are at *least* 20 bloggers on a subject for every print journalist, so the successful PR outreach is more complicated than it used to be. You need to find these folks, read what they're writing, and customize your pitch so it ties in to what they write about.

Referrals play a more significant role in the Intense Scrutiny category than in all other categories. The buying decision is so important, with so much at stake, that the credibility of the referrer plays a greater part in the buyer's decision to pursue a relationship with a specific vendor or company. The most credible referrer will be in a similar situation and/or industry, and will be someone that the buyer respects. Build a database of satisfied customers who don't mind being contacted by prospective customers, and keep track of how often their names are given out as a reference, so they don't get "reference fatigue."

Phone call by salesperson. If you're selling an Intense Scrutiny service, don't expect to make a sale on the first phone call. Don't even try to sell your services on the first phone call. That's guaranteed to be unsuccessful; it's like coming up to a complete stranger on the street and saying, "Hi, my name is Joe. Will you marry me?" Any sane woman would say "No!" and distance herself from Joe as quickly as possible. Unfortunately, this is the technique many salespeople use when they are trying to sell Intense Scrutiny services. You'd think, after the 1000th "No!" they'd get the idea.

Instead, offer a guide or white paper in the initial conversation, send it to the person *immediately* via email. Then call back after an appropriate time period. This is the right way to start an Intense Scrutiny relationship. You only take a second to introduce yourself, and you provide something of value right out of the gate. You tell the buyer you will call back tomorrow, and then you do. The buyer knows you will be calling back, and will at least glance at what you have sent. If the piece is helpful, you're on your way to having a meaningful conversation.

In the second call, don't focus on the piece you sent. It should stand alone, and unless the customer brings it up, there's no reason to discuss it. Instead, this is the time to start asking an open-ended question, such as:

- What's your biggest challenge right now in this area?

- What have you been trying to do to solve the problem, and how has it been going?

- If you could describe the perfect solution to this problem, what would it look like?

Listen very, very carefully to the customer's answers. Take detailed notes, so you can refer back to exact phrases that the customer used earlier in the conversation. Don't be boring. This is not a survey—it's a conversation between two people, one of whom has a problem and one who may have the solution to that problem.

One of the most powerful tools you can use, as a salesperson, is to keep the full range of possibilities in mind, from "I can't help you—what we offer isn't what you need," to "I have exactly what you need, start to finish." Being willing to admit that you don't have the answer will keep you from trying to convince the customer you have an answer when you really don't. It will also keep you from jumping in too soon, when in fact the biggest and best opportunity might come later in the conversation.

Many overly eager salespeople make this mistake. They are so glad to get a prospect on the phone, they try to sell anything and everything, right off the bat. It doesn't work because the customer knows perfectly well that the salesperson will not be able to suggest a good solution until he thoroughly understands the problem. Usually the salesperson interrupts the customer as he is trying to describe his problem, and the call goes south from there.

Nothing—*nothing*—is as important as letting the customer describe the entire problem, and making sure you understand that problem. This is much like an interviewing process, where you ask the customer to describe the various aspects of his problem. As you listen, ask questions about the areas where he may be glossing over something. Drill down for more detail. You want to understand his problem, and you want him to know that you care about his problem. Why? Because:

- The customer will be able to relax, after explaining his problem completely, knowing that you now understand the entire problem. He will be grateful to you for giving him the opportunity to unburden himself, without judgment or interruption.

- The customer will be more likely to believe that your solution will work for him, because you completely understand his problem.

- The customer will trust you more than another salesperson who didn't have the patience to listen to the whole problem. And, you can assume that at least 85% of the competing salespeople will not wait to hear the whole story before they launch into their canned pitch.

- Because you cared enough to listen to everything he had to say, the customer will feel valued and respected.

- You will see the whole picture, including what is important and what is not, what has been tried, what worked and what didn't, what the political scene looks like, who has the power to make a decision (and who doesn't), how much budget is available to solve the problem, what the best solution should look like, and so on.

- The customer will see you as an ally in his fight to solve the problem.

That's the best possible outcome in any Intense Scrutiny sales call. The customer comes to believe that you are on his side, that you understand his struggle, and that you are only going to recommend solutions that will work for him. Of course, that's exactly what you have to do—you can blow the whole interaction if you start to recommend solutions that will *not* work for him.

If you don't have the solution—and you can't think of any way to make anything you offer work for him—you should say so. He will appreciate your honesty and lack of pushiness. Because you have now earned his trust, he will actually start asking questions to see if there might be any way to make your solution work. Sometimes the customer may be able to see a way to make it work that you might not have thought of, or he may be willing to change his own requirements so that your solution has a chance of success.

There are big rewards waiting for the salesperson who doesn't jump in with a solution before hearing and understanding the whole problem.

What salespeople tend to forget, as they desperately try to meet quota each month, is that customers *want* solutions. If a salesperson comes along who actually listens to him, and understands him, the customer will go out of his way to buy from that salesperson. The salesperson has earned his reward through his courteous and respectful behavior.

ONCE YOU HAVE GOTTEN THE ATTENTION OF THE INTENSE SCRUTINY BUYER, YOU WILL NEED TO START ANSWERING HIS MANY QUESTIONS.

The buyer of Intense Scrutiny services will come to your site with an incredible number of questions. The more questions you can answer on your website and in your content, the better. You should have a library of useful and regularly refreshed content on your site.

The customer should be able to download your content easily without entering a lot of information. You can always get more information later on. Just ask for their name, email address, company, title, and phone—either before they download or after, on a thank you screen.

Is there a danger in giving away too much information? As with many things in business, it's a tradeoff. My experience has proven to me that you will get more sales by providing more information than you will by providing less—especially now, when buyers expect to get the majority of their questions answered on the Web. If your site is the site that answers most of their questions, chances are much greater that you will become the vendor of choice. Yes, competitors will copy some of it. But if you make it easiest to buy, and continue to provide fresh, relevant content, you will always be a step ahead of your competitors.

You shouldn't ask about the immediacy of their need. You don't really need this information, because you should treat every inquiry as if it is an immediate inquiry. Asking for the timing of their need can cause salespeople to cherry-pick the leads, putting other leads aside. This is a mistake. Anyone who is doing their research is already engaged in their buying process. If you get in on the ground floor, you will have more opportunities to establish credibility and build trust than the competing salesperson who enters the conversation later on.

Salespeople should be equipped to answer any question that the customer might have. The answers should be available in a searchable database, and via a tree menu (a list of categories and sub-categories). Sometimes it's easier to get to content via tree navigation than it is to use the search function offered on the website, especially when the search returns too many results. You don't want your salesperson verbally vamping on the phone, trying not to sound stupid, while desperately searching through 1,299 irrelevant results.

The questions in the database should *not* be made up by internal company people. The database should contain the real-life questions asked by customers, questions revealed in customer interviews, discussion groups and social media sites, and customer service queries. Additional questions will arise in the recorded conversations between salespeople and customers.

In my opinion, to make sure these requirements are met, two positions should be added to marketing departments:

- **An "Answer Generator"**—a writer who does nothing but research customer questions and answer them, in writing, getting the answers approved by the internal company experts. The answers can then be published on the website, in the company's intranet, and in the answer database used by salespeople and any selling partners. They can also be used by other copywriters who are creating content for the company, and by those monitoring discussion groups and social media sites.

- **A "Metrics Maven"** who owns the tracking or metrics part of marketing and sales. This person, working with management, decides what should be measured, then creates the measurement infrastructure, including the tools and vendors used for measuring, the reports for management, the analysis of the findings, recommendations for improving poor results, and strategies for further exploiting the successful efforts. At the very least, the Metrics Maven should be measuring incoming leads and conversion rates for those leads.

The efforts of these two people would have a significant and measurable impact on your ability to generate revenue (not to mention your ability to keep your costs down). All of the people who need answers—customers, salespeople, employees, and partners—would not have to search endlessly, guess, or fake it. The answers would be right there. Customers could get what they need to make a decision, employees would get what they need to get their work done or answer a question for a customer, and partners would be able to sell more effectively for you.

Tracking this activity properly will help you decide which type of content works best, and you will start generating more of that type of content. This will lead to more sales.

HIRING: AN INTENSE SCRUTINY BUYING PROCESS

The employer looking for an employee goes through an Intense Scrutiny buying process. There are some differences, of course; the "salesperson" is the candidate himself (although a headhunter might be involved in the process as well). The contract is the employment contract. But so many other aspects are the same.

There is a team involved in the decision, it takes time, the monetary commitment involves thousands of dollars and the intended relationship is long-term. The employer has many questions, and tries to get them answered through as many resources as possible—including references—and the candidate's social media sites such as personal blogs, Facebook, Twitter, and LinkedIn.

If you are an employee rather than an employer, keep this social media reality in mind. You are building a picture of your character with every post and every comment. One immature or profanity-laced post can cause an employer to decide that she doesn't want a person like that working inside her firm.

It's so easy to be sarcastic and silly when posting online, especially with the short-post, "only among like-minded friends" channels such as Twitter and Facebook. But it only takes one negative, offhand remark to keep a prospective employer from pursuing your candidacy, and hiring you for that job you always wanted. Think about what each post says about you before hitting the submit button.

A TYPICAL INTENSE SCRUTINY BUYING PROCESS

The Intense Scrutiny buying process is complex. Those of you selling Intense Scrutiny products and services already know this; but it's still instructional to look at it from the buyer's perspective. Most Intense Scrutiny sellers simply drop the ball at some point in the process. They make it so difficult for the buyer that the sale can stall for months, as the buyer keeps waiting for the seller to provide what is needed, and the seller simply does not.

Let's assume that Robert is an IT manager for a large pharmaceutical company. We'll call that company BigPharma. He has a data integration problem, one that has come up because his company has acquired a smaller company (LittlePharma) with a product line that is complementary to that of BigPharma. Robert needs a short-term solution—the ability to start accessing the data that currently resides in the other company's databases—but he also has a long-term goal of completely integrating the two systems over time, so that the data no longer resides on two systems.

Robert knows that he could hire a programmer and assign him to this project, but he doesn't think that's a good idea. He would rather talk to an outside vendor who has had experience with integration issues, and who also offers tools that facilitate the smooth integration of non-compatible data systems. The project is too important to assign to someone who might miss the "gotchas" inherent in integration of this type, and who might miss some subtle but critical business issues that could keep the data from integrating as it should.

Robert will try to recall an integration vendor who has contacted him in the past. If the name of the company is easily associated with "integration," he is more likely to remember the company. In any case, he will go to Google and type in "data integration vendors" or "database integration services" or "data integration tools." If the company he's already trying to remember comes up in the top few search results, he will go there first, because he will be more comfortable talking to a company he already knows than one that he has not interacted with before.

Let's interrupt Robert's buying process for a second to examine what is driving Robert. Obviously, he has a problem to solve. That's clear. But what about the less obvious drivers?

What about, for example, the black-mark-on-the-whiteboard syndrome? When I've worked inside larger corporations, one thing I noticed was that each person who works in a large company is issued an invisible whiteboard that gets hung around his or her neck on their first day. Each mistake they make, from that point forward, becomes a black mark on their whiteboard.

Everyone knows what everyone else's whiteboard looks like, and the black marks are never erased. The corporate memory doesn't have an erase function. If someone accumulates too many black marks, this person will be discounted by everyone else. In meetings, Mr. Blackmarks can make a recommendation; it might even be a good recommendation. But those black marks will cause others in the room to either ignore that suggestion or, if the situation has gotten completely out of hand, they will roll their eyes.

That whiteboard plays a major part in the decision-making process of people like Robert, especially in the case of an Intense Scrutiny type of purchase, where a bad decision can lead to a very messy and costly fiasco. Robert does not want this integration project to sully his whiteboard. In other words, he will do everything he can to avoid embarrassment. This desire to avoid embarrassment is one of the main drivers in all Intense Scrutiny buying decisions, and yet it is often ignored by people selling Intense Scrutiny products and services.

Another factor is Robert's personal history with decisions like this. Has he made good, solid decisions in the past? Or, is his history a mixed bag? Has he gained a reputation for being a poor decision-maker, to the point where others are constantly questioning his rationale and getting involved because they're concerned it won't turn out well? In that situation, he will tell you he's the main decision-maker, but as you work with Robert, you will quickly realize how little respect Robert has from others in the organization. Robert's reputation will become a serious barrier to the sale.

As I mentioned in the Heavy Scrutiny section, you should not make the all-too-common mistake of snubbing the champion, even when you've realized that his power is limited. Continue to treat him as if he has the power, but treat the others as if they also have the power. This is a delicate balancing act, but it pays off. The champion may have a low level of power in the organization, but he still has a goodly amount of influence over the sale. If you make him angry, he can and will find a way to keep you from getting the business.

Regardless of his own personal power level, Robert also has specific pressures from a variety of sources. Perhaps the CEO has made it clear that the data integration is a top priority for him. Perhaps Robert's direct boss, the CTO (Chief Technology Officer) has already mentioned that he has a preferred vendor in this space. It might even be a vendor that Robert doesn't trust because he's heard negative things from other IT managers. Even if that is true, Robert will have a difficult time overcoming the CTO's bias.

All of these issues will affect Robert's buying. These issues—and the questions associated with them—must be identified and addressed in order for a sale to be made.

Robert is most concerned about what will happen after the contract is signed. The proof that he made a good decision will only materialize because you kept the promises you made during the buying process.

It will be your job to *prove*, beyond a shadow of doubt, that you won't let Robert down. This can be done in three ways: by giving completely trustworthy answers to all of Robert's questions, by referring Robert to other customers who have already purchased from you, and, if possible, letting Robert "test" your product or service on a small scale before taking the big leap. Of course, once Robert is convinced, and he has convinced the others in his organization, you *must* keep all of your promises.

The smartest Intense Scrutiny salespeople make sure they talk to the other decision-makers as soon as possible in the buying process. Their goal is to determine the concerns that these important influencers have. Then they are able to help Robert make his case.

Not trained, not curious, not successful

While I was writing this chapter, I was called by a salesperson I'd met at an Inbound Marketing Summit conference. Her company provides search-engine-friendly content for companies. She sells an Intense Scrutiny service.

I have clients who need that kind of content. I am always looking for vendors who can provide it. In other words, this salesperson had reached someone who was very interested in what she had to sell.

Incredibly, she made me do all the work—and I *still* couldn't get to the next step in my buying process. The call failed. She actually kept me from buying. Not because she was irritating or rude, but because she was completely unable to help me proceed with my buying process.

She called and introduced herself. Then she asked me if she could help me with anything—before giving me any reason to believe that she could. She was making the classic mistake that so many salespeople make when attempting to sell an Intense Scrutiny service. She approached me, a perfect stranger, and said, "Hi, my name is Betsy. Do you want to buy what I'm selling?"

I tried asking questions about her services, but she didn't have any answers. I gave up on that approach. I asked her to send me more information, but instead she promised to send me an email inviting me to attend one of the monthly webinars her company puts on. Then she invited me to call her any time with questions. So far, I knew what kind of service she sells, I knew I might be interested, and all I got for the time on the phone was an invitation to attend a webinar and a promise to answer any more questions—even though she hadn't answered any questions so far.

What was missing? Why couldn't we connect?

To begin with, no one in management had prepared this young woman for the calls she was making. No one had even suggested that customers might want to have a conversation while they were on the phone with her. No one had told her the questions that might be asked and how she should respond to those questions. No one had explained the goal of the call should have been to find out what the customer needed, and see how the company's services could match up with that need. Instead, she had a vague idea that if the customer was interested, she should invite the person to a webinar.

That concept alone is terribly flawed. Given that we were on the phone, talking to each other, why would I want to go to a webinar sometime in the future to get my questions answered? Why not answer my questions … *now?* Why set me back to the beginning of a buying process, sitting through a long-winded webinar, aimed at generic customers, when I was on the phone with the salesperson now, expressing an interest, and asking late-stage-buying-process questions? By the time a salesperson gets involved in the Intense Scrutiny purchase, the buyer is not asking early-stage questions. The buyer is asking specific questions that the salesperson *should* be able to answer because her organization has prepared her to do so.

When she got on the phone, she did not engage in a conversation with me. She didn't ask me any questions. She wasn't at all curious about what I'm doing now to help clients create content.

Those of us who have learned how to sell Intense Scrutiny products and services are honestly curious about what our clients are trying to do, what they've done in the past to solve their problem, and what they think about the solutions they've already tried. We always ask a lot of questions. Always.

And, when we start getting answers, we don't prematurely launch into our pitch. In my first call with a new client, I can easily stay in "ask questions and listen" mode for 40 minutes before I start talking about solutions, which is why the first hour is always free.

Curiosity leads to revenue. The more you know about your customer—what they're trying to accomplish, what they've tried so far, what they wish someone would offer—the more you can understand how you might be able to help them. That is the true essence of sales success.

WHAT YOU'RE REALLY SELLING AND HOW TO SELL IT

When you're selling an Intense Scrutiny service, you're really selling the promise of a series of steps that you will take after the person agrees to buy. It's a process or a series of projects, which will be delivered by people. It is not simply a product or service; it is an *experience*.

The customer's most pressing question is, "What's going to happen to me after I buy?" The customer wants you to describe what the experience is going to be. In other words,

- What are the projects going to be?

- How will they be carried out?

- Who will carry them out?

- How well has this worked for others?

These are the questions you must answer, to the buyer's satisfaction, before you can make the sale.

All of your answers, no matter where they appear or how they are delivered, need to describe what is going to happen after the customer says, "Yes." Be very specific. Describe the steps that you and the customer will go through.

Your descriptions should include how your services will be custom-tailored to the specifics of your customer's situation. You also need to spell out the role the client will play as you provide your services.

Make a list of every step in the process of providing services. Write succinct descriptions of those steps. Post these steps on your website and in your selling materials. Make sure your salespeople can describe them in detail, at the drop of a hat. Your potential customers should be able to get their questions answered and know exactly what's going to happen to them after they buy.

Budget allocation for the Intense Scrutiny product or service

The bulk of your budget should be spent on answering questions, because that is the part of the process most important to your buyer. However, with an Intense Scrutiny product/service, selling doesn't stop with the first sale. You will continue to sell ongoing or additional services.

20% on attracting people to your content
15% on generating content that customers will find interesting and helpful
30% on answering questions—primarily on your website
15% on tools used by salespeople (presentations, proposals, webinars, seminars, events, contracts)
15% on ongoing customer contact, investigating and pursuing new opportunities in your current customer base
5% on monitoring and tracking your efforts

As with all of the budget allocation recommendations in this book, this is a list of things that should be done and the importance that should be attached to them, so that nothing is overemphasized and nothing is overlooked.

HOW TO KEEP YOUR COMPANY ON THE ROAD TO REVENUE

MANAGEMENT STRATEGIES FOR MAKING AND MAINTAINING THE SHIFT

Now you have a method for finding out what customers want to buy from you and how they want to buy it. And, you understand the level of scrutiny that your customer will apply to the purchase. Soon you will be calling customers, gathering data, and holding your big meeting. You will map out how to make it easier for customers to buy. You will put the finishing touches on the details of your own shift to a customer-centric company.

You will be steering away from wasting money on methods that won't work, confidently embarking on things that will work, using the guidance you receive from your customers, and following the methods explained in this book. You, your customers, employees, and partners will all be happier, and the competition will be tearing their hair out.

Since I've helped quite a few companies make The Shift, I've seen what you are going to encounter along the way.

This chapter contains the advice that will ensure you stay on the customer-centric, revenue-growing path as you start to employ the Roadmap method.

BE SURE YOU WANT TO DO THIS BEFORE GOING AHEAD

You're motivated to increase your revenue, or you wouldn't have read this far. But once you start this process, you may find yourself balking a bit.

For example, one CEO I worked with was perfectly happy with his lifestyle and the income he was making. Making the necessary changes to increase revenue, while he agreed that they should be done, just seemed like too much work. Another was comfortable making some changes, but not others—even though it was obvious that those additional changes would increase his revenue. A few just couldn't accept the concept that "my customers think they know more than I do about running my business," which, of course, misses the point. You still get to run your business, but in a way that makes more sense to the customer.

If you are motivated enough to do the interviews, but then find yourself hesitating to make the obvious and necessary changes, ask yourself why you are hesitating. Talk to your trusted advisors about it.

Perhaps you're the type of person who excitedly starts big projects, but gets bored quickly and doesn't follow through as well as you should. (Ask your spouse.) You may be afraid of doing things in a new way. You may be concerned that you won't do them well once you start.

If you built the business up from nothing, and you've still got the fire, you will be fine. But, if you're too tired, or too comfortable, or you came to your position through a series of fortunate circumstances, you simply may not have the energy to fix what needs fixing.

You need to be honest with yourself about your own level of motivation, because as you move forward, you will be required to motivate others. If they sense a doubt in you, they will think, *Oh, this is just another management fad. In six months this will blow over, and we'll be on to the next one.* They won't get excited. They'll just go through the motions.

Sometimes what is broken is something you created, so the first step in fixing it is to swallow your pride. This will take some character on your part. You can take comfort in the fact that after the changes have been made, you'll have even more to be proud of.

Once you start making changes, you'll start getting positive feedback and encouragement—from customers, who will buy more; from business partners, who will sell more; and from employees, who will be thrilled to see the company moving in the right direction and bringing in more revenue.

Here's a little extra incentive for you. As you examine your own level of motivation, you should be aware that whatever your customers know, your competitors know also. Sometimes your competitors know just by watching you, but often they learn about your weaknesses through customers.

The same prospective buyers who are considering purchasing from you are also considering your competitors. Customers are not shy about mentioning one company's weaknesses to a competing salesperson during their buying process. Customers often use this as a negotiating tactic. "Company X says they can do this in ten days, which seems like a long time to me. Can you do it faster?" The customer's question has given your competitor a new piece of information about you: It takes you ten days to deliver. If the competitor can deliver in seven days instead of ten, now they have a definite advantage over you.

Over and over, I have seen more aggressive and opportunistic CEOs gain market share against a less-motivated competitor, exploiting one weakness at a time, until the less-motivated company is marginalized—and eventually eliminated. You don't want to be the losing company. It's no fun. In fact, it's one of the most painful things that can happen to any company owner or top manager.

The interviewing method used in this book will tell you what your competitors already know. If you fix what needs fixing, you will be removing the opportunities that your competitors could otherwise exploit. All you have to do is face up to the reality that the customers are revealing to you, and make the necessary changes.

MAKE SURE YOU INVEST THE TIME AND EFFORT NECESSARY TO CONVINCE OTHERS IN YOUR COMPANY THAT THIS IS THE RIGHT THING TO DO

Common sense is surprisingly uncommon. Even when the course of action is obvious—and obviously beneficial—human beings have an incredible capacity to do just the opposite.

Take losing weight, for example. We all know "how"—eat less, exercise more—but we don't do it. As a general rule, we eat more and exercise less.

Creating a customer-centric company will be just like trying to get all of your employees to eat less and exercise more. They will resist you—overtly or covertly. They will agree, in meetings, and maybe even enthusiastically, that certain things need to change. Then, they will go back to their desks and continue to do what they have always done. The truth is, they will have to be *sold* on doing the right thing, and then *managed properly* to make sure they actually do it.

Employees are actually your first customers. They, too, have a buying process. Understanding what motivates them will help you convince them to do the right thing. For example:

- **Your CFO** is going to be most interested in the *cost* of making The Shift to a customer-centric company. You and your CFO will need to discuss the costs of making The Shift, which things you can stop paying for, and how the costs will be offset by increased revenue.

- **Your salespeople** will want to know how quickly they can start using the new methods, so they can close more sales. Your answer is that you will get there sooner if they help you describe and diagram the customers' buying process. They can continue to help after the big meeting, too—by telling you whenever they encounter a new barrier to the sale, or when they know they need a new selling tool.

- **Your marketing people** will wonder how they are going to create all the new tools you're going to need, while still meeting all the deadlines they're meeting now. Your answer: They will be able to stop working on some projects—the ones that don't fit into the Action Plan. Together, you will work on this with them, so that you end up with a reasonable workload.

- **Your product managers** will be concerned about how your research is going to affect the decisions they've already made about the products—including product functions and market positioning. Your answer is that you will work together to reorganize priorities and product development efforts, to satisfy the customer requirements and preferences uncovered in the customer interviews.

In each case, your approach should be that you *will* be making The Shift, and you need your employees' help. Work with them. Discuss ways to make it happen as inexpensively and efficiently as possible. In fact, you'll be doing many of the types of things you've always done, but now you can do them knowing that the customer will appreciate and reward your efforts.

DON'T CHEAT THE PROCESS

This book describes a method that always works—if you do it as described. If you attempt to short-change or shortcut the process, you will be acting on inaccurate data that will mislead you. You will be making decisions that are not in sync with what customers are really thinking and how they will actually behave. Instead of being on the road to revenue you'll be taking a wrong turn— into a rocky road that may turn into a dead end.

It will be temping to avoid talking to customers, or charge ahead without making sure everyone is on board, or invite people to the big strategy meeting without ensuring that they've read this book. All of these shortcuts will create a less-than-optimum result. You'll never realize the full benefits of the Roadmap method.

To make sure your meeting participants read *Roadmap to Revenue*, initiate discussions about the book before the meeting. Everyone will get the message that they have to read it. If someone hasn't read it, you'll know about it via their responses.

Some people will want to resist the changes because they are afraid that The Shift to a customer-centric organization will lead to layoffs. To solve this problem, when you first announce the fact that you are going to be interviewing customers, make it clear that the goal is to *grow* the company using the input from customers. While your research will surely uncover ways to improve processes, it will also identify new opportunities to satisfy customers—thereby creating new projects and jobs. Make it clear to everyone that the employees who most enthusiastically embrace the "customer first" concept will be most likely to be appreciated, retained, rewarded, and promoted.

You may be in a big hurry to increase your revenue because of financial pressures, but taking the necessary time now will get you off that stressful treadmill once and for all, and get your whole company moving in the right direction. The stress will start to lift, as you replace it with the new-found confidence that comes from *knowing* what customers are thinking, what they care about, and how they are trying to buy what you can provide.

You can't cheat the process of fixing what you find lacking, either. If customers are unhappy with something, and it comes through loud and clear in the interviews, fix it. Really fix it. Don't just pay lip service to it, gloss over it, or fix it partially. Dig in there, figure it out, and make whatever changes you have to make.

STOP THINKING ABOUT "MARKETING AND SELLING"

The customers' buying process is the key to increased growth. Your marketing people and salespeople should be dedicated to making it easier for the customer to understand what is being sold and to make a purchase. Everything else is just a waste of time, effort, and money.

If you really want to change departmental psychology, so that your efforts are obviously centered on the customer's buying process, needs, and perceptions, avoid titles with "marketing" and "selling" in them altogether. Companies are now using titles such as "Chief Revenue Officer," and "Customer Experience Manager." These titles more accurately reflect the new reality of the interaction between companies and their customers, and will help you eliminate the problems that occur because of departmental parochialism.

IGNORE YOUR COMPETITION—FOR THE MOST PART

You can pay some attention to your competition, but only *after* you have found out what customers want and how they want to buy. Look at what your competitors are doing and see if they are doing a better job of supporting the buying process. The idea is to learn from them and incorporate their smart ideas into your system.

Only your customers can steer you in the right direction. If you pay more attention to a competitor than you do to your customers, you are sure to lose.

Furthermore, as I mentioned earlier, your company is unique. There is no company in the world like yours. A very common cause of company failure is the assumption that "it worked for them, so it will work for us." But you're *not them*. No other CEO thinks like you do or makes decisions the way you do. No other CEO has the same vision, the same experiences, the same preferences, and the same character. No other company has hired the same mix of people you've hired. No other company does business exactly the way you do. Even if another company tried, they couldn't create a company exactly like yours.

Yes, you might be selling something that is almost the same (or even exactly the same) as what someone else is selling. That only means that you must be even more aware of the one-of-a-kind additional value that you can provide your customers through everything else associated with your product or service—including your people, processes, passion, and policies.

SIMPLIFY, SIMPLIFY, SIMPLIFY

Don't be afraid to make major changes to a product or service that is too difficult to explain. Consider turning it into separate modules or simplifying it drastically. A product or service that meets a specific need beautifully will sell more than one that meets many needs insufficiently.

Customers prefer doing business with efficient, well-run companies. Those companies are *always* run by a CEO who is *constantly* looking for new ways to simplify operations.

USE THE FLIP METHOD, NOT THE DRIP METHOD

The best way to change a system or process is to set up the new way of doing things, then flip the switch, and start doing it the new way. This is far more effective than the drip method, where you try to get there incrementally. The flip method isn't always possible, of course—especially in larger companies— but it is the best way to proceed in smaller companies.

Decide what you need to do. Set up the new process or system. Train everyone who needs to be trained on operating the new process or system. Load the old data into the new system. Then flip the switch.

If it's difficult to get the old data into the new system, and you can live without seamless access, don't even try to get the old data into the new system. Keep the old data in the old system, and access it via the old system. It will be somewhat inconvenient and less relevant from a reporting perspective, but it will save you a lot of money, time and aggravation if you just start fresh with the new system.

MANAGE YOUR CONTENT PROPERLY—AND GIVE IT THE ATTENTION IT DESERVES

Your company is now your website. As far as your customers are concerned, that's all they see until they actually start using your product or service. What you say in your website (and in related content, such as emails and white papers) will have a huge impact on your marketplace success.

Your content is actually the "product" you deliver first, for free. If they like that first product, they will be more confident that they will like what you sell. If they don't like your content, they won't want anything further to do with you.

Looking at it another way, your content is a trail of cookie crumbs that they follow to the consummation of their purchase. If the cookie crumbs don't taste good, they won't make it to the cash register. They'll spit those crumbs out and look for different crumbs that taste better.

The buying process can't proceed without content. The content has to answer the questions they have at every stage in their buying process.

The content should be appropriate to the audience. Copy for a female grooming product should have a completely different tone than one for an industrial machinery product. You would think this is obvious, but we have seen copywriters be "chirpy" when describing an industrial machine. It's even possible to be too chirpy with a female grooming product aimed at teens, believe it or not, by leaving out the essential information that the buyer needs in order to make a buying decision (facts about ingredients, usage, etc.). The only way to know how to talk to your customers in your content is to have real customers in your head while you are writing the content.

Substandard content will only repel potential customers. It will kill your chance of making that sale—and any subsequent sales that could have come from that customer. Substandard content is content that:

- Has errors and typos—hasn't been properly proofed

- Is incomplete, confusing, and/or misleading

- Talks down to the buyer

- Is full of hype instead of facts

- Is copied from someone else's site

- Doesn't "start where they are" or ignores the reality of the customers' situation

- Is just poorly written—so that sentences don't hang together, or the author's voice gets in the way of successful communication

- Describes the customer's problem in great detail, without really describing the solution. This method is used frequently by sellers offering educational content—such as a 6-week course in Internet marketing. It is also inappropriately popular for copywriters selling Heavy and Intense Scrutiny products and services, where they go on and on about the problem, but never actually describe how they will fix it. In the case of educational content providers, it's understandable—the answer is in the content they're selling, and they're not about to give that away. In the case of those selling Heavy and Intense Scrutiny products and services, a reluctance to explain how their product or service will solve the problem forces the customer to look elsewhere for a solution.

You would think, given that your company is now your website, that top executives would pay more attention and devote more resources to their content. Instead, most of them are still behaving as if their company is a brick-and-mortar operation, because that's what *they* see every day. They drive to a building, park in the parking lot and interact with employees all day.

The website is almost completely off their personal radar. It's an afterthought, something out there that they pay little attention to. They don't relate on a strategic level to the marketing communications people, the webmasters, and the nerds who are running the Web. They also don't realize how much content matters—when in fact, for almost all of their sales, it is the *only* thing that matters.

The CEOs who "get it" spend a lot of time on their own websites. Writer and speaker Gerry McGovern often talks about Dermot Mannion, the CEO who came into Aer Lingus in 2005. The company had almost gone bankrupt in 2002, and managed to stay alive through drastic cost-cutting. The CEO in charge of that phase left, and was replaced by Dermot, who was fixated on making the website as usable as possible. The first thing he did every single morning was try to book a flight on his company's site, as well as on five or more competitors' websites. His experiences enabled him to drive the Web team to continue making improvements to the site until it became truly easy to book a flight.

Before he came on the scene, the website home page was dominated by a "billboard" for the airline—showing friendly flight attendants and a responsible-looking pilot, and planes. This is a common mistake made by companies who hire ad agencies to drive their website design. Agencies know how to create billboards, so that's what they put up on the site. As much as half of the home page is dominated by a large, unclickable graphic containing pretty pictures that belabor the obvious. What a waste.

Now, thanks to Dermot's insistence on making it as easy as possible to book a flight, when you go to the site, the first thing you see is "Book a Flight." The rest of the site is incredibly task-oriented. Even the "About Us" section is a place where you can get all kinds of information that will help you, the airline customer, do what you need to do: contact a customer service rep, check on your bags, check the punctuality of the airline, and so on.

Content matters. Your content is your sales team. It should be relevant, interesting, educational, respectful, professional, and friendly. It should be refreshed often, so you can use that content to bring new people to your site as well as giving current customers a reason to return to your site. Fresh content will also improve your search engine results.

Find good writers and pay them well. Shift money from some other aspect of your marketing budget, if you must, in order to make sure that your question-answering content is rich and relevant. Make sure that your writers interview real customers. Don't let them write until they have personally conducted those interviews.

Leverage your content. Make sure it works as hard as it can. Demos created for your websites can be sent to prospects as an email attachment. An audio or video interview of someone in your company (or a customer) can be posted on social media sites and your website. Send a link to the video interview via an email to your prospect and customer list.

Different people learn differently. Don't be afraid to explain something one way in one place and another way in another place. Deficiencies in one explanation will be covered by strengths in the other.

In technical companies, the best way to educate salespeople is to shoot videos of the technical people demonstrating product functions. Those same videos can be used over and over, educating new salespeople as they join the company, without requiring any more time from the technical expert.

Salespeople should be tested randomly and frequently to make sure they have retained the information in the videos. The sales manager should develop a set of questions for each video, and ask each salesperson one of the questions in the weekly sales meeting. Anyone who fails to answer the question properly will be embarrassed enough (and directed by management) to hit the videos again.

Look for new ways to organize the facts about your product or service, or to describe them in a more meaningful way. If you sell a variety of products or services, categorize them in the ways that are most relevant to customers.

MAKE BETTER USE OF YOUR CRM (CUSTOMER RELATIONSHIP MANAGEMENT) SYSTEM

Equip your salespeople with a solid sales or CRM system. Manage their activity very closely. They must call customers back when they say they will. They must keep checking in with the customer. They must be able to answer questions, and if they can't, they should be able to get the answer from someone else in the company or a database within *minutes*—and get that info back to the customer right away. Product and service experts should be responsible for training salespeople and answering their questions. These *experts* are the ones who should be inconvenienced when the salesperson doesn't have the answer— not the salesperson or the customer.

Interestingly, when CRM systems were first introduced, their creators suffered from the classic "not checking with the user first" trap. Companies spent millions buying CRM systems and getting them up and running, only to find that the salespeople didn't use them. The data entry process was too cumbersome. Salespeople preferred their own custom-made tools. Managers, assuming that they'd be seeing wonderful data after the system was installed, found that they had very little data, in spite of the investment they had made in the CRM system.

It took several years for this situation to change. It wasn't until a later generation of systems on the market made it easier to enter data, and the systems were accessible via the Web, that salespeople finally abandoned their self-made systems and started to actually use the CRM systems their companies had provided for them.

Salespeople should set up their email folders so they "light up" (the folder name becomes bold) when a customer responds to one of their emails. They should use the same subject line—whenever possible—when they send out certain types of emails to customers, so that the response lands in the special folder. The salesperson should jump on those emails the minute they come in. Customers expect immediate response; the company that responds immediately is most likely to make the sale.

CONTINUE TO INTERVIEW CUSTOMERS

After that initial interviewing effort, it will be tempting to stop interviewing customers. Big mistake.

There is no more reliable way to keep your company on track and to uncover new revenue opportunities than to keep interviewing customers. You'll always be the first out of the gate with the right solution. When you go head-to-head with a competitor, you will walk away with the order. Your competitors will wonder how you manage to beat them to the punch, time after time.

GET AGGRESSIVE ABOUT GATHERING CUSTOMER INTELLIGENCE THROUGH DAILY INTERACTIONS WITH CUSTOMERS; STORE THAT INFORMATION IN A USEFUL WAY, AND ACT ON IT PROMPTLY

Make sure you tell everyone in the company—and vendors associated with the company—that you are now going to be focusing on the customers' buying process. Ask them to help you gather intelligence about the way that customers buy.

Create an intranet, shared spreadsheet, or database where this intelligence can be entered. Evaluate the entries there weekly (or even daily, depending on the "rhythm" of your business). Take action on what you have learned.

Make sure you get back to the person who made a good suggestion or provided valuable customer input. Let them know you are taking action. Reward them in some way. At the very least, publicly recognize their contribution. Make sure they know you appreciate it.

These actions will create a community of people who are thinking hard about providing what the customer needs. All of this activity will lead to higher revenues. Customers will sense the difference and respond positively.

HIRE SECRET SHOPPERS

After you've put some Buying Process Roadmap elements in place, hire a secret shopper and see how it's working. Make adjustments as needed.

If you're selling a Heavy or Intense Scrutiny product or service, it will be more difficult for the secret shopper to be credible. Instead, have an outside sales consultant listen to recorded sales calls and coach your salespeople in the areas where they need improvement. Record your customer service calls as well; listen to several of them every week. Make changes and improvements as needed.

If the product or service you're selling involves a contract, go over the contract with several existing customers to identify what is confusing or too wordy, and make the necessary changes.

BE CONSTANTLY ON THE LOOKOUT FOR COMPANY-CENTERED THINKING

Company-centered thinking is a natural force, like gravity. It never rests. It will always be trying to pull you back into the old ways of thinking and behaving.

When you see company-centered thinking, don't let it gain any traction. Let everyone know that you have found it, and make sure everyone knows that you won't accept that kind of behavior anymore. Reward the people who do the best job of incorporating customer preferences into their activities.

Firing the worst offender will encourage the people who are doing a good job. Some of the other resistors and backsliders will get the message and fly right. Anybody who doesn't clean up their act after seeing the consequences of resistive behavior isn't someone you want around. Let them go to work where customers don't matter.

REGULARLY REPEAT THE ROADMAP PROCESS TO CONTINUE TO GROW YOUR REVENUE

Go through the Roadmap process twice a year. Interview customers, create the report, and have another strategy meeting. Identify any new barriers to your customers' buying process. Measure whether or not you are properly supporting that buying process. Make the necessary changes to your business to stay in step with customers.

Doing this regularly will have the added advantage of keeping your competition on the run. As they see what you are thinking and doing in the marketplace, they will imitate it. However, you will always be one step ahead of them, because you will be keeping up with what *customers* are doing and making adjustments in sync with current customer perceptions, preferences, needs, and trends. No matter how hard they try, your competitors will always be one step behind you.

IMPLEMENT GREAT IDEAS—THE RIGHT WAY

So far, we have talked mostly about making improvements to an existing business or product line, as a result of your customer research. Sometimes, though, your research will lead to a Great Idea—and you'll want to act on it.

The Great Idea may be a new product or service you want to introduce, or you may wish to make a major change in a current product or service. You may want to change the very nature of your business, or buy another business.

Because the idea will be new, it will be difficult to acquire customer input. However, the strong appeal of a Great Idea can taint your perceptions of reality. It is even more necessary for you to obtain customer input. Without customer input, it's easy to be led astray.

There are dozens of people around you who have a vested interest in "liking" your latest Great Idea (or any idea that you've decided to pursue), because if you pursue that idea, they will have a job or be hired to do some project work.

Even venture capitalists, who are believed to be a good proving ground for an idea, are poor judges of an idea's validity. They only need one out of 20 (or even 100) companies to hit pay dirt. *Their odds are not your odds.* Your success rate has to be one out of one, and you're betting everything you have.

Great Ideas have created millions of great companies, large and small. I personally love Great Ideas—coming up with them, helping company owners and managers come up with them, and carrying them out. Great Ideas are exhilarating. There's nothing inherently wrong with Great Ideas, no matter where they come from.

However, Great Ideas, if not handled correctly and seen in the proper perspective, can literally ruin your company. You can imagine, given that I've spent much of my career in the high-tech business, that I've seen my share of failures that started with Great Ideas. I've also been called in after companies have done all the wrong things as they attempted to profit from their Great Idea, and they needed help setting things right.

One the most common killers of companies is the Great Idea that makes perfect sense in the conference room, on the detailed profit projection spreadsheets, in the venture capital meeting, to all the employees and vendors brought on board, and to all the friends and relatives of the passionate, convinced—and convincing—entrepreneur. The company is built on the promise of the Great Idea being a hit.

It all makes perfect sense, in the Great Idea Scenario. All of this activity takes place without involving the customer, to everyone's detriment.

The customer isn't in the shower with the entrepreneur when he has the Great Idea. The customer—a real, live, intelligent human being who has his or her own needs, problems, and limited resources—isn't consulted as the business plan is being drawn up or the financial projections are constructed. The customer is missing when the product is designed or the service is formulated. The customer is still not present when employees are hired and the business takes brick-and-mortar form. The customer isn't involved when the website, systems, processes, and policies are created.

It isn't until the company is well down the road, burning through the venture money, that the product or service is finally released, and the customers are allowed to play their appointed role in the Great Idea Scenario.

That's when reality hits—like a two-by-four, right between the eyes. Real, live customers are not as crazy about this Great Idea as the entrepreneur, the VCs, the employees and the vendors.

Something about it just doesn't make sense to them, for any number of reasons which are valid to them:

- It's too much work

- They'd rather "do nothing" than pay that much to solve the problem

- They're already solving that problem, in another way

- They're happy with a cheaper solution, which is "good enough"

- They come to the website, and they don't like what they see. They leave.

- The solution is too confusing. Customers only have a limited amount of time and patience to figure out what is being sold, how it works, whether it would solve their problem, and whether it is worth the risk to try it out. If it takes too long—and a lot of research says that seven seconds is all you have when they come to one of your website pages—they won't stick around.

- The idea just seems silly

- They like the solution, but when they try to buy it, the buying process is too difficult

- They buy the solution, but they are disappointed. They warn others to stay away, creating a negative backlash in the marketplace that overwhelms the company's hype.

Whatever the reason, the real customer isn't acting the way everyone *assumed* he would act in the Great Idea Scenario. He's not being the nice, compliant deep-pocketed, trusting, risk-taking customer who does his part, and buys the product or service the way he is expected to.

Stupid customers! Don't they know this is the best thing since sliced bread? What's the matter with them?

Scrambling ensues. What to do? Usually more money is thrown down the marketing hole. We saw a great deal of this sort of thing in the dot-com boom and bust, where high-priced agencies were hired to create edgy campaigns. The campaigns themselves may have gotten attention, but the sales never reached the levels that could save the companies running the campaigns.

This is a good time to say that the hubris associated with these companies and their creative agencies was thick enough to cut with a knife. Before the customer becomes involved in the Great Idea Scenario, the entrepreneur feels like nothing can stop him, and he's already counting his millions. The Scenario has him becoming the next Bill Gates or Richard Branson. He's a genius in his own mind, and all those associated with him get drunk on the same Kool-Aid.

After everyone realizes that the sales are just not happening, someone in the company or associated with the company may suggest that customers be consulted. If this is done soon enough, and managers actually take action on what they learn, failure can be averted.

You won't make this kind of mistake, because now you know better. Now you know how to turn the customers' desires and buying process into a machine that gives the customer what he wants—at a price he is willing to pay. Now you know how to become the kind of customer-centric company that everyone holds up as a model. Now you know that the customer must be consulted early and often, and that the customer's voice is the voice that should be driving you, inspiring you, and giving you great ideas.

EMPLOY CUSTOMER AND LOGISTICS FILTERS (ANTIDOTES TO THE GREAT IDEA SCENARIO SYNDROME)

As you continue to interview and interact with customers, you should also be building and refining two mental filters. Using these filters will keep you from falling prey to the Great Idea Syndrome. I call these filters the Customer Filter and the Logistics Filter.

Run your ideas through your mental Customer Filter, then your mental Logistics Filter. If the idea survives these filters, it's time to run the idea by real potential customers and the logistics people who will be carrying out the work.

The Customer Filter

Your mental Customer Filter consists of a series of questions:

- How would our customer(s) react to this?

- Would it actually help them? Would it solve a real problem that they are struggling with?

- Would they think it was a good idea? Why?

- How would a customer explain the idea to another interested customer? Would it be easy to explain?

- Would they consider this solution to be affordable in terms of time, resources and money—relative to competitive and alternative solutions?

If your filter doesn't get clogged as you subject the idea to these questions, you still must check with real customers. Otherwise, you can easily rationalize the answers, guess wrong, overlook something important, or minimize something that is actually very important to the customer.

The Logistics Filter

Most entrepreneurs, and many managers inside companies, have a serious problem with logistics. They love to snap their fingers and say, "Make it so," leaving their employees and vendors to work late into the night trying to solve problems that should have been anticipated and dealt with much earlier in the process.

Not thinking things through is the most common cause of inefficiency inside companies, and the biggest drain on profits. When something isn't thought through, people often end up doing things twice or three times, to accomplish one task. The first and second attempts are failures. They run full speed in one direction, then hit a logistical dead end. They are then forced to revise what they were doing and run full speed in another direction. It usually isn't until the third attempt that it is accomplished properly.

Meanwhile, the deadline that was set, early on in the process, never moves. The stress mounts. Employees and vendors doing all this frantic work get frustrated, discouraged, and angry. The fiascos accumulate, and after a while, that's how the whole company is operating. The best people will be the first to leave. This downhill slide will accelerate.

You will retain the best employees and vendors, and make higher profits, if you always think things through. Everyone will recognize and appreciate good planning and thorough organization. The Logistics Filter will help you.

The Logistics Filter also consists of a series of questions:

- How is this going to work—from start to finish? What are all the steps involved? (Diagram them.)

- Who is going to be responsible?

- Who is going to be involved? Do they have time to do this? Are they capable of doing a good job?

- Is it the sort of thing we are already good at? Do we have the resources, systems, and processes already in place to make this work?

- How long will it take?

- How much will it cost? (Whatever you're thinking about the cost, triple it. First, there's what you *think* it will cost, if things go as you expect them to go. Then, there are the rush charges you will incur as you fall behind schedule. You'll say "do it anyway," because you believe that your future obscene profits will pay for everything. Then, there are the costs you simply hadn't anticipated. All this will add up to three times what you thought it would cost.)

- Who's going to maintain it? What's required to maintain it?

- What do we have to stop doing, if we start doing this?

- How will we make the transition from the old to the new?

- What could go wrong?

- What will we do when something goes wrong?

After you have run the idea through your own *mental* Customer and Logistics

Filters, run the idea by *real potential customers.*

Ask them:

- What do you think of this?

- Will it actually help you? Will it solve a problem you want to fix?

- Do you think it is a good idea? Why?

- How would you explain the idea to another interested customer? Would it be easy to explain?

- Would you consider this solution to be affordable in terms of time, resources and money—relative to competitive and alternative solutions?

Customers will think of things that you hadn't thought of. At the very least, their input will help you refine the idea so that it will work smoothly for customers. At the most, you will abandon an idea that would have failed in the marketplace.

Yes, you will need to have customers sign a non-disclosure agreement (NDA). Use wisdom and caution in your selection of customers to contact. Choose people whom you know to be trustworthy. In my experience, it is extremely unlikely that you will regret revealing the idea to a customer. On the contrary, the usual outcome is that the customer is flattered that you asked, and ends up buying the product or service from you when it's finally available.

Most entrepreneurs avoid running an idea by customers or potential customers because they are secretly afraid that the customer might not like it. They assume that once it's out in the market, they will be able to talk the customer into liking it. After all, the entrepreneur has been able to convince everyone else around him. What he doesn't take into account, though, is that all those other people he's "convinced" have a personal, vested interest in the idea being pursued. Those interested folks think that they will at least have a job until it flops, and if it turns out to be a hit, they'll be in on the ground floor—stock options, an impressive resume, fast promotions as the company grows, and other enticing visions.

Entrepreneurs, bolstered by all this self-serving encouragement, plow ahead, thinking that once they get the idea out in to the market, the customer can be convinced that it's a great idea. After all, entrepreneurs have shelves full of marketing books that tell them how to sell anything to anybody.

If the idea does not appeal to customers, the product or service just won't make it in the market. Customers will give it the Big Yawn. If your customer decides the product/service isn't worth his money, you're toast—no matter how brilliant or determined you are. The best thing to do with an iffy idea is to abandon it. You'll have another idea soon enough. Dump the losers. Save yourself for the blockbusters.

If the potential customers for your idea have confirmed it's worth pursuing, using the Customer Filter, run the idea by the people who will have to do the work.

Ask them the Logistics questions (repeated here for your convenience):

- How is this going to work—from start to finish? What are all the steps involved? (Diagram them.)

- Who is going to be responsible?

- Who is going to be involved? Do they have time to do this? Are they capable of doing a good job?

- Is it the sort of thing we are already good at? Do we have the resources, systems, and processes already in place to make this work?

- How long will it take?

- How much will it cost?

- Who's going to maintain it? What's required to maintain it?

- What do we have to stop doing, if we start doing this?

- How will we make the transition from the old to the new?

- What could go wrong?

- What will we do when something goes wrong?

Using the Customer and Logistics Filters, and running the idea by real customers and the people who will be doing the work, will help you detect the fatal flaws in what seemed like a Great Idea.

Owners and managers who rush headlong into the latest idea without first sifting the idea through the Customer and Logistics Filters are doomed to fail. They expend a lot of energy selling others on how great the idea is. They make decisions without thinking things through. Giving orders gets ahead of what the orders *should* be—and would be—if the planning and critical thinking got done before the orders were given. People are yanked away from working on the previous Great Idea. These scatter-brained managers don't think about the consequences, and their people suffer for it. The company lurches violently from one idea to the next, like a dog on a leash being yanked around by an owner with an emotional problem. The company wastes energy, good will, resources, and funding on projects that are never completed.

On the other hand, successful owners and managers can get enthusiastic about a Great Idea, but as soon as they have it—or hear it—they immediately start asking themselves the customer and logistics questions. They present it to real customers and real workers, and see what they think.

They "test" the idea, looking at it from every angle, playing devil's advocate, until they are satisfied that it will work. They work out the details—ahead of time. They take the time and effort to provide clear instructions to everyone who has to carry out the plan.

Everyone in the company knows that the boss will be asking the customer and logistics questions whenever they propose an idea. They, too, will think about those issues when they come up with an idea that *they* think is a Great Idea.

Consultants bearing hammers

Be especially careful of the author/consultant who takes a marketing idea that's been kicking around for years, and then "owns it" by giving it a catchy name and writing a book about it. He then tries to make a career out of the idea, promoting it everywhere he can, regardless of its applicability. The only marketing problem solved by books like these is the marketing problem the *consultant* has—promoting himself.

I've been called in a number of times to rescue a company that tried to apply one of these silver bullet solutions to their situation. I remember one company that sold software to lawyers. They tried to apply the "crossing the chasm" model to their situation. They spent two days with a consultant trying to apply the "chasm" model. Finally, even the consultant had to admit that the model didn't fit. There is no "chasm" for this type of product. A chasm only exists when you are going from early adapters to a mass market—and there is no "mass market" for software sold to lawyers.

Many of these silver bullet ideas have been around since the rise of cities. They have survived because there are occasionally situations where they are helpful. Chances are, though, that your situation is different, and the silver bullet will not work. **Your situation is what your customers *tell you* it is.**

These consultants have one tool—a hammer. As far as they're concerned, every problem is a nail. If your problem happens to be an egg, they will *still* apply their hammer. You're left to clean up the mess, and your original problem remains unsolved. The consultant moves on, flashing his hammer around in the next victim's conference room, wearing the Armani suit that you paid for.

Next time you find yourself reading one of those books, ask yourself if you have talked to a customer lately.

In other words, if you want to increase your top line revenue, stop searching for a silver bullet and start talking to customers. Your customers are the ones who will give you money when you start providing what they need.

STICK TO YOUR SCRUTINY CATEGORY

Your chances of success will be far greater if you only offer products and services that fall into the Scrutiny category you're already in.

Companies selling Heavy Scrutiny products and services are all set up for a buying cycle that is very slow. The time that transpires between the first contact to a closed sale can take months. The company's rhythm is in sync with the slow buying process. On the other hand, companies selling Light Scrutiny products/services are good at making a sale after a couple of seconds. Their rhythm is quite different.

Your people and the processes you've put in place are all set up for your accustomed rhythm. The speed with which you make decisions, and the decisions you make, are affected by your company's rhythm. If you start trying to sell a product or service in another Scrutiny category, using the resources you have in place, you will be at a distinct disadvantage in the marketplace. Your experienced competitors' selling process will be in sync with the speed of your new customers. Your wrong-speed selling process will cause you to start out in last place and fall further behind from there.

If you want to offer a new product or service that is outside of your normal way of doing business, set up a separate division or a company that is designed to work with its customers' speed and Scrutiny level.

Hire people with experience in that industry or marketplace. Face the fact that you won't be as good a judge of their character and experience as you are in your current business. Realize that there will be things you don't know—

things that you *assume* will work a certain way, but they won't. Many of the things you take for granted or learned long ago in your current business won't apply to the new business. You can easily be blind-sided. Heck, you *will* be blind-sided. Expect it.

For all of these reasons, you are always better off implementing ideas that logically flow from the way you do business now, preferably ideas that worked well in the same industry or a closely-related industry, ideas that keep you in your familiar Scrutiny category. You will be able to apply the same knowledge, experience, people, processes, and rhythm to the new business. Your two businesses may have customers in common. All of this will give you an advantage over any competitors who are just starting out.

Put another way, it is much more likely that a candy bar company will succeed when it comes up with a new type of candy bar than if the company started to offer consulting services. Conversely, a consulting company that comes up with a new consulting service is much more likely to succeed than if it decided to start making candy bars.

These are extreme, Light-to-Intense Scrutiny examples, but the warning still holds when the difference is not so great. A company selling Medium Scrutiny products or services can easily fail if it tries to sell a Heavy Scrutiny product or service.

Successful companies suffer when they attempt to jump to another Scrutiny category without realizing what they are doing—and the pitfalls they are about to encounter. The new venture fails, and, even worse, the original company is so depleted and distracted by the attempts to make the failed venture work, that the original company never returns to its former state of prosperity.

What about those situations where an industry is literally drying up? We all saw that happen to the travel agent industry, with the introduction—and universal adoption—of book-it-yourself sites such as Expedia and Travelocity. What if you find yourself facing the virtual elimination of your industry?

My advice is the same. When you realize you must change to a new type of business, your chances of success will be far greater if your new endeavor is in the same Scrutiny category.

If you do decide to launch a product/service or open a business in a different Scrutiny category, at least you are now aware of the difficulties you may encounter. You are also aware of the characteristics of the four Scrutiny categories, which will help you manage the new effort more effectively.

COMMUNICATE EFFECTIVELY TO THE TROOPS

If people you are managing don't "get" what The Shift is all about, it's because you haven't communicated properly.

Communicating with the troops is something that very few managers do well. They make decisions, together, as a leadership team, but then they don't do a proper job of explaining to the troops what those decisions were—and why they ended up making the decisions they made. Instead, they come out of the meeting and start giving orders with no context. This is one of the main reasons why workers think bosses are so stupid.

In the absence of effective communication and official information, people make things up. Rumors and myths are spread, and even become part of the corporate culture. People start doing the wrong things for the wrong reasons, because they are acting on the rumors and myths.

To avoid this debilitating situation, force yourself to communicate formally and promptly in all situations. If you are communicating via email, write a succinct, informative email containing the background behind the decision, describing the decision itself, and what is going to happen because of the decision. Use a relevant subject line. Don't say, "latest thinking." Instead, say, "HR policy: New hiring method."

Subject lines are an incredibly important tool for managing by email. They are the "file tabs" that your employees are using to organize all of their work. Don't send out emails with nothing in the subject line. And don't send out emails with "stream of consciousness" subject lines. All projects progress more smoothly when the email subject lines associated with those projects are used properly.

As you start making The Shift from company-centered to customer-centric, the most important time to communicate is right after your big strategy meeting. Don't depend on an email for this. Gather the troops, either all together or department by department. As the CEO, you should do this yourself, for three reasons: You will know exactly what the troops were told, you will hear the questions that people are asking, and your very presence will communicate to everyone that The Shift is a Big Deal.

Relying on individual managers for this communication task can backfire, as some managers will either be poor communicators or will have a hidden agenda that they didn't reveal in the strategy meeting. You can't afford to have individual agendas get in the way of The Shift. As the CEO, you should be the person to set the tone and explain what is happening.

Tell everyone that you have conducted customer research and have learned that the company is doing a lot of things right. It's important for everyone to know this. They will have heard about the survey, and the big meeting, and will be wondering if the company has serious problems or if their jobs are in jeopardy. Set their minds at ease, right off the bat, and the rest of your message will be accepted more readily.

You can then say that you discovered things that everyone should be doing to make it easier for customers to find, buy, and use the company's products and services. Then show them the Buying Process Roadmap and the Action Plan, so they get the whole picture.

Employees really appreciate being brought into the inner circle of management thinking. They will be more willing to make relevant recommendations when they understand the goals of the company and the rationale for various decisions. They will appreciate the fact that the CEO cares enough to tell them what is going on. They enjoy working where managers care about all the people associated with the company—customers, employees, and vendors.

Meeting with employees in this way, after the Brainstorming and Planning Meeting, will build employee support for all of the steps you must take in order to make The Shift. Everyone in the company will know what the plan is. The foot-draggers will be obvious to all of those on board. They will be encouraged to get with the program.

ELIMINATE ADDITIONAL ROADBLOCKS

Here are some of the additional roadblocks you'll encounter and how you can eliminate them:

- **The people you are managing may have difficulty doing their part.** They may not understand. Or, they may understand, but not like the changes for some reason. What is required of them may not be in their character or it may be beyond their intelligence. Be patient. Work with each person individually if you have to. Listen, observe and understand their reluctance. Figure out what it will take to get this person on board. In management, you are always working with "imperfect instruments." It often takes a bit of time to figure out how to get the best performance out of each person. The goal is to have each person working hard, but to be operating within realistic limits. However, if someone refuses to get on board, even after receiving personal attention, he will drag down the rest of your team as well as your efforts to make The Shift. It's best to let this person go. Everyone else's attitude will suddenly improve.

- **The vendors you're working with are resisting your customer-centric direction.** Try to figure out what is causing their resistance, and if you can fix it, great. If not, look for a new vendor. As soon as you find one who will be an enthusiastic supporter of The Shift, test the new vendor. If the new vendor works out, fire the old one.

- **What you must fix takes more money or resources than you have.** Break the solution (and the cost) into modules. Attack one module at a time. Or, secure some financing specifically to make The Shift. Explain to potential investors what you have learned and what you must do, how you're going to fix the problems, and how making these changes will improve your revenue.

  Give the potential investor a copy of this book, so they will be able to see, in detail, what you are doing and how it's going to work. This will make it easier for the investor to support you.

- **An investor or board member is not comfortable with your new direction.** This is a tough problem, but it must be faced. Get these folks involved in the process as deeply as you can. Have them read this book. Show them the results of your research. Discuss the findings. If they come around then, feel free to invite them to the Brainstorming and Planning Meeting, if it's appropriate. If not, don't—they will be too disruptive.

  It is normal to be questioned by conscientious board members and investors; it's the way they make sure you are doing the right thing. That's not what we're talking about here. What we're talking about here is a stubborn, illogical, and vehement resistance to making The Shift.

  If they continue to hold their negative views in spite of all the evidence you've presented to the contrary, you will have to figure out what is motivating them to disagree with customers. It could be fear, arrogance, resistance to change, "not invented here" syndrome, or simply the desire to argue with the obvious. Watch for any clues you can find regarding their real motivation, and address it as soon as you figure out what it is. Call them on it. After you've confronted them with it, talk it out. In the end, you must take your customers' word over the word of any other person who influences your decisions, because your customers are your only true source of revenue.

Unfortunately, there are some jerks who actually hate customers. In the investment community, I'd estimate that the number is about one out of every twenty individuals. They will do everything in their power to stonewall the process. The will resist the whole idea that the customer is more powerful than they are. They may behave as if they agree, but will disparage the effort behind your back. They will be constantly on the lookout for opportunities to obstruct the process. You will simply have to out-number them (and any of their sycophants). It will be a constant struggle.

An investor who is dead-set against a customer-centric policy will not support The Shift to a customer-centric company. If this happens, your best option is to use your new profits to buy out the investor, or find a new customer-centric investor to buy out the obstructionist. At the very least, when it is obvious what he is doing, call him on it in meetings. This will give everyone else in the room permission to ignore him and move on without him.

- **What customers are asking for is something you are not willing to do.** Sounds crazy, but it happens. Perhaps they are asking for more attention than you are willing to give them ("let them use voicemail!"), or the change they are asking you to make is something you decided not to do a long time ago. There are hundreds of reasons for not doing what the customer wants you to do. I only have one response: Do you want to sell more, or not? Swallow your pride or stifle your resistance, and decide to make the change in spite of your own personal reaction. The ability to eat a little humble pie will reward you handsomely as you strive to meet customer needs. Everybody will think better of you for it.

- **What customers are asking you to do will compromise another goal.** Let's say your website navigation is confusing. Your customers have made this very clear. But your search engine optimization vendor has insisted that you use the phrases you're using in your website menus in order to increase the traffic coming to your site. Should you continue to confuse customers when they get to your site? Of course not. Why go to all that effort to bring them to your site, if all they're going to do is scratch their heads and click away? Instead, figure out what the navigation should say—so it's easy for customers to understand—and then tweak the names just slightly to include some search terms. Or, find other ways to incorporate your search phrases into your content. Sacrificing usability to make a programmer's job easier is an old, tired, unprofitable game. Your customers, not your programmers or website designers, should drive your decisions.

- **Your budgets and your budget categories don't make it easy for you to make the necessary changes.** Change your budgets and your budget structure. Imagine what you would do if you were a startup coming into your industry, unencumbered by existing systems and processes. You wouldn't hesitate to do what is right. Assume that there are always new competitors coming into your industry, and they are not handicapped by "the way we've always done it." You are competing against companies that are unencumbered.

THE GOOD NEWS

Every single time I have guided a client through The Shift, the problems we discovered in the customer interviews were all fixable. (Since I don't work with jerks, "replace the CEO" was never on the customer list of grievances.)

In many cases, the problems involved company and product positioning, processes, usability, and content. Addressing these problems started the revenue trending in the right direction. On the rare occasions when people were a problem, it was usually because a person was in the wrong position, a new person was needed, people weren't being properly trained, or someone in the ranks thought that customers were a pain.

Product design came up less frequently as an issue in the interviews than you would expect, even though product usability, like content, is not typically a high enough priority for most CEOs. Products are often launched with many of the functions customers want, but the product isn't very usable at first.

Photoshop, the graphic design software, is a good example of this. When it was first introduced, all of the pixel-manipulation functions were there, but only the cleverest and do-it-all-day designers could figure out how to operate the program in ways that gave them the image results they sought. Since it was introduced more than 20 years ago, each new version improved the usability of the pixel manipulation functions, to the point where any office worker can now use the program with ease. The companies that have made usability a top priority, such as Apple, enjoy a distinct advantage in the marketplace.

I don't know what your customers will tell you. You don't either. But you will know after you have made the calls.

The entrepreneurs and CEOs I have worked with see everything in a new light after we present our findings and recommendations. They have a series of "ah-ha" thoughts, which lead to new ideas and approaches, which lead to new revenue. They see why some things were working and other things were not. They have a new basis for making decisions and leading their people. They gain a renewed sense of purpose and resolve.

This conversion is what gets me up in the morning. There is nothing more satisfying than starting to work with entrepreneurs or CEOs who have been struggling, wracking their brains, searching desperately for the answer. It's wonderful to be able to show them where the answers are, and then get to work on the changes that increase their revenue.

It is one of the ironies of business life that the answers they seek aren't outside, but right there, as close as their customer list. Yes, they will still need to come up with great ideas, and make sound decisions, and manage their companies wisely. But they aren't struggling anymore. They aren't desperate. They know what to do. As they start taking the right steps, they start to see the right results. They become calm and confident.

Their customers find the company when they go looking, get all the answers they need, decide to buy the product or service, get it, use it, like it, and tell others about their good experience. Success builds on success. Momentum is created that makes life more difficult for competitors (poor, poor competitors). Investors are rewarded, handsomely. Employees are happy; they're making a difference, working in a company that provides valued products and solutions, and that takes good care of customers.

As you've discovered, this book is not a light, entertaining business book. Making The Shift to a customer-centric focus is fairly heavy going. Your to-do list won't be short.

However, the Roadmap to Revenue system is linear and logical. It will put you on a straight path. You will be able to find out what needs to be done, which is often half the battle. Once you have properly followed the method, your course will be clear. You will be able to make changes with confidence, knowing that you're doing the right thing, and that your efforts will pay off.

Non-linear activity is expensive. Wrong turns and dead ends can be fatal. Most products have a limited market opportunity window, and you can't spend the first two years of a three-year market window fumbling around in the dark. That's what most companies do. When they finally figure out what they *should* be doing, it's too late.

Sometimes a CEO who spends a year trying "this and that" may get lucky. It happens. But the chances of it happening are very slim. It's like show business; for every mega rock star, there are millions of young performers struggling for local gigs who never get past the neighborhood saloon stage.

Once you start to make The Shift, your company and your customers will be working in concert. You will be providing what the customer needs, and the customer will get his or her problems solved.

After you understand what is really driving your customers, each idea you have will be evaluated in the context of your customers' world. You will know if an idea is going to rub customers the wrong way. You will know when an idea is going to make sense to the customer. Your Great Ideas will be much more likely to work.

MAKING THE SHIFT FROM COMPANY-CENTERED TO CUSTOMER-CENTRIC REQUIRES MATURITY, DISCIPLINE, AND COURAGE

You must be intolerant of the tendency to slip into old, self-centered habits. As the leader of your company, you are the one who must make sure everyone stays on the Road to Revenue, and set the tone for every interaction with customers.

Doing the right thing for the customer is the essence of business success. Your customers want to buy what they need. Your job is to make it easy. Good luck, and may your customers be with you.

EMAIL ME IF YOU HAVE QUESTIONS

I wrote this book so that any company owner or manager could put these techniques to work. I've left nothing out in the description of the method. There are no hidden, untold secrets. I've tried to answer all the questions you might have about the method.

Of course, one can't put all of one's experience into a book, but I have tried my best to give you every chance of success.

I don't mind telling you the secrets of the method, because I know that the method works and it will help you. I also know that many of you will want to do everything yourselves. Great. Everything you need to know is here.

Some will want to bring me in to conduct the research and recommend the right course of action. Happy to help. Either way, with or without my direct involvement, following the Roadmap to Revenue method will grow your sales.

As you start your unique journey on the road to higher revenue, you may have questions that I can answer. Feel free to contact me at Kristin@Zhivago.com. Write "Book Question" in the subject line so it's easy to distinguish your *wanted* email from the unwanted email in my inbox.

I'll help you any way I can.

ABOUT THE AUTHOR

Kristin Zhivago is a Revenue Coach to companies of all sizes. She has more than 40 years of experience helping CEOs and entrepreneurs sell more—by understanding what their customers really want to buy from them and how they want to buy it. Clients have included IBM, Johnson & Johnson, Dow Jones, Siemens, Lexmark, and Bazaarvoice, and hundreds of other companies.

Zhivago's articles have appeared in numerous business publications and sites since she started writing a monthly column for *Marketing Computers* magazine in 1984. She published a newsletter for technical marketers called *Marketing Technology* from 1991 to 2004. In 2004, Zhivago started writing an advice blog for CEOs and entrepreneurs called the Revenue Journal (www.RevenueJournal.com).

Zhivago conducts highly personalized workshops for corporations and associations around the world. For every workshop, Zhivago interviews attendees and their customers prior to the event. Attendees come to these events with deep, perplexing concerns. They walk out with a completely new perspective on their marketing and selling—and a logical, sensible, concrete set of next steps that they can use to remove the barriers to higher revenue growth.

Zhivago founded Zhivago Management Partners, Inc., in Silicon Valley in 1979. The company moved to Jamestown, Rhode Island in 1996.

ORDERING INFORMATION

Roadmap to Revenue: How to Sell the Way Your Customers Want to Buy can be purchased in bulk. Quantity discounts are available. For more information, please contact the publisher: BookSales@BristolAndShipley.com.

Bristol & Shipley Press
381 Seaside Drive
Jamestown, RI 02835

To email the author, send an email to Kristin@Zhivago.com.